MAKE ANY MOMENT
A STUDY MOMENT

Download your free Fully-Featured Mobile app!

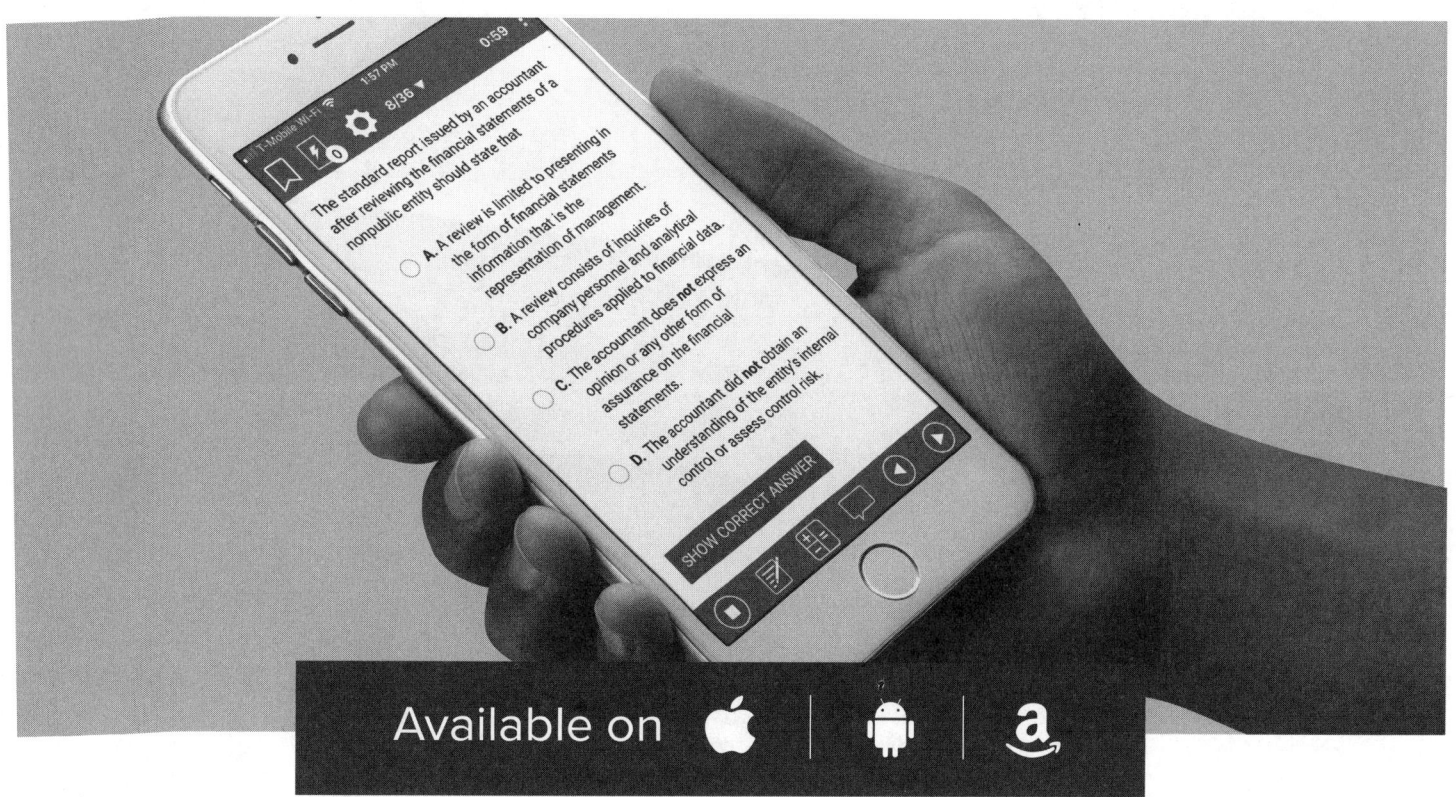

MAXIMIZE YOUR STUDY TIME WITH CONVENIENT ACCESS TO ALL YOUR COURSE MATERIALS.

- Streamline your studies across multiple devices
- Practice Multiple Choice Questions & Task-Based Simulations
- Stream lectures and view eTextbooks
- Assess real-time progress metrics with SmartPath Predictive Technology™
- Download course materials for offline access
- Flip through Digital Flash Cards for a quick review

BEC

Business Environment and Concepts

Written By:

Roger Philipp, CPA, CGMA

UWorld
9111 Cypress Waters Blvd
Suite 300
Dallas, TX 75019
accounting.uworld.com/cpa-review

Permissions

The following items are utilized in this volume, and are copyright property of the American Institute of Certified Public Accountants, Inc. (AICPA), all rights reserved:

- Uniform CPA Examination and Questions and Unofficial Answers, Copyright © 1991, 1992, 1993, 1994, 1995, 1996, 1997, 1998, 1999, 2000, 2001, 2002, 2003, 2004, 2005, 2006, 2007, 2008, 2009, 2010, 2011, 2012, 2013, 2014, 2015, 2016, 2017, 2018, 2019, 2020
- Audit and Accounting Guides, Auditing Procedure Studies, Risk Alerts, Statements of Position, and Code of Professional Conduct
- Statements on Auditing Standards
- Statements on Standards for Accounting and Review Services
- Statements on Quality Control Standards
- Statements on Standards for Attestation Engagements
- Accounting Research Bulletins, APB Opinions
- Uniform CPA Examination Blueprints
- Independence Standards Board (ISB) Standards

Portions of various FASB and GASB documents, copyright property of the Financial Accounting Foundation, 401 Merritt 7, PO Box 5116, Norwalk, CT 06856-5116, are utilized with permission. Complete copies of these documents are available from the Financial Accounting Foundation. These selections include the following:

Financial Accounting Standards Board (FASB)
- The FASB Accounting Standards Codification ™
- Statements of Financial Accounting Concepts
- FASB Statements, Interpretations, and Technical Bulletins

Governmental Accounting Standards Board (GASB)
- GASB Codification of Governmental Accounting and Financial Reporting Standards and GASB Statements
- GASB Concepts Statements
- GASB Interpretations and Technical Bulletins

The following items are utilized in this volume, and are copyright property of the International Financial Reporting Standards (IFRS) Foundation and the International Accounting Standards Board (IASB), all rights reserved:

- IASB International Reporting Standards (IFRS), International Accounting Standards (IAS) and Interpretations

---

Copyright © 2021
By Roger Philipp CPA, CGMA
On behalf of UWorld
San Francisco, CA
USA

All rights reserved.
Reproduction or translation of any part of this work beyond that permitted by sections 107 and 108 of the United States Copyright Act without the permission of the copyright owner is unlawful.

Printed in English, in the United States of America.

ABOUT THE AUTHOR

Roger S. Philipp, CPA, CGMA
Founder and Instructor, UWorld Roger CPA Review

Roger Philipp, CPA, CGMA, is one of the most celebrated motivators and instructors in the accounting profession. Roger believes you should enjoy what you do—in life, business, and learning. Guided by this philosophy, he strives to create dynamic and engaging instruction that makes learning concepts enjoyable. This focus has helped aspiring accountants across the globe reach career success for almost 30 years.

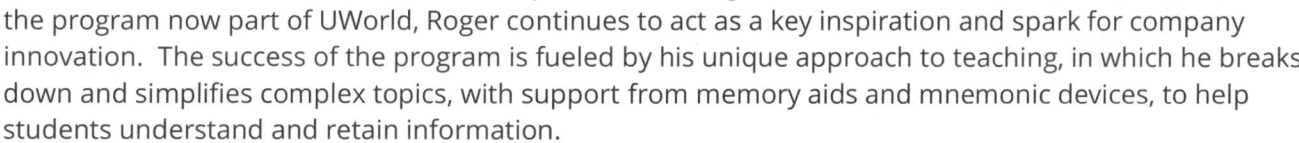

Roger launched Roger CPA Review in 2001 with the goal to create a CPA review course that would alter the landscape of accounting education. With the program now part of UWorld, Roger continues to act as a key inspiration and spark for company innovation. The success of the program is fueled by his unique approach to teaching, in which he breaks down and simplifies complex topics, with support from memory aids and mnemonic devices, to help students understand and retain information.

Roger's early career began in public accounting at Deloitte & Touche, where he earned his CPA designation, before transitioning to educational instruction. He was a lead instructor at Mark Dauberman CPA Review, before starting Roger CPA Review. Roger attributes his entrepreneurial success to the many doors his CPA license opened, as well as his passion for making professional education engaging and relevant for optimum effectiveness. In recent years, Roger was featured as one of Accounting Today's Top 100 Most Influential People in Public Accounting.

Today, Roger is a member of the AICPA, CalCPA, and has served on the Board of Directors for the American Professional Accounting Certification Providers Association (APACPA). He resides in San Francisco with his wife and co-founder of the company, Louisa, and their three children. He enjoys traveling with his family, enjoying the arts, and volunteering at his local food bank.

Acknowledgements

Keeping the course materials updated and accurate would not be possible without the contribution of our content expert **Jae Johnson**, CPA. Jae has been the driving force behind the updates and improvements for this year's textbooks.

Business Environment & Concepts

Table of Contents

Introduction Intro-1

BEC 1	Economic Concepts	1-1
BEC 2	Corporate Governance, Internal Control & Enterprise Risk Management	2-1
BEC 3	Business Processes & Information Technology	3-1
BEC 4	Data	4-1
BEC 5	Financial Management & Capital Budgeting	5-1
BEC 6	Decision Making	6-1
BEC 7	Cost Accounting	7-1
BEC 8	Planning, Control & Analysis	8-1
BEC 9	Final Review	9-1

Introduction

Table of Contents
Lecture 0.01 – Course Introduction 1
Lecture 0.02 – BEC Introduction 1

Lecture 0.01 – Course Introduction

Lecture 0.02 – BEC Introduction

Welcome to your UWorld Roger CPA Review Course!

Greetings Student,

It is an honor to be your partner on your CPA Exam journey. Your success is our success, which is why we are 100% dedicated to providing you with a learning experience that inspires, delights and delivers results with optimum efficiency. With the power or our new alignment with UWorld, enhanced question explanations, the strength of our SmartPath Predictive Technology™ and the profession's leading video lectures, you'll be on your way to the CPA in no time.

This course is structured for a variety of student types. Each topic is broken down from the beginning and taught as if the student has little to no prior knowledge of the particular topic at hand. Therefore, whether you are a first-time review student who has never attempted an exam part, or a seasoned professional returning to the exam after an earlier attempt, you will be prepared.

As you work through the material, you will be able to gauge your competency on each topic using SmartPath Predictive Technology™, a tool that provides targets based on the performance of previous students who have passed the CPA Exam. We recommend that you achieve each target in order to be fully prepared to take the exam.

Ultimately, you control your destiny. As your instructor Roger Philipp, CPA, CGMA always says, "The CPA Exam is not an IQ test. It is a test of discipline. If you study, you will pass!" You will find on the next page our **"Guide to Using Your Course."** This will provide you with our recommended approach to preparing with this course and its support features.

We wish you all the best on this journey and are here to guide you along the way.

Sincerely,

The UWorld Roger CPA Review Team
#TaketheSmartPath

Follow us on social media for CPA Exam tips and tricks at @RogerCPAReview.

Subscribe to our blog to get the most up-to-date CPA Exam information, as well as plenty of advice on careers, education and the CPA Exam at accounting.uworld.com/blog/cpa-review.

Guide to Using Your Course

 Plan

Before you start studying, log into your course and navigate to the Study Planners (located under "Study Resources"). Choose between a 3, 6, 9 or 12 month planner, and customize to meet your needs. It is important to follow your planner steadily so that you can work through all of the material before your exam date. If you miss a day, make it up!

 Learn

In this program, you will build your foundation in core CPA Exam concepts as you work through practice questions and simulations that match the actual exam.

> **Tip:** Download the app! This gives you access to everything your course offers while on-the go.

When you first log into your course you will be presented with the QBank. This is where you will setup custom practice sessions to work through problems. When you are still learning the material, we recommend turning on *Tutor Mode*. This will provide you with clear and concise expert-written answer explanations directly after answering each question. Pay attention to these because this is where much of the learning happens! You should have a grasp on *why* you have answered each question correctly or incorrectly. This *learn by doing* method is called *active learning* and is proven to help students obtain and retain information.

 Improve

As you work through your course, keep track of your performance and progress using SmartPath Predictive Technology™. SmartPath is a data-driven platform that provides recommended targets based on previous successful students. This is an important tool to help you gauge whether you are *exam-ready*. Your ultimate goal is to hit both targets per course chapter: (1) number of question attempts and (2) score.

> **Tip:** Don't over-study! SmartPath™ helps determine when you can move on to the next topic.

If you are having trouble with some of the concepts and/or falling short of reaching your targets, there are tools to help you improve:

- Video Lectures – You have access to the profession's most motivating and effective lectures from Roger Philipp, CPA, CGMA. Lectures break down difficult topics into simplified concepts and provide helpful memory aids. These are especially recommended for visual and audio learners.

- Textbooks – The text is a companion to the video lectures. Some students find benefit in following along and taking notes in the textbooks while watching the lectures. You can also use these as a reference if you need further explanation of a related question.

- Digital Flash Cards – Create your own flash cards within the courseware and flip through them whenever you need a quick drill (this is a great option with the mobile app!). To create a flash card from your practice question content, simply highlight the relevant text and the option to create a flash card will appear. Depending on your program package, your course may also be pre-loaded with an "Expert Deck" of flash cards covering the most heavily tested topics.

↺ Review

As you get ready for exam day, review your SmartPath data to ensure you have hit all targets. Revisit any areas marked "Needs Improvement." If it is included in your program package, use the Cram Course to do a final review of the most heavily tested topics.

Finally, we recommend taking at least one full practice exam before exam day (go to QBank > Create Test, and then choose the "Exam Sim" tab.) This allows you to hone your test-taking skills in an environment that follows the same 5-testlet, 4-hour structure of the exam.

Plan Your Time!

Ensure success on the exam by following our recommendations for time allocation:

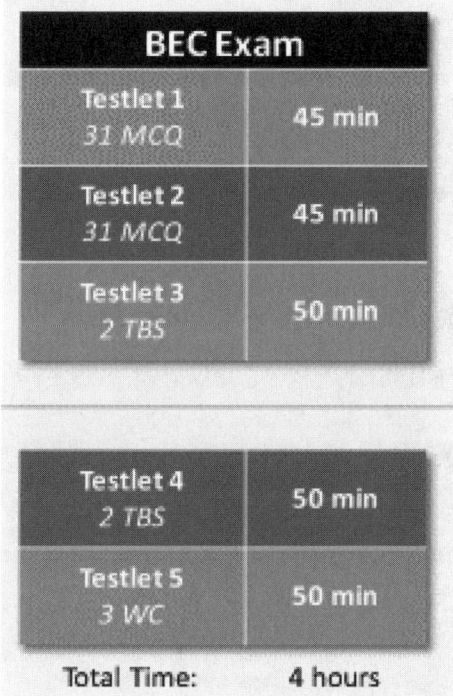

Things to consider:
- Allocate 75 seconds per multiple choice question
- Allocate 10 - 15 minutes for each written communication question
- Allocate 15-25 minutes for each task-based simulation, depending on complexity
- Plan to use no more than 10 minutes per research question (none in BEC)
- Take the standard 15-minute break after the 3rd testlet – it doesn't count against your time.

Introduction   accounting.uworld.com/cpa-review

CPA Exam Blueprints

This course is based on the CPA Exam Blueprints, which are created by the American Institute of Certified Public Accountants (AICPA) to help candidates know what skills and content topics will be tested on the CPA Exam.

Not only are the CPA Exam Blueprints intended to assist candidates in preparing for the exam, but they also take into account the minimum level of knowledge and skills necessary for initial licensure once candidates become CPAs.

We have already used the blueprints to guide our course materials, so you are already on the right path. However, if you'd like to reference the blueprints to better understand what's required on the exam, we've provided a helpful guide below.

Overview of the CPA Exam

The blueprints provide an overview of how much time candidates have for each section and how many questions by question type each section contains. Question types include Multiple Choice Questions (MCQ), Task-based Simulations (TBS), and Written Communication (WC).

Section	Section Time	MCQs	TBSs	WC
AUD	4 hrs	72	8	-
BEC	4 hrs	62	4	3
FAR	4 hrs	66	8	-
REG	4 hrs	76	8	-

Scoring Weight for All Question Types

Here candidates can see how the question types for each section are weighted and account for their overall score.

Section	MCQs	TBSs	WC
AUD	50%	50%	-
BEC	50%	35%	15%
FAR	50%	50%	-
REG	50%	50%	-

Skill Allocations

Each exam section has a Skill Allocation framework based on the revised Bloom's Taxonomy of Educational Objectives. These are the skills that CPA candidates need to learn and successfully demonstrate on the CPA Exam.

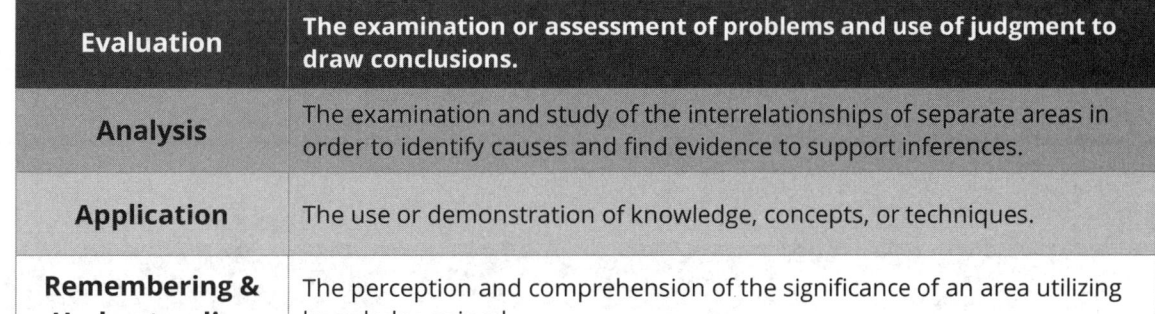

Evaluation	The examination or assessment of problems and use of judgment to draw conclusions.
Analysis	The examination and study of the interrelationships of separate areas in order to identify causes and find evidence to support inferences.
Application	The use or demonstration of knowledge, concepts, or techniques.
Remembering & Understanding	The perception and comprehension of the significance of an area utilizing knowledge gained.

Skill Levels to be Assessed on Each Section of the Exam

To break it down even further, here are how each of the skills above will be assessed on every section of the exam.

Section	Remembering & Understanding	Application	Analysis	Evaluation
AUD	30-40%	30-40%	15-25%	5-15%
BEC	15-25%	50-60%	20-30%	-
FAR	10-20%	50-60%	25-35%	-
REG	25-35%	35-45%	25-35%	-

Summary Blueprint Snapshot

Below is an overview of the content and skill allocation for each section of the exam.

AUD Content Area Allocation	Weight
I. Ethics, Professional Responsibilities and General Principles	15-25%
II. Assessing Risk and Developing a Planned Response	20-30%
III. Performing Further Procedures and Obtaining Evidence	30-40%
IV. Forming Conclusions and Reporting	15-25%

AUD Skill Allocation	Weight
Evaluation	5-15%
Analysis	15-25%
Application	30-40%
Remembering and Understanding	30-40%

BEC Content Area Allocation	Weight
I. Corporate Governance	17-27%
II. Economic Concepts and Analysis	17-27%
III. Financial Management	11-21%
IV. Information Technology	15-25%
V. Operations Management	15-25%

BEC Skill Allocation	Weight
Evaluation	-
Analysis	20-30%
Application	50-60%
Remembering and Understanding	15-25%

FAR Content Area Allocation	Weight
I. Conceptual Framework, Standard-Setting, & Financial Reporting	25-35%
II. Select Financial Statement Accounts	30-40%
III. Select Transactions	20-30%
IV. State and Local Governments	5-15%

FAR Skill Allocation	Weight
Evaluation	-
Analysis	25-35%
Application	50-60%
Remembering and Understanding	10-20%

REG Content Area Allocation	Weight
I. Ethics, Professional Responsibilities & Federal Tax Procedures	10-20%
II. Business Law	10-20%
III. Federal Taxation of Property Transactions	12-22%
IV. Federal Taxation of Individuals	15-25%
V. Federal Taxation of Entities	28-38%

REG Skill Allocation	Weight
Evaluation	-
Analysis	25-35%
Application	35-45%
Remembering and Understanding	25-35%

How Skills are Applied to Exam Tasks (A Sample)

Each blueprint area is broken down further by content topic, skill, and representative task. This helps candidates identify the topics and subtopics they will be tested on in each section and which skill they will be required to demonstrate as they answer questions regarding those topics. Lastly, the representative task gives detailed, specific information on what they will be expected to perform on the exam related to those topics. (As the AICPA points out, the representative tasks are not an all-inclusive list of items that will appear on the exam.)

To see how the content topic, skill, and representative tasks are presented in the blueprints, here is an excerpt from the AUD section:

Content group/topic	Skill				Representative task
	Remembering and Understanding	Application	Analysis	Evaluation	
A. Nature and scope					
1. Nature and scope: audit engagements	✓				Identify the nature, scope and objectives of the different types of audit engagements, including issuer and nonissuer audits.
2. Nature and scope: engagements conducted under Government Accountability Office Government Auditing Standards	✓				Identify the nature, scope and objectives of engagements performed in accordance with Government Accountability Office Government Auditing Standards.
3. Nature and scope: non-audit engagements	✓				Identify the nature, scope and objectives of the different types of non-audit engagements, including engagements conducted in accordance with the attestation standards and the accounting and review services standards.
B. Ethics, independence and professional conduct					
1. AICPA Code of Professional Conduct	✓				Understand the principles, rules and interpretations included in the AICPA Code of Professional Conduct.
	✓				Recognize situations that present threats to compliance with the AICPA Code of Professional Conduct, including threats to independence.
		✓			Apply the principles, rules and interpretations included in the AICPA Code of Professional Conduct to given situations.
		✓			Apply the Conceptual Framework for Members in Public Practice included in the AICPA Code of Professional Conduct to situations that could present threats to compliance with the rules included in the Code.
		✓			Apply the Conceptual Framework for Members in Business included in the AICPA Code of Professional Conduct to situations that could present threats to compliance with the rules included in the Code.
		✓			Apply the Conceptual Framework for Independence included in the AICPA Code of Professional Conduct to situations that could present threats to compliance with the rules included in the Code.

Conclusion

We hope you found this guide on how to read and understand the blueprints helpful. As we mentioned before, the UWorld Roger CPA Review course curriculum is directly mapped to and guided by these blueprints, so there is no need for you to spend considerable time studying the blueprints, as your course will guide you through the material. Rest assured that the practice questions in this course are designed to challenge critical thinking skills, ensuring you are thoroughly prepared to pass the CPA Exam.

To see the full AICPA Blueprints, visit
https://www.aicpa.org/becomeacpa/cpaexam/examinationcontent.

BEC 1 – Economic Concepts

Table of Contents

Lecture 1.01 – Microeconomics: Supply & Demand 1
- OVERVIEW 1
- DEMAND 1
- PRICE ELASTICITY OF DEMAND 3
- INCOME ELASTICITY OF DEMAND 4
- CROSS-ELASTICITY OF DEMAND 5
- SUPPLY 5
- PRICE ELASTICITY OF SUPPLY 7
- MARKET EQUILIBRIUM 7
- SOME GOVERNMENT ACTIONS THAT AFFECT EQUILIBRIUM 8
- CONSUMERS 9
- PRODUCTION COSTS 10
- RETURNS TO SCALE 11

Lecture 1.02 – Market Structure & Industry Analysis 12
- OVERVIEW 12
- PERFECT (OR PURE) COMPETITION 12
- PURE MONOPOLY 13
- MONOPOLISTIC COMPETITION 13
- OLIGOPOLY (OR OLIGOPOLISTIC COMPETITION) 14
- INDUSTRY ANALYSIS 15

Lecture 1.03 – Macroeconomic Impacts on Business 17
- OVERVIEW 17
- MEASURES OF ECONOMIC CONDITIONS 17
- MEASURES OF PRICE INFLATION 18
- CAUSES OF INFLATION 18
- MULTIPLIER EFFECT 19

Lecture 1.04 – Business Cycles & Economic Indicators 20
- OVERVIEW 20
- INDICATORS OF ECONOMIC ACTIVITY 21
- UNEMPLOYMENT 22

Lecture 1.05 – Interest Rates & Government Involvement 23
- INTEREST RATES 23
- GOVERNMENT INVOLVEMENT IN THE ECONOMY 24
- OBSTACLES TO INTERNATIONAL TRADE 26
- EFFORTS TO REDUCE TRADE BARRIERS 27

Lecture 1.06 – Financial Risk Management 28
- FOREIGN EXCHANGE RATES 28
- FOREIGN EXCHANGE RISK 28
- MITIGATION OF OTHER FINANCIAL RISKS 30
- GLOBALIZATION 31

Economic Concepts

Lecture 1.01 – Microeconomics: Supply & Demand

Overview

Economics is the study of how we allocate scarce resources to satisfy unlimited wants. **Microeconomics** is the study of the decisions of, and interactions among, various individual economic agents (households and firms).

- Both households and firms act as buyers in the economy, providing **demand** for products (or goods) and services (including labor).

- Both households and firms act as sellers in the economy, providing the **supply** of products and services.

- The interaction of demand and supply determine the price, quantity produced and consumed, and the allocation of products and services.

Demand

A **demand curve** shows the *inverse relationship* between the price and the quantity of a product or service that a group of consumers are willing and able to buy at a particular time (ie, the quantity demanded). For instance, as the price of a product increases (eg, from 10 to 20), the quantity demanded by buyers decreases (eg, from 50 to 30).

> Remember that the **Demand** curve, starting with a D, slopes **Down**, also starting with a D.

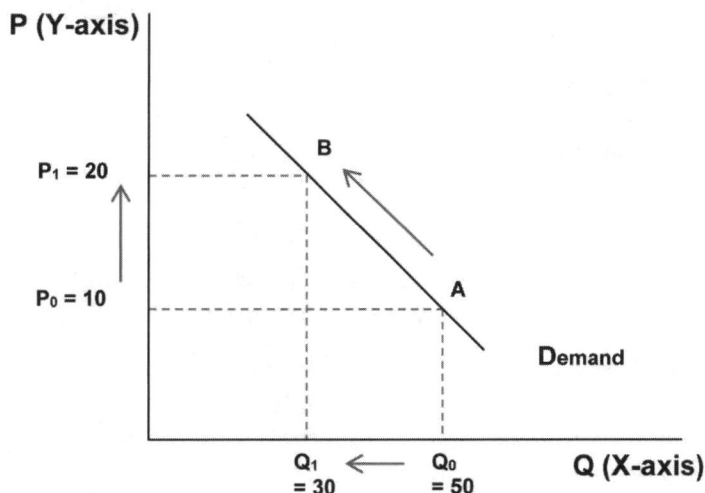

> 👉 Economists are very specific about the usage of the terms "demand" vs. "quantity demanded." The term "demand" refers to the demand curve that can be plotted on a graph with quantity demanded on the x-axis (horizontal) and price on the y-axis (vertical). The demand curve may also be thought of as a schedule listing multiple combinations of prices and quantities demanded (eg, those for points A and B in the graph). Thus, economists would not say that higher prices decrease "demand." Instead, economists would say that at higher prices, "quantity demanded" is lower. As prices increase, one moves along the demand curve to find lower quantities demanded.

Price and quantity demanded have a reliably **inverse relationship**; however, the precise placement of the demand curve on the graph may change regularly. These changes are known as **demand curve shifts**. A demand curve shifts if there are changes in relevant factors *other than a change in price*. Economists use a variety of terms to describe demand curve shifts:

- **Changes in the demand curve where quantity demanded becomes larger for each and every price** are described as "the demand curve shifted upward," "the demand curve shifted outward," "the demand curve shifted to the right," or "demand increased."

- **Changes in the demand curve where quantity demanded becomes smaller for each and every price** are described as "the demand curve shifted downward," "the demand curve shifted inward," "the demand curve shifted to the left," or "demand decreased."

Below we show an upward demand curve shift from D_0 to D_1. Note that at a price of 20, consumers are willing and able to purchase 50 instead of 30 units. Alternatively, for a quantity of 30, consumers are willing and able to pay a price of 27 instead of 20.

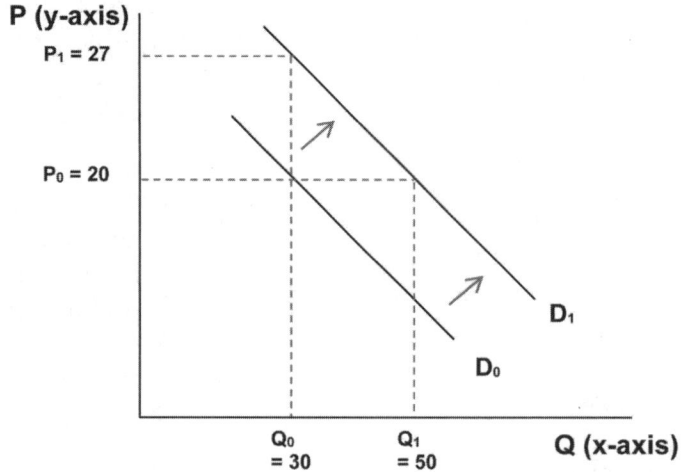

There are various reasons why demand curves may shift. Some factors exhibit a **direct relationship** with the demand curve, meaning that increases in that factor cause the demand curve to *shift upward* (or demand to increase). Examples are:

- **The price of a substitute good** – When product A may be an acceptable alternative to product B, an increase in the price of product A will make product B more attractive (eg, some consumers will shift from buying product A to product B). For example, an increase in the price of hamburgers will increase the demand for hot dogs.

- **Expectations of price changes** – Consumers are more likely to buy now if they think prices will increase in the future. For example, if cigarette taxes are expected to double next year, some buyers will bring forward some of their purchases, increasing demand this year until the tax increase goes into effect.

- **Income** (for **normal goods**) – For many goods (eg, cars or smartphones), when incomes increase (wealth increase), demand increases. Below we point out that not all goods are "normal goods."

- **Extent of the market** – New consumers may increase demand, therefore increasing the size of the market. For example, the removal of trade barriers by foreign governments will increase the demand for American products that can be exported. A baby boom will increase demand for baby food. A large inflow of immigrants from a country to the U.S. will increase demand for that country's ethnic food in the U.S.

Other factors exhibit an **inverse relationship** with the demand curve, meaning that increases in that factor cause the demand curve to *shift downward* (or demand to decrease). Examples are:

- **The price of a complement good** – When products are normally used together, an increase in the price of one of the goods decreases demand for the other. For example, an increase in the price of chips will cause a downward shift in the demand for salsa.

- **Income** (for **inferior goods**) – For some goods (eg, used cars), when incomes increase (wealth), demand decreases as consumers shift their spending to other goods (eg, new cars).

- **Consumer boycotts** – An organized boycott will, if effective, temporarily decrease the demand for a product. For example, members of unions commonly refuse to buy from businesses that are involved in labor disputes.

Changes in consumer tastes may affect demand but whether demand increases or decreases as a result depends on whether the change in tastes favors or disfavors the specific product. These are said to have an indeterminate relationship. The theory of *derived demand* predicts that demand for the resources used to produce product A is derived from the demand for product A.

Price Elasticity of Demand

Barring shifts in the demand curve, a firm expects the quantity demanded for its product to decrease as the price increases. A smaller level of sales (ie, quantity demanded) could reduce the firm's total revenue (= price * quantity). Alternatively, a higher price could increase the firm's total revenue. Whether total revenue will increase or decrease when prices change turns out to depend on the price elasticity of demand (aka, "elasticity of demand"). This concept measures how responsive the quantity demanded (of a good or service) is to a change in price.

Price Elasticity of Demand (Ed) = Percentage change in **Quantity demanded** / Percentage change in **Price**
(Elasticity of Demand)

Elasticities are commonly computed using the "arc method" or relative to the midpoint (or average) between conditions before and after a change, instead of relative to conditions "before" the change.

$$Ed = \frac{\frac{\text{Change in quantity demanded}}{\text{Average quantity demanded}}}{\frac{\text{Change in price}}{\text{Average price}}}$$

Using the formula above, price elasticities of demand technically yield negative answers (either the change in quantity demanded or the change in price will be negative while the other is positive). When interpreting price elasticities of demand, it is customary to ignore the negative sign (or to report its absolute value).

If Ed is greater than 1, demand is **elastic**, and total revenue will decline if the price is increased. If Ed is less than 1, demand is considered **inelastic**, and total revenue will increase if the price is increased. If elasticity is equal to 1, demand is said to be "**unit elastic**," (unitary) and total revenue is not sensitive to price changes. For example, goods that represent a larger fraction of consumers' budgets tend to be elastic (automobiles) and those that represent a smaller fraction of consumers' budgets tend to be inelastic (table salt).

> Assume a firm can sell (ie, it faces a quantity demanded of) 110 units for a product that is priced at $9 per unit. Thus, its total revenue currently would be 110 × $9 = $990. The firm is considering a price increase of $2 per unit or 20% (under the arc method).
>
> If the 20% price increase caused quantity demanded to decrease from 110 to 80 or by 30 units (30/95 (avg Q dem = 31.6%), price elasticity would be: 31.6% / 20% = 1.58, and demand would be elastic. Thus, total revenue would decline to 80 × $11 = $880.
>
> If the price increase caused quantity demanded to decrease only from 110 to 100, or by 10 units (9.5%), price elasticity would be 9.5% / 20% = 0.48, and demand would be inelastic. Thus, total revenue would increase to 100 × $11 = $1,100.
>
> | | | **Elastic** | **Inelastic** | **Unit elastic** |
> |---|---|---|---|---|
> | Unit price | $9 | $11 | $11 | $11 |
> | X units | x 110 | x 80 | x 100 | x 90 |
> | Total Rev. | $990 | $880 | $1,100 | $990 |
> | | | | | |
> | % ch Qt | | .316 | .095 | .20 |
> | % ch Pr | | .20 = 1.58 | .20 = .48 | .20 = 1.0 |

Elasticities are often larger if more time elapsed while the compared changes took place. For instance, in the short run, consumers may not be able to reduce their consumption of gasoline significantly when there is an increase in gasoline prices; ie, consumers' gasoline purchases are less responsive to price changes in the short term; consumers' demand for gasoline is more inelastic over the short term.

Over longer periods, however, they can switch to more efficient cars, change their work arrangements to reduce driving needs, and reduce their consumption of gasoline. The longer they have to adjust, the more they can reduce their gasoline consumption in response to price increases; ie, consumers' gasoline purchases are more responsive to price changes in the long term; consumers' demand for gasoline is more elastic over the long term.

Income Elasticity of Demand

Income elasticity of demand measures the effect of changes in (consumer) income on changes in the quantity demanded of a product. All elasticities (not just price elasticity of demand) may be computed using the arc method.

Income Elasticity = Percentage change in **quantity demanded**
of Demand Percentage change in **income**

A positive income elasticity indicates a **normal good**, which means that as consumer income increases, the quantity demanded of the normal good also increases. A negative number indicates an **inferior good**, so as income increases, the quantity demanded of the inferior good will decrease. For example, if incomes increase and the quantity demanded of new cars also increases, new cars are a normal good. However, incomes increase and the quantity demanded of used cars decreases, used cars are an inferior good.

Cross-Elasticity of Demand

Cross-elasticity of demand measures the change in the *quantity demanded of* a good to a change in the *price* of another good, and is used to determine if two different goods are **substitutes** (butter and margarine), which would result in a direct relationship (positive number), or **complements** (chips and salsa), which would result in an inverse relationship (negative number). If the coefficient is zero, the products are **unrelated**.

Cross-Elasticity = Percentage change in the **quantity demanded** for product **X**
of Demand   Percentage change in the **price** of product **Y**

> For example, if the price of butter increases by 10% and the quantity demanded of margarine increases by 12%, .12 / .10 = 1.2, then their cross-elasticity of demand is positive and they are *substitutes*. However, if the price of chips increases by 10% and the quantity demanded of salsa decreases by 12%, -.12 / .1= -1.2, then their cross-elasticity of demand is negative and they are *complements*.

Supply

A **supply curve** shows the *direct relationship* between the price of a product or service and the quantity that a group of producers and/or sellers are willing to supply at a particular time (ie, the quantity supplied). For instance, as the price of a product increases, the quantity supplied by sellers increases.

Remember that the s**UP**ply curve slopes up.

> Economists are very specific about the usage of the terms "supply" vs. "quantity supplied." The term "supply" refers to the supply curve that can be plotted on a graph with quantity supplied on the x-axis (horizontal) and price on the y-axis (vertical). The supply curve may also be thought of as a schedule listing multiple combinations of prices and quantities supplied (eg, those for points C and D in the graph). Thus, economists would not say that higher prices increase "supply." Instead, economists would say that at higher prices, "quantity supplied" is higher. As prices increase, one moves along the supply curve to find higher quantities supplied.

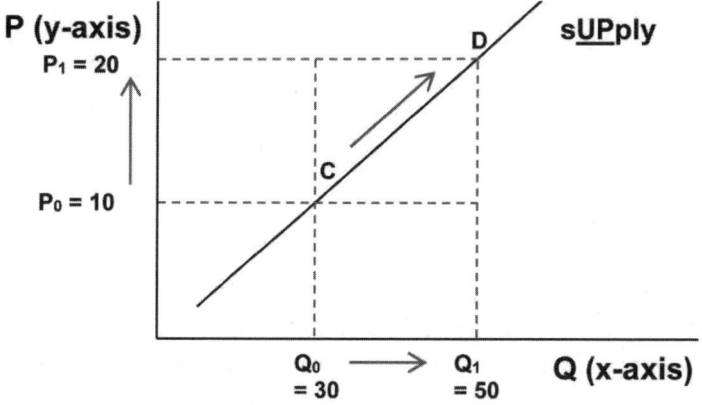

Just as in the case of demand, the **supply curve shifts** if there are changes in relevant factors other than a change in price. Economists use a variety of terms to describe supply curve shifts:

- **Changes in the supply curve where quantity supplied becomes larger for each and every price** are described as "the supply curve shifted outward" (not upward), "the supply curve shifted to the right," or "supply increased."

- **Changes in the supply curve where quantity supplied becomes smaller for each and every price** are described as "the supply curve shifted inward" (not downward), "the supply curve shifted to the left," or "supply decreased."

Below we show a supply curve shift to the right from S_0 to S_1. Note that at a price of 20, sellers supply 70 instead of 50 units. Alternatively, for a quantity of 50, sellers charge a (lower) price of 10 instead of 20.

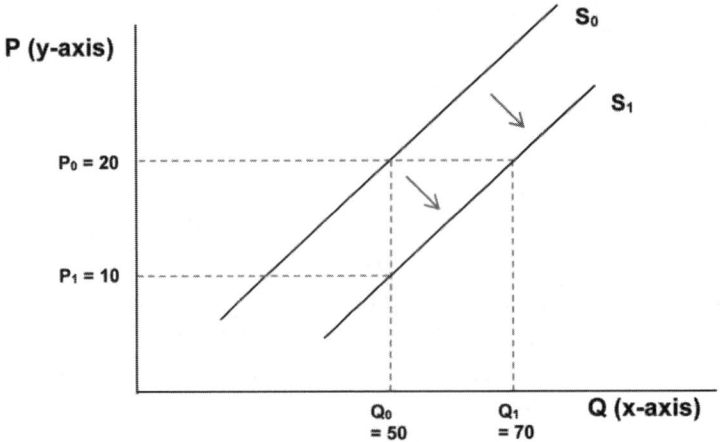

Some factors exhibit a **direct relationship** with the supply curve, meaning that increases in that factor cause the supply curve to shift outward (or supply to increase). Examples are:

- **Number of producers** – More producers normally increase the quantity supplied of a product at a given price. Entry by foreign suppliers into the U.S. auto market increases the supply of cars in the U.S.

- **Government subsidies** – Additional funding permits producers to purchase more inputs and, thus, increase quantity supplied at any given price.

- **Price expectations** - If producers expect higher prices, producers will increase their quantity supplied at any given price.

- **Technological advances** – Technological advances generally reduce production costs; hence, producers generally will increase their quantity supplied at any given price with an increase in technological advances.

Other factors exhibit an **inverse relationship** with the supply curve, meaning that increases in that factor cause the supply curve to *shift inward* (or supply to decrease). Examples are:

- **Increases in production costs (eg, production taxes)** – If producers' costs increase, producers will decrease their quantity supplied at a given price.

- **Prices of other products** – If producers may produce both product A and B, and producing A becomes more profitable, producers will decrease their quantity supplied of B at any given price.

Price Elasticity of Supply

A measure of how sensitive quantity supplied of a good or service is to a change in price or cost. Tells us how a change in prices will affect the quantity supplied by firms.

Price Elasticity of Supply (Es) = Percentage change in **Quantity Supplied**
(Elasticity of Supply)   Percentage change in **Price**

Owners of factors of production (labor, natural resources, capital, and entrepreneurship) aim to shift those factors to their most productive uses. These efforts are reflected in **economic rents** or **surpluses**, which are the excess of the payments for these factors when used most productively over their best alternative use (ie, opportunity cost).

Opportunity cost is also known as the benefit given up from not using the resource for another purpose (the foregone benefit of a rejected alternative *not* selected).

For example, if a worker accepts a job paying $60,000 instead of another offering $50,000, the worker would have received an economic rent of $10,000 from accepting the higher paying job, and faced an opportunity cost of $50,000 by doing so.

For suppliers themselves, **economic profit** refers to the excess of the profits they are receiving over the **normal profit rate** in the economy. Economic profits usually result in more suppliers entering the market, and economic losses will usually result in suppliers exiting the market.

Market Equilibrium

Generally, as long as governments do not interfere, prices, quantities supplied, and quantities demanded adjust to an equilibrium level, where there is adequate supply to satisfy buyers and adequate demand. Point E, where the demand and supply curves cross in the graph below, identifies such an equilibrium point. At the equilibrium price: **quantity demanded = quantity supplied**, so all the goods offered for sale will be sold.

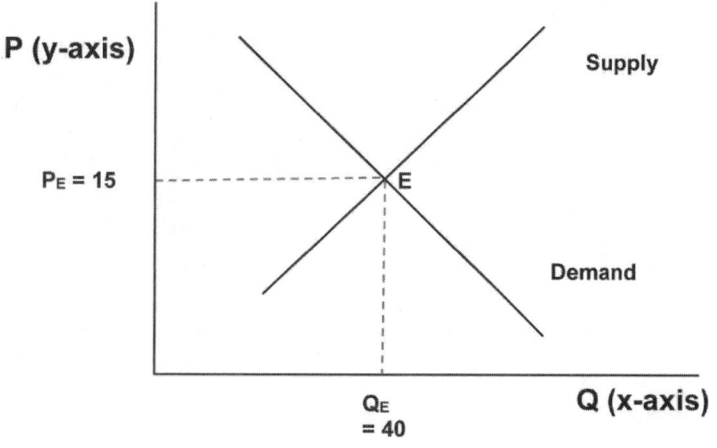

Some Government Actions that Affect Equilibrium

If governments impose a **price ceiling** (eg, setting the maximum legal price at which a product or service may be sold at $7) below equilibrium (ie, $15), the quantity demanded (ie, 56) will exceed quantity supplied (ie, 24), resulting in *shortages of goods* (ie, 56 – 24 = 32 is the number of units that consumers would like to purchase at that price but are unable to; the lower line in the graph below represents the price ceiling and helps identify the various quantities).

For example, some cities set maximum rents that result in apartment shortages.

If governments impose a **price floor** (eg, setting the minimum legal price at which a product or service may be sold at $17) above equilibrium, the quantity supplied (ie, 52) will exceed quantity demanded (ie, 28), resulting in unpurchased *surpluses of goods or services* (ie, 52 – 28 = 24 is the number of units that suppliers would like to sell at that price but are unable to; the upper line in the graph below represents the price floor and helps identify the various quantities).

For example, a minimum wage for unskilled workers results in higher unemployment rates for unskilled workers.

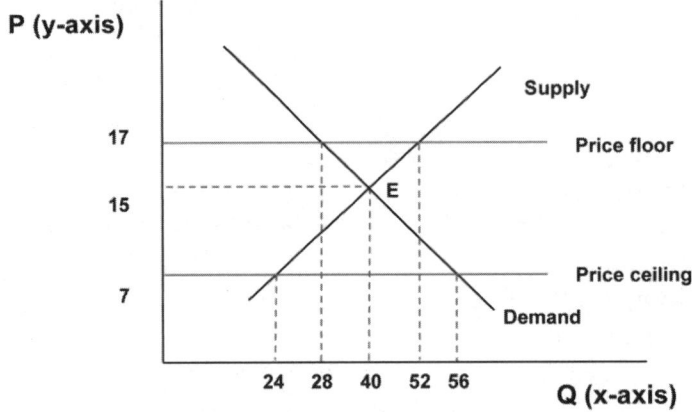

Shifts in demand and supply lead to somewhat predictable changes from an initial combination of equilibrium price and equilibrium quantity to a new combination:

Comparing an Initial and a New Equilibrium Resulting from an Increase in Demand

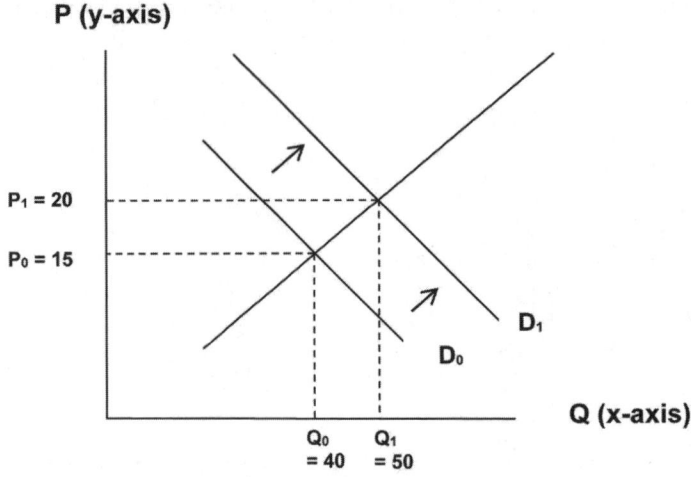

Comparing an Initial and a New Equilibrium Resulting from an Increase in Supply

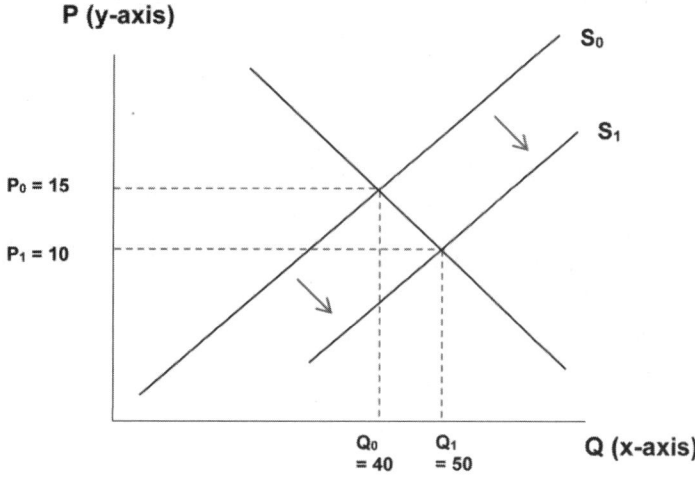

Below we summarize the changes in equilibrium price and quantity resulting from various shifts in supply and demand curves:

Demand	Supply	Equilibrium Price	Quantity Purchased
Increase	No change	Increase	Increase
Decrease	No change	Decrease	Decrease
No change	Increase	Decrease	Increase
No change	Decrease	Increase	Decrease
Increase	Increase	**Uncertain**	Increase
Decrease	Decrease	**Uncertain**	Decrease
Increase	Decrease	Increase	**Uncertain**
Decrease	Increase	Decrease	**Uncertain**

Consumers

Microeconomics assumes that consumers seek to maximize their *satisfaction* (aka, **utility**). That is, people will spend money on one thing rather than another such that the **marginal utility** of spending money on the product or service chosen will be greater than from the forgone alternatives.

According to the **law of diminishing marginal utility**, the more a consumer consumes of a particular product, the less satisfying the next unit of that product will be. For example, the twentieth cookie doesn't taste nearly as good as the first one.

A consumer maximizes total satisfaction when the last dollar spent on each product generates the same amount of marginal utility. That is, if the marginal utility per dollar is greater from product A than product B, the consumer will:

- Increase consumption of product A, reducing its marginal utility per dollar, and
- Decrease consumption of product B, until marginal utility per dollar is equal for both products A and B, and ultimately across all products.

Consumers do not have unlimited amounts of money to spend. The available income of a consumer after subtracting mandatory payment of taxes (or adding receipt of government benefits, if applicable) is known as **personal disposable income.** Consumers have only two choices with each dollar of personal disposable income: they can either spend (consume) it or save it.

- The **marginal propensity to consume (MPC)** is the percentage of the next dollar of income that the consumer would be expected to spend (change in consumption / change in income).

- The **marginal propensity to save (MPS)** is the percentage of the next dollar that the consumer would be expected to save (change in savings / change in income).

- Since these are the only choices, the two calculations must add up to 100%, MPS + MPC = 1.

$$\text{MPS} = \frac{\text{Change in Savings}}{\text{Change in Disposable income}} \qquad \text{MPC} = \frac{\text{Change in Consumption (spending)}}{\text{Change in Disposable income}}$$

Production Costs

- **Total costs (TC)** – The sum of fixed and variable costs (TC = FC + VC). *Average total costs* (ATC) are total costs divided by the number of units produced.
    - **Fixed costs (FC)** – Costs that won't change (eg, rent) even when there is a change in the level of production.
        - *Average fixed costs* (AFC) are total fixed costs divided by the number of units produced.
    - **Variable costs (VC)** – Costs that rise as production rises (eg, materials used in the manufacture of the product).
        - *Average variable costs* (AVC) are total variable costs divided by the number of units produced.
        - Over periods of time that are long enough, all costs are *variable*, since firms may change how much they use of any input (hire more or fewer hourly or salaried workers, expand factories, etc.). In the long run, even if a firm may adjust its level of usage of all inputs, it may find that increases in production may reduce, have no effect on, or increase their per unit (or average) costs.
- **Marginal cost (MC)** – The increase in cost that results from producing one extra unit.
    - Only variable costs are relevant since fixed costs won't increase in such circumstances.
- **Marginal Revenue (MR)** - The change in total revenue (TR) associated with the sale of one more unit of output.

To **maximize profits**, managers would choose levels of production (output or quantity) such that their company's **marginal revenue equals** their **marginal cost**. If the marginal revenue of producing one extra unit exceeds its marginal cost, it is profitable to increase production.

In the following graph, MR = MC for a quantity of 50.
- The total cost (TC) is $1,200 (ATC × Q = $24 × 50).
- The firm would set the price at the maximum possible level given the demand curve (30), not at the marginal revenue (of about 12).
- Total revenue (TR) is $1,500 (P × Q = $30 × 50). Profit is $300 (TR − TC = $1,500 − $1,200).
- Note that the profit maximizing quantity does not involve the minimum level of ATC (ie, where MC crosses ATC), but a slightly higher level (24).

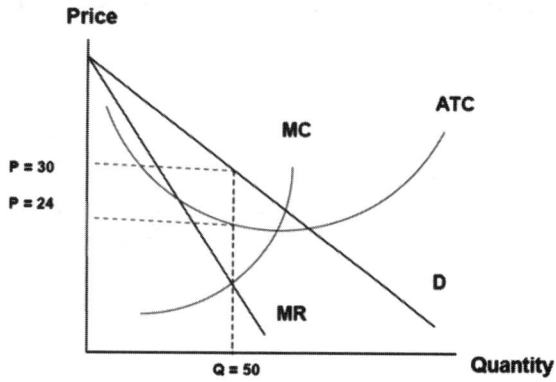

Returns to scale

Returns to scale are the increases in units produced (output) that result from increases in production costs (ie, costs of inputs).

Returns to scale = Percentage increase in **output** / Percentage increase in **input**

- At lower levels of production (and use of inputs), many firms face returns to scale **greater than 1**, or **increasing returns to scale**. Alternatively, these firms may be described as facing **economies of scale**, or increased efficiencies from producing more units of a product. This may result from:
    - Spreading fixed costs over larger numbers of units
    - Being able to save on transaction and transportation costs by buying in larger quantities
    - Having employees specialize in different tasks and improve their abilities
    - Automatic procedures that are performed repetitively

- Larger levels of production (and use of inputs) may eventually result in returns to scale **smaller than 1**, or **decreasing returns to scale**. These firms may also be described as facing **diseconomies of scale**, or increased inefficiencies. This may result from:
    - Increasing volumes of inventory stored, making retrieval more difficult
    - Increasing the number of employees working, making effective supervision more difficult
    - Hiring lower skilled workers, resulting in more errors and a lower product acceptance rate

- Between increasing and decreasing returns to scale, firms may operate in ranges of levels of production (and of use of inputs) where they face **constant returns to scale**. Over this range, increasing production would not affect their average costs.

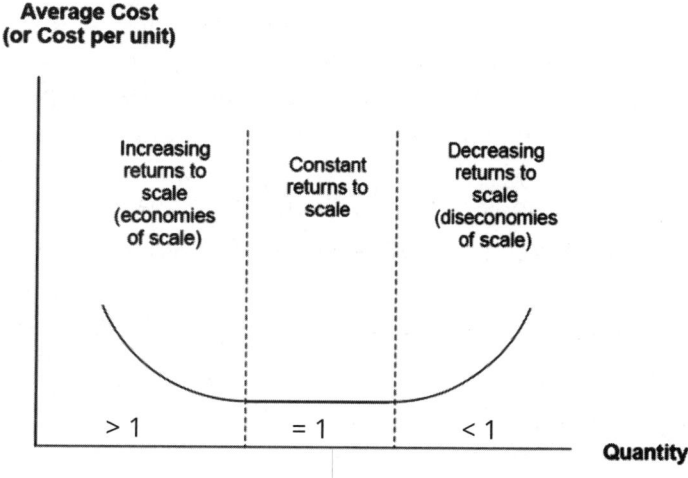

Lecture 1.02 – Market Structure & Industry Analysis

Overview

Economics defines an **industry** as a group of firms that produce products or services that consumers would identify as similar enough to be considered substitutes. To better understand how firms and industries operate, economists have developed several key models of market structures that illustrate varying levels of competition. Ranging from most to least competitive, these models are:

- Perfect competition
- Monopolistic competition
- Oligopoly (or oligopolistic competition)
- Pure monopoly

Perfect (or Pure) Competition

While few, if any, industries or markets may actually be perfectly competitive, having a model of perfect competition is useful in terms of assessing how close or far various industries may come to being perfectly competitive. Perfect competition would involve a situation with large numbers of sellers, where each individual seller is too small to affect the overall market price, easy entry and exit of suppliers (no barriers to entry/exit), a homogeneous (standardized or identical) product, and an absence of non-price competition (such as advertising and perceived quality differences).

Some commodities markets (wheat, soybeans, corn, etc.) are commonly mentioned as coming closest to being perfectly competitive. In a perfectly competitive market, an individual firm effectively faces a horizontal demand curve and prices are perfectly elastic: The firm can sell as many goods as it can produce at the equilibrium price but no goods at a higher price. In other words, the firm is a *price taker*. Thus, for the individual firm, the equilibrium market price is its marginal revenue curve for all production levels. The individual firm faces an incentive to expand quantity produced until its marginal costs rise to equal the equilibrium market price (which is the firm's marginal revenue curve).

While each individual firm alone has no effect on the overall market price and the demand curve for each individual firm is horizontal, the *market demand curve* is downward sloping. Therefore, quantity demanded increases if entry of more suppliers lowers prices and quantity demanded decreases if exit by some suppliers raises prices. If the equilibrium market price is high enough that individual firms earn economic profits, large numbers of new suppliers will enter the market, lowering prices until firms earn only normal profits (ie, an economic profit of zero). If the equilibrium market price is so low that individual firms incur economic losses, large numbers of the most marginal (ie, least efficient) suppliers will exit the market, lifting prices until the remaining firms earn normal profits.

To recap, an industry would be *perfectly competitive* if it met the following conditions:

- It includes a large number of sellers, each of which is too small to affect the overall market price.
- All firms sell a homogeneous (ie, largely identical) product (eg, wheat, soybeans, corn, etc.).
- There is no non-price competition (eg, no advertising).
- Firms may enter or exit the market very easily (ie, there are no significant barriers to entry, ceilings or floors).

Economic Concepts   BEC 1

- Each individual firm faces a demand curve that is perfectly elastic (horizontal).

Pure Monopoly

In this model, there is only one firm that sells a product or service for which there are no close substitutes. Monopolies may exist as a result of public policy or of "technical" conditions. Common examples of monopolies resulting from public policy include the local monopolies that cable companies operate in most areas or the national monopolies that each drug manufacturer has for each given product for which it has a **patent**, which ultimately is a *barrier to entry*.

For markets where there is no relevant range of output, where decreasing returns to scale set in, **natural monopolies** may exist as economies of scale would permit the largest firm to underprice, and eliminate, all others. Companies with lower costs may seek to engage in **predatory pricing**, charging temporarily low prices to drive their competitors out of existence, only to increase their prices as monopolists once they have eliminated their competitors. Unless restricted by regulation, a pure monopoly would have great pricing power and, producing only to the level where marginal revenue equals marginal costs, would result in economic profits (earnings higher than normal profits), with substantially higher prices and lower output than under more competitive market structures in both the short and long runs.

Various laws have been passed to reduce anticompetitive market practices, including:
- **The Sherman Act** (1890) prohibited price fixing, boycotts, market division, and restricted resale agreements among suppliers.
- **The Clayton Act** (1914) prohibited stock mergers that reduce competition, price discrimination, and common directorships among competing firms.
- **The Robinson-Patman Act** (1936) prohibited discounts to large purchasers not based on cost differentials.
- **The Celler-Kefauver Act** (1950) prohibits acquisition of the assets of a competitor if it would reduce competition.

To recap, an industry would be a *pure monopoly* if it met the following conditions:
- There is only one producer.
- No close substitutes are available.
- There is blocked entry (patent or Government franchise-public utility).
- The firm's Demand curve is substantially downward sloping (almost vertical).

Monopolistic Competition

In this model, large numbers of firms produce heterogeneous products and engage in a great deal of nonprice competition. Entry and exit are relatively easy, but not as easy as under perfect competition. The products offered by different firms are close substitutes, but not identical. Examples might include mom-and-pop restaurants, groceries, hairdressers, etc.

Firms' efforts to differentiate their products in the minds of their customers give firms some control over prices; that is, individual firms' demand curves and the marginal revenue curves are not completely horizontal as in perfect competition, but are slightly or somewhat downward sloping. Thus, as firms produce to the point where marginal revenue equals marginal costs, this model yields prices that are somewhat higher and quantities that are somewhat lower than under perfect competition.

In this model, however, easy entry and exit generally tends to eliminate large economic profits. Thus, prices are generally substantially lower and quantities substantially higher than in pure monopoly situations. Again, products and services under monopolistic competition tend to be priced somewhat higher than in a perfectly competitive market, but substantially lower than in a pure monopoly.

To recap, an industry would be *monopolistically competitive* if it met the following conditions:

- It includes a large number of sellers.
- Firms sell heterogeneous products.
- There is lots of non-price competition (advertising, products with slightly differing features, actual quality differences).
- It is relatively easy to enter and exit the market.
- Each individual firm faces a demand curve that is slightly or somewhat downward sloping.

Some customers may be willing to pay higher prices than others. **Price discrimination** works most effectively when consumers are split into distinct segments. For example, consumers buying prestige shampoo for humans generally are willing to pay more than consumers buying shampoo for horses—even if the formula is the same; with different packaging, the producer may charge more to purchasers intending to use the shampoo on humans. A seller may contrive segmentation where none naturally exists, with coupons or early bird sales. For instance, a seller may give significant discounts to the first 100 shoppers on the day after the Thanksgiving holidays or small discounts to buyers with coupons placed in strategically chosen periodicals.

Oligopoly (or Oligopolistic Competition)

In this type of market structure, significant barriers to entry ensure that there are only a small number of (typically large) firms. Barriers to entry may result from a variety of reasons: Developing new products or factories may be very costly or involve substantial lags from development to sales (eg, automobiles and aerospace) or setting up the infrastructure to service large numbers of customers may be costly (eg, car dealerships). In some cases, government licensing effectively creates oligopolies (eg, cell companies, etc.). In oligopolistic competition, products may be homogeneous (such as a given grade of oil) or heterogeneous (such as the airline manufacturing market). In oligopolistic markets, since there are few competitors, the actions by one firm are likely to affect the decisions of other firms (**game theory**), and the market as a whole.

Because the actions of rivals cannot be easily predicted in such a strategic setting, there is not a single model that describes well all markets with few firms. In some cases, a company's decision to gain market share by lowering its prices may result in other companies matching its pricing (ie, there would be a **price war** and market shares might not change appreciably). Thus, oligopolistic firms often attempt to engage in non-price competition (by product differentiation or providing high levels of service). In other oligopolistic markets, a small number of smaller firms simply base their pricing on that of a larger firm that acts as a pricing leader.

Governments seek to regulate oligopolistic competition variously, for instance, by forbidding formal quantity agreements among competitors, known as **cartels** and price fixing (or collusive pricing). A concentration ratio is a measure of the total output of an industry by a certain number of firms in that industry, such as the 4 or 8 largest. The Herfindahl index (concentration ratio) is a measure of the size of firms within an industry. These measures indicate the degree to which an industry is oligopolistic. Under oligopolistic competition, products and services tend to be priced

Economic Concepts

substantially higher than under monopolistic competition, since barriers to entry cause economic profits to remain, but pricing is typically somewhat lower than under pure monopoly.

To recap, an industry would be *an Oligopoly* if it met the following conditions:
- A small number of large sellers
- Barriers to entry (cost or patents)
- Non-price competition exists.
- Rival actions are observed.
- The firm's Demand curve is Kinked.

Industry Analysis

To analyze their industry, firms may use **competitor analysis** to understand and predict the behavior of a major competitor. The two components of competitor analysis are collecting information and using that information to understand, predict and respond to that competitor. Firms must also analyze their **target market,** which involves determining who their customers are and why they are purchasing their products.

Strategic planning involves organizations' efforts to identify their long-term goals and to determine how best to reach those goals. To develop **business strategies**, managers commonly engage in formal analyses of their *strengths, weaknesses, opportunities, and threats* (ie, **SWOT** analyses).

Formal strategic planning typically involves several steps. A typical first step involves creating (or updating) an organization's **mission statement**, which outlines the long-term purposes of an organization. The purposes of different organizations vary across the different types of organizations, ranging, for instance, from for-profit, family, mutual or cooperative, government, or charitable organizations (eg, delivering profits to owners, delivering a quality product to consumers, serving unmet needs of specific groups, etc.). Some organizations create a values statement first, from which the mission statement flows.

After the organization has a mission statement, it may set its **goals and objectives**. The boundary between goals and objectives is definitional and different organizations may use different terms but, in general, goals are expressed in general terms (eg, deliver good returns to investors) and objectives (often several objectives per goal) set specific targets (eg, increase ROE from 15% to 20% within 5 years).

Next, organizations determine what **actions** should be taken to meet their goals and objectives and establish mechanisms to collect data to be able to engage in **assessment** of whether the goals and objectives were met. Once data has been collected, organizations review whether their actions were successful and restart the cycle, perhaps revising strategic plans, but specifically using the data and assessment results to develop new action plans.

To successfully implement their strategies, firms must ensure that formal strategies are not simply developed by an ad hoc committee and then not implemented, but rather that management is on board with the development and implementation of its business strategies. **Business strategies** are commonly classified as product differentiation or cost leadership strategies.

- **Product differentiation strategies** involve developing a range of slightly different products that are more attractive to one's target markets or simply to ensure that they differ substantially from competitors' offerings. This strategy will (1) make the firm's sales less responsive to changes in the prices charged by other competitors, (2) allow the firm to charge different prices (ie, some higher)

for different products, and (3) ultimately allow the firm to charge higher prices than otherwise (and potentially higher than those of one's competitors). Products may differ in many ways:
- *Physical differences* – individual features, quality, appearance
- *Perceived differences* – image, brand name, advertising
- *Customer support differences* – return policies, technical support

- **Cost leadership strategies** concentrate on *cutting the costs* of producing, selling, and distributing a firm's range of products. These strategies include:
  - *Process reengineering* – In-depth redesigns of firms' existing processes to improve performance.
  - *Lean manufacturing* – Identifying and removing the misuse of resources in the firms' existing production processes.
  - *Supply chain management* – Sharing relevant information in the chain of sales that ranges from the final consumer to the various levels of suppliers, independently of whether each step took place within one's firm or not. For example, all steps of the chain, from retailers to wholesalers to suppliers and supplier's suppliers, might be able to operate with leaner inventories overall if each party shared more readily its plans and forecasts.

Lecture 1.03 – Macroeconomic Impacts on Business

Overview

Macroeconomics is the study of the economy as a whole. Key concerns in macroeconomics include unemployment, inflation, and long-term economic growth. Other subsidiary concerns in macroeconomics include lending growth, interest rates, exchange rates, the trade balance, and government budget deficits and debts.

Macroeconomics studies the roles of households (consumers), (nonfinancial) businesses, governments, the financial sector, and foreign economies in causing and/or alleviating undesired fluctuations in domestic economic conditions. For example, governments may influence economic decision making through taxes (including tariffs on trade) that favor or disfavor certain activities, through their spending of tax revenues, and through regulatory policies that encourage or discourage various activities.

> Note that the AICPA is no longer testing macroeconomics in general. They are, however, still testing how macroeconomic concepts, such as inflation and interest rates, affect industries and businesses; therefore, we still need to cover some of the basics.

Measures of Economic Conditions

- **Gross Domestic Product (GDP) or Nominal GDP** – This is the total dollar value, at current (or nominal) market prices, of all the "final" goods and services produced **within one country's borders**, regardless of the citizenship of the individual residents or the country of headquarters of the companies involved during a period of time (typically a year). The word "final" refers to the fact that GDP aims to avoid double counting of inputs used in the production of other products.

- **Real GDP** – Real GDP (aka, inflation-corrected GDP) is the total dollar value of all the final goods and services produced, expressed using a price level that is constant over time.

  o **Potential GDP** – This estimates the degree to which the economy is either underutilizing resources or "overheating." If, for instance, actual real GDP falls short of potential real GDP, resources will be underused (unemployment rates will be higher). If actual real GDP exceeds potential real GDP, the economy will be overheating (resulting in unsustainably low unemployment rates, boom conditions in various markets, and eventually price inflation).

  o Similar to potential GDP are the concepts of "natural" or **"nonaccelerating-inflation" rate of unemployment (NAIRU).** If the actual unemployment rate falls below NAIRU, boom conditions follow in the short term and problems, such as higher inflation, eventually follow.

- **Gross National Product (GNP)** – GNP is the total dollar value of all goods and services produced by a country's **residents**, regardless of where they were produced. GNP differs from GDP in that GNP includes, for instance, earnings of U.S. companies abroad, and excludes earnings of foreign companies within the U.S.

- **Inflation** – Commonly reported on an annual basis, inflation is the percentage rate of increase in the price level of goods and services. Rising inflation means that individuals have less purchasing power over time.

  o With respect to financial statements, inflation tends to distort accounting measures that do not change over time (eg, assets and depreciation entered using historic values). Other accounting measures, such as revenues (prices), costs (wages and interest), and resulting earnings, are affected more simultaneously.

- o **Hyperinflation** is similar to inflation, except that the value of the currency is decreased at a much faster rate, so prices increase much more rapidly.
- **Aggregate Demand & Supply** – Aggregate demand and supply curves describe the relationship between the overall levels of prices and production of goods and services of an entire economy.
  - o An **aggregate demand curve** represents the relationship between (1) **total expenditures** by consumers, businesses, government, and the foreign sector and (2) the **price** level. The standard assumption is that looser fiscal policy (ie, larger government budget deficits) and looser monetary policy (ie, lower interest rates) increase aggregate demand.
  - o An **aggregate supply curve** represents the relationship between (1) **total goods and services produced** and (2) the **price** level, at a given point of time. The standard assumption is that tighter fiscal policy and tighter monetary policy will decrease aggregate demand. We'll review fiscal and monetary policy in more detail below.
- **Deflation** – This is negative inflation, or a general decline in the price level (ie, not a decline in the prices of just a few goods). Periods of weak economic growth (like the 1930's in the U.S.) are sometimes accompanied by bouts of very low inflation or outright deflation, and by low nominal interest rates.
  - o Businesses may not want to take loans when they are uncertain about how well the economy will perform (ie, will sales justify the loan?).
  - o The most accepted solution for deflation is *to increase the money supply*.

Measures of Price Inflation

There are three common measures of price inflation:

- The **consumer price index (CPI)** compares the price of a fixed basket of goods and services that a typical urban consumer might purchase in an earlier base period (eg, 100 in 1982-84) and the price of the same basket of goods and services at later times. The CPI is commonly used to convert "nominal" figures that are not readily comparable across years into "real" figures that use the same level of prices and are therefore more comparable.

  > A worker earned and spent $40,000 in 2002 when the CPI was 180. The same worker earned (and spent) $50,000 in 2012 when the CPI was 230. Converting the $40,000 from 2002 into 2012 dollars, one finds that the income in 2002 purchased the equivalent of $51,111 in 2012 (= $40,000 × 230 / 180). Thus, the worker's real income is 97.8% ($50,000 / 51,111) of what it used to be (ie, it fell by 2.2%)

- The **producer price index (PPI)** compares the price of a fixed basket of goods, inputs, and materials purchased by producers at the **wholesale** level, instead of focusing on the prices paid at the retail level by consumers.
- The **GDP deflator** is the most comprehensive measure of price levels, including prices paid by all parties included in GDP instead of only consumers. The GDP deflator is the index used to convert nominal GDP into real GDP.

Causes of Inflation

Demand-Pull Inflation

When aggregate spending increases, the **aggregate demand curve (AD)** moves to the **right**, causing the market equilibrium to occur at higher price levels. **Excess demand** bids up the cost of labor and other resources. Excess demand may be a result, for instance, of improved expectations by consumers or businesses, of the foreign sector, or from government fiscal and monetary policy that turned out to be too loose. According to this simplified model, the equilibrium point occurs at **higher** levels of both **prices and quantity**.

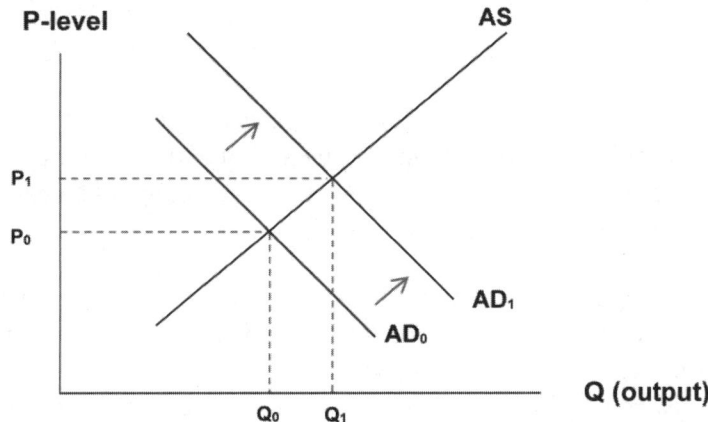

Cost-Push Inflation

As suppliers face **increases** in input **costs** (eg, oil), the **aggregate supply curve** shifts to the **left**, causing market equilibrium to occur at a **higher price** level and **lower quantity**.

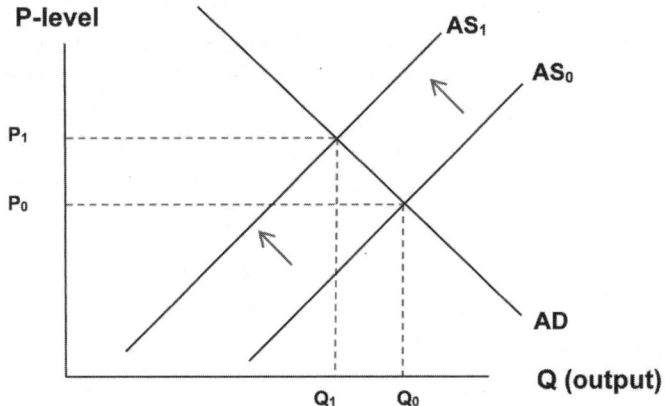

Multiplier Effect

If an economy is producing below its potential, increases in spending by consumers, businesses, the government, or the foreign sector may cause increases in output that exceed the increase in spending. This is called the **multiplier effect.** It mobilizes otherwise idle or unemployed resources, as the first round of increased spending becomes income to previously underutilized suppliers, who in turn spend more, increasing the income of other suppliers, etc.

In a simplified macroeconomic model, the size of the multiplier effect depends on the percentage of increased income that consumers are likely to spend—the **marginal propensity to consume (MPC)**—and the related percentage of increased income that they will save—the **marginal propensity to save (MPS).**

Lecture 1.04 – Business Cycles & Economic Indicators

Overview

Business cycles are fluctuations in economic production (output) typically lasting several years. Some business cycles have been shorter (barely a couple of years) and others longer (over a decade). Some business cycles are deep, involving large fluctuations and others relatively shallower.

By convention, each business cycle includes one **recession** (or contraction) and one **expansion**. Each recession begins at the **peak** (or maximum level of output) from the previous expansion and ends at its **trough** (or minimum level of output for the recession). Each expansion begins at the trough of the previous recession and ends at the next peak.

The early stages of expansions are called **recoveries**. Recoveries are commonly described as having become full expansions when the previous peak is passed. Over the long term, nearly all measures of economic activity and personal well-being have grown or improved enormously in virtually every capitalist economy. However, growth has not taken place at a steady pace, but typically alternates between longer periods of strong growth and shorter periods of decline.

Terms used in connection with the business cycle include:

- **Expansion** – Typically extended period (ie, several years) of increased economic production. The early stages of many expansions (ie, recoveries) during the second half of the twentieth century were marked by fast declines in unemployment rates. However, declines in unemployment have grown increasingly slower (ie, so-called **jobless recoveries**) following each of the last three recessions (ie, those of 1990-1991, 2001, and 2007-2009). The final stages of many expansions during the twentieth century were marked by booming economic conditions, including GDP above potential and higher rates of inflation. Increased spending will cause a positive shift in the demand curve to the right (higher equilibrium GDP). Technological advances will also cause a positive shift in the supply curve, also resulting in a higher equilibrium GDP.

- **Recession (or Contraction)** – Typically briefer periods (ie, several months or only a few years) of decreased economic production. Formally, the business cycle dating committee of the National Bureau of Economic Research (NBER, technically a non-profit) determines the beginning and end of recessions and expansions based on a variety of parameters. As a rule of thumb, economists describe recessions as periods of at least two consecutive quarters of negative growth in real GDP. During the twentieth century, **many recessions followed efforts by the Federal Reserve (see section below on monetary policy) to restrain higher inflation rates through increases in interest rates**. The declines in economic production during recessions are accompanied by declines in employment and increases in unemployment rates (Okun's law provides a commonly-mentioned rule of thumb relating declines in GDP and increases in unemployment). At the end of recessions, GDP is well below potential. Periods of decreased aggregate spending will shift the demand curve to the left and result in a lower equilibrium GDP. Trade wars cause a negative shift in the supply curve and also cause a decline in GDP.

- **Depression** – A recession that is either particularly deep or long lasting. There is no formal agreement as to the boundary between recession and depression. For perspective, the Great Depression of 1929-1933 involved declines in real GDP of 27% and increases in unemployment rates from 3.2% to 25.2%. Since unemployment rates had declined only to 9.9% by 1941, the Great Depression is often dated as having spanned 1929-1941. In contrast, the recent Great Recession was the deepest recession since World War II and involved declines in real GDP of 4.7% and increases in unemployment rates from 4.7% to 10.1%.

- **Recovery** – The early stages of an expansion, commonly thought to become a full expansion when the peak from the previous expansion is passed.

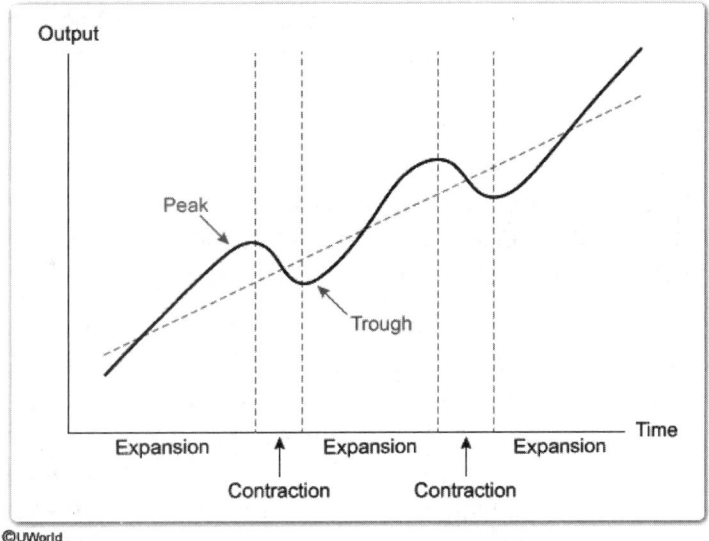

Indicators of Economic Activity

Economists track many indicators to gauge, evaluate, and predict current and future economic conditions. These indicators may be classified into three broad categories:

- **Leading Indicators** – Seek to predict whether expansions (or recessions) are likely to end within the next few months. Economists have experimented with many indicators for these purposes, but their effectiveness, of course, varies across business cycles. Some commonly used leading indicators include:
    - Changes in **stock market** prices
    - Average hours worked per week
    - **New orders for durable goods**
    - Average initial claims for unemployment insurance
    - Building permits
    - **New private housing starts**
- **Coincident Indicators** – Normally move up and down simultaneously (coincide) with economic expansions and recessions. Examples include **industrial production** and manufacturing and trade sales.
- **Lagging indicators** – Only move up and down months after economic conditions change. Examples include the **average prime rate** for bank loans, the **average duration of unemployment,** and the **unemployment rate**.

Increases in economic growth do not necessarily result mechanically in increases in job growth in the short term. For instance, if businesses are afraid that growth is temporary, they may rely on overtime from existing employees rather than hiring new workers. However, in the long term, subject to long and variable lags, economic growth does tend to result in job growth. In a sense, sustained declines in the **unemployment rates** serve as one of the most important lagging indicators of economic recovery.

Unemployment

Economists commonly identify three or four **types of unemployment:**

- **Frictional unemployment** – affects workers who are unemployed as a result of the normal turnover of workers between jobs or of new entrants into the work force. Some of these workers may leave their employers voluntarily searching for something better. In other cases, employers may have discontinued employment, but the employees find new work relatively quickly. In a mobile society and given unavoidable "imperfections in the labor market," or "search costs" (ie, the time needed to find and compare alternative jobs and to decide that it is not worth waiting for something else better), market economies unavoidably always have some level of this type of unemployment, even in "full" employment.

- **Structural unemployment** – affects workers who lose their jobs as a result of changes in the demands for goods and services (eg, manufacturers of horse buggies when automobiles took off) or of technological advances that reduce the need for their current skills (eg, car mechanics unused to electronics in automobiles). Addressing this type of unemployment normally requires retraining. The problem underlying this type of unemployment is not deficient aggregate demand, but the speed with which workers may be retrained to meet new demands and technologies.

- **Cyclical unemployment** – involves job losses resulting from the fluctuations in the business cycle. This type of unemployment is the key concern during recessions and decreases during expansions.

Note: The "*Full*-employment," "natural," or "nonaccelerating-inflation" rate of unemployment (NAIRU) rates, are the rates below which unemployment may not fall sustainably without causing boom conditions that eventually may result in higher rates of inflation. If we identify only the three types of unemployment above, NAIRU would largely be the sum of *frictional and structural* unemployment.

- **Institutional unemployment** – Some economists identify this type of unemployment as that affecting workers who cannot find employment as a result of government restrictions on the economy, eg, wage floors for younger workers, restrictions on the ability of small businesses to launch, etc. Since injections of aggregate demand may not help these workers and result in inflation, this type of unemployment would also be part of NAIRU. Differences in NAIRU across countries often result from different institutional frameworks and, thus, from different levels of institutional unemployment.

Lecture 1.05 – Interest Rates & Government Involvement

Interest Rates

Interest rates refer to the prices that:

- Borrowers (households, businesses, governments) pay in exchange for "funds" (eg, loans and bonds)
- Lenders (or depositors) receive in exchange for forgoing the use of their funds for various periods of time (eg, mortgages vs. certificates of deposit)

Interest rates are determined by the demand and supply of funds. Businesses, for instance, may demand funds (loans) if they expect the return on their projects to exceed the interest rate they pay. Governments and households (eg, students and younger home buyers) are, of course, also large demanders of funds (borrowers).

The supply of funds is affected by past and current saving by households (eg, older ones) and many firms, but also by government monetary policy. Increases in the demand for loans (whether by households, businesses, or governments) put upward pressure on interest rates.

Types of interest rates include:

- **Nominal interest rates** – Those regularly quoted by financial institutions. Setting interest rates, financial institutions and markets will include "premiums" to protect themselves against expected problems, such as inflation, loan defaults ("credit risk"), etc. Of course, actual levels of inflation and loan defaults often vary from those expected when interest rates are originally set.

- **Real interest rates** – Those adjusted for inflation. Calculations of real interest rates often seek to incorporate the rate of inflation that is expected in the future. In practice, such expectations typically largely mimic recent historical experience.

- **Risk-free interest rates** – Those that would be charged to borrowers if lenders had an absolute certainty of being repaid (ie, no credit risk). Financial markets largely treat the rates paid on conventional United States Treasury securities (or Treasurys, ie, it is not spelled Treasuries) as indicators of risk-free interest rates. The U.S. Treasury issues securities through a large range of maturities (from 4 weeks to 30 years) in both a conventional format (where the buyer bears inflation risk) and in an inflation-indexed format (ie, TIPS, where buyers are compensated for deviations in the CPI). Interest rates on conventional U.S. Treasurys are indicators of risk-free rates plus an inflation premium. Interest rates on TIPS are indicators of risk-free rates. The difference between conventional and TIPS Treasurys for a given maturity are indicators of expected inflation over that maturity (even though there are also, typically small, liquidity premiums involved). For instance, if 10-year conventional Treasurys yield 2.0% and the 10-year TIPS yield -0.5%, then the expected inflation rate (plus the difference in liquidity premiums) over the next ten years would be 2.5%.

- **Federal funds rate** – The rate that commercial banks charge and pay one another for short-term loans of reserves (ie, unlent cash, also called "federal funds") at the Federal Reserve System (the U.S. central bank, commonly called the "Fed"). In recent decades, the Fed has conducted monetary policy largely through "open market operations," ie, setting a target rate for the federal funds rate and buying and selling short-term U.S. Treasurys (bills) to ensure that the actual (effective) rate in the federal funds market matched its target. Below, in the section on monetary policy, we explain the details further.

- **Prime rate** – The rate banks charge their most creditworthy business customers on short-term loans. Throughout the last two decades, most banks have routinely set their prime rates at a 3% premium over the federal funds rate.

Government Involvement in the Economy

While the proper role and extent of government involvement is likely to be debated indefinitely, governments are very likely to continue to regularly intervene in many aspects of the economy for the foreseeable future through **fiscal policy, monetary policy,** and **regulatory policy**.

Fiscal Policy

Fiscal Policy involves governments setting, applying, and changing levels of taxes, subsidies, and government spending. Many economists argue that, if (1) economic production (GDP) is below potential, (2) the financial sector is failing to lend funds adequately, and (3) unemployment rates are too high, then governments may successfully use **deficit spending** as **expansionary fiscal** policy to increase aggregate demand and, thus, output. Deficit spending involves increasing spending levels without increasing tax revenues by an equivalent amount, or lowering tax revenues without decreasing spending by an equivalent amount.

The (federal) **deficit** is the amount by which (federal) government expenditures (or spending or outlays) exceed (federal tax) revenues (or inlays) within a period of time (typically, reported for one year, or one month). The U.S. government finances its deficits through the sale of U.S. Treasurys (called bills, notes, and bonds depending on their maturity). The (federal or national) **debt** is the total amount of outstanding U.S. Treasurys or the sum of past deficits (subject to some adjustments as some government agencies hold securities issued by other branches of government).

Conversely, if (1) economic production is above potential and (2) there are concerns about boom economic conditions and current or upcoming rates of inflation that are too high, then governments may run budget surpluses as **contractionary fiscal** policy (increase taxes) to reduce aggregate demand and, thus, inflation. Historically far rarer, (federal) surpluses involve revenues exceeding expenditures.

Types of taxes include income and payroll taxes (like those for social security and Medicare) and international trade tariffs (all of the above chiefly used by the federal government), sales (consumption or excise) taxes (chiefly used by state governments), and property taxes (chiefly used by local governments). Current income taxes use "progressive" tax rates that are higher for those with higher incomes and zero or, even negative, for those with lower incomes. Some economists argue that income taxes reduce incentives for individuals to work and, conversely, that switching to consumption taxes would increase incentives for individuals to save.

Monetary Policy

Monetary Policy involves efforts by the central bank of the U.S., the Federal Reserve System (or "Fed") to manage credit conditions, interest rates, and the money supply. Like other elements of macroeconomic policy, the key goals of monetary policy include (1) maximizing economic growth, (2) minimizing unemployment rates, (3) minimizing inflation rates, and (4) minimizing economic and financial fluctuations, ie, ensuring financial stability, minimizing boom-bust cycles, avoiding financial crises, and minimizing failures of financial institutions. The Fed has several tools at its disposal to carry out **expansionary monetary policy** (eg, to reduce unemployment rates) and **contractionary monetary policy** (eg, to reduce inflation rates). Some of these tools include:

- **Reserve requirements (ratio)** – The Fed may affect the total amount of lending in the economy (eg, tighten/loosen credit conditions) by changing (ie, increasing/decreasing) the percentage of customer's deposits that the Fed requires banks to hold in reserve (ie, not to be loaned out). In recent decades, the Fed has rarely changed reserve requirements; ie, it has effectively not used them as a tool of monetary policy.

- **Discount rate** – The Fed may affect the total amount of lending in the economy (eg, tighten/loosen credit conditions) by changing (ie, increasing/decreasing) the interest rate (called the discount rate) that it charges banks for short-term emergency loans. Except in, fortunately, still relatively rare crisis conditions, few banks request these types of loans to avoid the stigma of informing the Fed (their regulator in many cases) that they need "emergency" help. Thus, in recent decades, the discount rate has largely not been a key tool of monetary policy.

- **Open-market operations** – In recent decades, the Fed has conducted monetary policy largely through "open market operations," ie, setting a target rate for the federal funds rate and buying and selling short-term U.S. Treasurys (bills) to ensure that the actual (effective) rate in the federal funds market matched its target. When the Fed is concerned about high unemployment rates, it can engage in expansionary monetary policy by lowering its target for the federal funds rate, buying government securities on the open market, thereby increasing the amount of reserves available for banks to lend (the money supply).

When the Fed is concerned about boom conditions or current or expected high inflation rates, it can engage in contractionary monetary policy by increasing its target for the federal funds rate, or selling government securities on the open market, or both, thereby decreasing the amount of reserves available for banks to lend (the money supply).

Until the financial crisis, the federal funds rate was routinely substantially above 0%. Under such conditions, many observers interpreted monetary policy as largely involving changes in interest rates. At that time, increasing (reducing) interest rates (ie, akin to the *price* of credit) would typically make credit conditions tighter (looser), that is, reduce (increase) the *quantity* (or the rate of increase) of money (and eventually lending).

During the years following the financial crisis of 2008, the federal funds rate was almost zero (the Fed could technically have insisted on banks formally charging one another negative interest rates, but it did not). Thus, when, for instance in 2013, the Fed engaged in open market operations to buy Treasurys, and increase the *quantity* of money, the Fed did not formally affect the federal funds rate (a *price*); ie, the federal funds rate remained at almost zero and did not formally become negative in nominal terms. Since Fed open market operations then did not formally affect the level of the federal funds rate (ie, a *price*), but only affected the *quantity* of money, these types of policies are widely known as **quantitative easing**.

Another difference between Fed open market operations before and after the financial crisis is that before the crisis, the Fed bought almost exclusively Treasurys and now the Fed buys large amounts of real estate-related securities (albeit issued by Fannie Mae and Freddie Mac, institutions currently managed by the federal government).

Monetary policy may impact economic conditions because looser (or tighter) credit conditions may affect the decisions of individual economic agents (eg, households and businesses). Looser credit conditions (eg, lower interest rates and more readily available credit) tend to stimulate consumer and business spending (and thus aggregate demand). Tighter credit conditions (eg, higher interest rates and less readily available credit) tend to discourage consumer and business spending, of course. Because monetary policy is beset with long and variable lags that may be several years long, achieving the many goals of monetary policy sustainably is not easy in practice.

Economists use a variety of measures to track credit conditions, including interest rates, lending volumes, surveys of underwriting standards, and monetary aggregates such as the **monetary base, M1,** and **M2**. While the theoretical relationship between money, output, and prices (subject to lags) still stands, (1) far deeper financial markets, (2) the large role of the U.S. dollar abroad, (3) regulatory changes, and (4) technological innovations have jointly reduced the relevance of short-term changes in monetary aggregates in predicting the short-term impacts of monetary policy.

Regulatory Policy

Governments may further influence economic activity through regulations affecting environmental issues, labor issues (eg, immigration and minimum wage laws), occupational health and safety, energy policy, healthcare, bank capital, lending practices, etc. On one hand, governments may choose to channel resources from disfavored sectors to favored sectors. On the other hand, governments could seek to reduce the likelihood of financial crises, for instance, by requiring banks to develop thicker capital cushions over time, or by adjusting minimum permissible mortgage down payments if other housing bubbles surfaced in the future.

Obstacles to International Trade

While all countries on average theoretically benefit from international trade, large fractions of goods and services are not traded across international borders. There are many barriers to international trade; some are "natural," such as transportation and information costs, and some are the result of government policy.

Government Trade Controls

Historically, the most common type of trade barrier had been **tariffs** (ie, taxes on imported goods). Domestic industries that are losing market share to foreign competitors (eg, textiles, furniture) often advocate for **trade restrictions**. Below we summarize some effects of trade restrictions.

- **Domestic producers of protected goods** – Positive. The demand curve they face shifts to the right as the availability of substitute goods has been reduced. They sell more goods at higher prices. Managements and unions typically sought the restrictions as both parties benefit from higher sales and prices, with some of the gains passed on to owners, managers, and workers (in the form of higher wages and more job security than they would have otherwise).

- **Domestic users** – Negative. The supply curve they face shifts to the left, forcing them to pay higher prices and being able to buy fewer goods.

- **Domestic producers of exported goods** – Negative. The demand curve they face shifts to the left, as their consumers are made worse off overall by the higher prices they pay on protected goods. Since these negative impacts are diffused across many industries and the positive impacts of protection are concentrated on the protected industries, often each individual protected industry can lobby effectively for its protection without major opposition from all the other industries that are hurt only by a small amount (per industry).

- **Foreign producers encountering protection elsewhere** – Negative. The demand curve they face shifts to the left, resulting in lower sales and prices.

- **Foreign users of protected goods** – Positive. The supply curve shifts to the right, as their producers will have to do more selling in their own market. They buy more goods at lower prices.

Efforts to Reduce Trade Barriers

Learning from the negative effects of **trade wars** during the interwar period and the Great Depression, many governments have moved to reduce many trade barriers and to coordinate some aspects of their economic policies.

The **World Trade Organization (WTO)** is an international organization that:

- Provides a forum to continue to negotiate greater liberalization of international trade policies
- Provides a forum to resolve international trade disputes
- Seeks to help prevent trade wars and the growth of other trade barriers

Since World War II, many have increasingly reduced their reliance on tariffs as a means of trade protection. However, just as they moved away from tariffs, many countries continue to experiment and switch to other less transparent means of protection, such as import quotas, embargoes, and foreign-exchange controls.

- **Import quotas** place limits on the quantity of a good that may be imported during a period.
- **Embargoes** are total bans on importing either a number of goods or nearly all goods from a country.

As an example of how protection efforts can become blurred and complex, during the 1980s, the U.S. auto industry realized that the U.S. government was formally restricted by its international agreements from imposing tougher explicit restrictions on Japanese competitors. Thus, the U.S. auto industry pushed the U.S. government to push the Japanese government to push the Japanese auto industry to self-impose "voluntary" quotas, called **"voluntary export restraints" (VER)**. One key result of these policies was Japanese companies switching from producing in Japan to setting up factories in the U.S. to sell in the U.S.

Many governments also attempt to manipulate trade through **foreign-exchange controls.** These policies may restrict the types of domestic parties that may use foreign currencies, their amounts, and their uses. Governments may use these policies to favor some industries over others. Some countries operate multiple exchange rates, requiring more or less favored domestic parties to use the various rates for different purposes.

Dumping involves a manufacturer exporting a product to one country at a price that was unjustifiably low and harming the domestic producers of that country. Companies operating in different countries (with different currencies) may engage in **dual-pricing** strategies, for instance, charging customers in new markets lower prices to introduce them to their products, or charging customers in countries with more elastic demand curves lower prices (even though that may open them to accusations of dumping).

Many governments also use **export subsidies** to encourage the production and export of specific products. Subsidies may take many forms, some more or less overt, ranging from outright payments to favored tax treatment, or access to subsidized lending. If a WTO panel finds that one country is in breach of international trade rules (eg, by having illegal export subsidies) and the country refuses to correct the situation, the countries bringing the complaint may impose **countervailing duties** (ie, tariffs) for an equivalent amount on products from the offending country.

Lecture 1.06 – Financial Risk Management

Foreign Exchange Rates

The exchange rates between countries' currencies are very important to any company that faces foreign competitors, regardless of whether the company is an exporter facing competitors abroad or the company faces imports from foreign competitors domestically. When a foreign country's currency weakens, products from companies from that country become cheaper for purchasers in the U.S., providing those foreign companies' products an advantage.

Fluctuations in currencies' exchange rates are ultimately based on relative changes in the supplies and demands of those currencies. Companies considering decisions regarding short-term international trade and long-term international investments face these types of (nominal and real) **exchange rate risks**.

Repatriation is the process of converting a foreign currency into your own country's currency ($U.S.), at the current exchange rate.

Exchange rates may be expressed by dividing by either currency, for example, if €1 (ie, 1 euro) buys $1.25, the exchange rate may be expressed as €1 = $1.25, or $1 = €0.80. In a table listing multiple exchange rates for one currency, it is customary to express all exchange rates on the same basis, for example, how many units of the various foreign currencies does it take to buy $1. It is also customary to choose the "direction" of the exchange rates that ensures that most exchange rates are greater than 1 (ie, $1 = 80 yen, instead of $0.0125 = 1 yen).

Commonly cited exchange rates between currencies include:
- The **spot rate** is the exchange rate at which a financial party (a financial institution, a currency dealer, etc.) will exchange two currencies at this time (ie, "on the spot").
- The **forward rate** is the exchange rate at which a financial party will exchange two currencies at a specific future date (called the settlement date), for example, three months later.

In forward markets, one currency is at a premium (discount) if its forward rate is higher (lower) than the spot rate (both rates expressed per the foreign currency), that is, if it is expected to appreciate (depreciate). For instance, according to the spot rate, 1 Kuwaiti dinar may equal $3.57, and according to the 3-month forward rate, 1 Kuwaiti dinar may equal $3.53. In this case, there is a discount since the Kuwaiti dinar will be worth less in the future (ie, it will buy fewer dollars). The size of the forward premium (or discount) is expressed in annual terms as follows:

$$\frac{\text{Forward rate} - \text{Spot rate}}{\text{Spot rate}} \times \frac{\text{Months in a year}}{\text{Months in the forward period}}$$

$$\frac{3.53 - 3.57}{3.57} \times \frac{12}{3} = -4.5\%$$

Foreign Exchange Risk

Companies with operations in more than one country bear various types of **foreign exchange (or currency) risk**.

Economic Concepts

Translation Risk

A company with operations in countries with different currencies will likely have **assets and liabilities** in more than one currency. Creating financial statements (eg, balance sheets) that cover the whole company will require using exchange rates to convert the value of the assets and liabilities from one country's currency into the currency used where the company is headquartered.

Changes in those values resulting from changes in exchange rates involve **translation (accounting) risk** and are entered as gains or losses on the balance sheet as other comprehensive income (OCI). Companies may seek to manage their translation risk by **matching assets and liabilities** in each market where they operate.

For instance, a company operating a plant (or a distribution network) in a foreign country might finance those operations in the local currency (ie, through loans with local banks or by issuing bonds in that country's currency).

Transaction Risk

A company with operations in countries with different currencies will likely have streams of future **revenues and costs** in more than one currency. Thus, forecasting future earnings, expressed in the currency used where the company is headquartered, will involve one additional type of risk that is known as **transaction risk**.

Companies may seek to manage their transaction risk, similarly, by **matching** as many **revenues and costs** as possible in each market where they operate. For instance, a Japanese company selling cars in the U.S. would reduce the volatility of its earnings if its dollar-denominated revenues were matched by dollar-denominated labor costs, by producing some of those cars in the U.S. Short of matching revenues and costs by currency, companies also use derivatives, or **hedging contracts** to manage these risks.

- **Options** permit, but do not require, holders to buy or sell commodities (eg, a specific type of wheat) or instruments (a stock, bond, or currency), at a given price until some date (under an American option) or at some date (under a European option).
  - **Call options** permit the holder to **buy** a security at a fixed price.
  - **Put options** permit the holder to **sell** a security at a fixed price.
- **Forwards** are specifically negotiated contracts in which two parties agree to exchange (one party buys and the other sells) some quantity of a commodity or instrument (eg, currency) at a pre-set price on a future date. Forwards differ from options in that they do not just permit the exchange, but require both parties to participate.
- **Futures** are standardized versions of forward contracts that are traded (bought and sold) in exchange markets (like the Chicago Board of Trade or the Chicago Mercantile Exchange). Future contracts have standardized sizes (eg, $1 million) and dates (eg, the end of a quarter).
- **Currency swaps** contracts under which one party A agrees to make payments in one currency to another party B (eg, twelve monthly payments of 10 million pesos) and the other party B agrees to make payments to party A in the other currency (eg, twelve monthly payments of $1 million) independently of how spot rates change during that period of time.
- **Money market hedges** involve turning transaction risk (which may result in either gains or losses) into a loan. This strategy involves the cost of certain interest payments, but removes the possibility that currencies may change unfavorably. In our example above, a U.S. company expecting 12 monthly payments of 10 million pesos could take a loan whose repayment schedule was 12

monthly payments of 10 million pesos (or twelve separate loans with single payments each one month apart) and convert the peso proceeds from the loan(s) into dollars today using the spot rate.

Mitigation of Other Financial Risks

Asset-liability matching, derivative products, and other techniques may be used to hedge or manage a variety of financial risks.

Interest Rate Risk

Interest rate risk is the risk that changes in economy-wide interest rate levels may affect their earnings adversely. Typically, banks have assets with longer maturities (eg, long-term mortgage loans) and liabilities with shorter maturities. Thus, interest rate increases may leave banks with assets that reprice slowly and liabilities that reprice quickly. That is, assets continue to pay the low interest rates they started charging in previous years, while they will pay higher rates on most liabilities quickly.

Again, financial institutions may manage this risk by:
- Reducing the amount of assets with long maturities and increasing the amount of liabilities with long maturities
- Reducing the amount of fixed-rate long-term assets and increasing the amount of variable-rate long-term assets
- Using interest rate derivatives (including swaps), albeit the fees for interest rate derivatives grow larger and larger the further out one seeks to be protected

Credit Risk

Credit risk is the risk that the parties that one has lent to, or who owe payments, may fail to pay. Standard techniques to deal with credit risk include:
- Diversifying one's customers
- Selling future streams of payments; that is, turning from being a lender who "originates to hold" and earns profits from interest payments to being a lender who "originates to distribute" and earns profits from origination fees
- Implementing internal control mechanisms to ensure that credit standards are appropriately tight
- Requiring greater guarantees from borrowers (eg, requiring larger down payments or other forms of collateral
- Using derivatives, such as credit default swaps (CDS)

Companies, and other investors, holding bonds issued by third companies may purchase CDS that are essentially insurance products that protect against defaults on bonds in exchange for premiums. (Sophisticated) investors holding bonds (or debts) owed by companies for which CDS are not available may still purchase portfolios of CDS to protect themselves if not exactly against the default by their particular borrower, at least against the threat of an economy-wide surge in defaults (since defaults typically take place in waves when there are economy-wide problems).

Liquidity Risk

Liquidity risk is the risk that while they may be solvent on a long-term basis (ie, their long-term revenues outweigh their long-term costs), during a crisis situation, their short-term obligations might outweigh their access to liquid funds, forcing them to sell long-term assets at "**fire sale**

prices" or at depressed prices, effectively making them insolvent in the short term and, hence, indefinitely.

Companies may manage their liquidity risk by:

- Matching more the maturities of their assets and liabilities such that, as liabilities come due, some assets can be liquidated at full prices
- Maintaining a large cushion of liquid assets (cash and short-securities), albeit at the cost of foregoing returns on those assets
- Maintaining a variety of long-term lines of credit with a variety of providers
    - Of course, the greater the number of lines, the more secure that they are, and the longer they extend into the future, the higher the fees they will involve.

Market Risk

Market risk is the risk that sales of their products or the value of some of their assets may decline. To manage this risk, companies may:

- Shift their financing sources from debt to equity, since equity can accommodate more easily temporary declines in the value of their assets
- Diversify their income streams and the assets they hold, albeit greater diversification may be accompanied by losses in managerial focus
- Use hedging strategies, such as purchasing instruments whose value will increase should the company, its competitors, or the economy as a whole experience difficulty
- "Short" the S&P 500 stock index (for short-term market risk)

Country Risk

Companies also bear country risk when investing overseas. Country risk affects profits and the value of assets, as they have very little control over the political and financial risks associated with investing in a foreign country.

Globalization

Economists use the term globalization to describe how the economies of nearly all individual countries in the world are developing increasingly deeper connections in their markets for goods, services, labor, capital, and technologies. Globalization plays a role in many deeply transformative processes that have been ongoing for several decades now.

Increased Foreign Direct Investment (FDI)

Many companies from developed countries operate in multiple other countries, both developed and developing, operating factories, research facilities; call, service, and technical support centers; and distribution networks. Growing levels of FDI have contributed to the growing importance of intra-company international trade and to growing levels of international transfers of technology and knowhow.

Increased Foreign Indirect, or Portfolio, Investment

Seeking diversification in their portfolios, international investors have been shifting growing fractions of their savings into financial (or portfolio) assets (ie, stock and bonds) denominated in the currencies of other countries. This shift undoubtedly helps individual savers, and may help improve how well international savings flow to the countries with the most promising projects, but

BEC 2 – Corporate Governance, Internal Control & Enterprise Risk Management

Table of Contents

Lecture 2.01 – Corporate Governance — 1
- Overview — 1
- Board of Directors — 1
- Committees — 2
- Executive Oversight: Compensation — 3
- Executive Oversight: Monitoring Management — 4
- Sarbanes-Oxley Act (SOX) — 5

Lecture 2.02 – Internal Controls — 7
- PCAOB Integrated Audit — 7
- COSO's Internal Control Framework — 7
- Fraud Risk Management Program — 14

Lecture 2.03 – Enterprise Risk Management (ERM) — 18
- Components & Principles Overview — 18
- Governance & Culture — 19
- Strategy & Objective Setting — 21
- Performance — 22
- Review & Revision — 27
- Information, Communication & Reporting — 28

Corporate Governance, Internal Control & Enterprise Risk Management

Lecture 2.01 – Corporate Governance

Overview

It is the role of corporate governance to make certain that the objectives of the entity are met while the legitimate needs and concerns of all stakeholders are being addressed. Stakeholders may include stockholders, customers, suppliers, employees, regulators, and the communities that are affected by the entity's operations or activities.

Corporate governance consists of the systems that are applied to **control** and to **direct** a corporation. Those responsible for governance will depend largely on the size and nature of the entity. In a small organization, governance may be the responsibility of owner-managers. In larger organizations, however, the responsibility for governance is disbursed among a variety of individuals in a somewhat more structured environment.

In most publicly held companies, for example, stockholders are not directly involved in its operations. They elect a **board of directors** (BOD) who in turn are responsible for **strategic planning** as well as for the selection and **oversight** of the entity's management. The board will also **monitor management** to make certain that its decisions are consistent with achieving the entity's objectives.

Board of Directors

The **bylaws** (internal rules of the corporation) generally indicate the minimum and maximum number of directors, how they are to be selected and compensated, how often they are to meet, and the nature of their responsibilities. The typical **duties** of a BOD include:

- The board members have a **fiduciary duty** to:
    - **Act loyally** and in the best interest of the corporation and shareholders, which includes not putting their interests above the company's and acting without personal economic conflict.
    - **Act with a Duty of Care** and be diligent when making company decisions.
    - **Act with Due Diligence,** which means using reasonable care when entering into agreements or transactions with another party.
- Determining or revising the entity's mission and amending its bylaws
- Strategic planning and the development of broad objectives and policies
- Selection and oversight of the chief executive
- Securing the availability of financial resources
- Budget approval, and approval of major operating and financial proposals
- Accounting to stakeholders, including making certain that reliable financial information is reported by the entity
- Providing advice to management and determining its compensation
- Establishing dividend policies
- Reacquiring treasury stock

Business Judgment Rule

A director has some protection against liability when decisions do not provide the anticipated results. The business judgment rule was established as a result of case law, and it requires a director to fulfill a **fiduciary duty** to the entity by acting in good faith, being loyal, and applying due care. When they do so, the courts will not review their business decisions, regardless of the outcome. In general, directors will not be liable for their decisions unless they are guilty of fraud.

For example, if directors reasonably rely on information showing that dividends may be declared and declare such dividends when, in fact, the corporation was insolvent, the directors will not be held liable for the illegal dividends. (The shareholders will have to repay the dividends if the corporation was insolvent when the dividends were declared.)

Committees

The BOD will establish various committees to disburse the board's responsibilities.

- In some cases, committees are required to be made up of independent, or **outside directors**. These are directors who have no involvement with the entity other than in their capacity as a director.
- An **inside director**, on the other hand, has some significant involvement in the entity, often as a member of management, in addition to being a director. Some entities will apply the term **executive director** exclusively to the chief executive officer (CEO), while others will apply it to any director who is also an executive, or officer, of the corporation.

While there may be more, there are **three committees** that a publicly held company is required to maintain.

Nominating/Governance Committee

The nominating committee (aka, governance committee) is responsible for the overall corporate governance of an organization. The primary duty of the nominating committee is to determine who is suitable for service on the BOD. It is charged with developing and suggesting governance principles and policies to the board, overseeing CEO succession, enhancing the quality of nominees to the board, and making certain of the integrity of the nominating process.

Audit Committee

The audit committee is required to be made up of **independent directors** and at least one member of the audit committee is required to be a financial expert. A **financial expert** has:

- An understanding of GAAP and financial statements
- Experience preparing or auditing comparable financial statements and experience in applying financial statement or audit knowledge to the accounting for estimates, accruals, and reserves
- Experience with internal accounting controls
- An understanding of the functions of the audit committee
    - Need not be a CPA

Responsibilities of the audit committee include:

- Overseeing the **financial reporting** process
    - It is to make certain that reliable information that is useful to stakeholders is available on a timely basis.

- Appointing, compensating, and overseeing of the entity's **external auditors**, who are to report directly to the audit committee
- Overseeing the establishment of appropriate **controls**, including programs for the prevention and detection of fraud
- Maintaining a **code of ethics** for senior financial officers and making it publicly available
- Establishing procedures for dealing with **complaints** about accounting, I/C, or audit matters, and facilitating a process for employees (**whistleblowers**) to anonymously and confidentially express concerns about accounting related issues

Compensation Committee

The compensation committee, made up of independent directors, is responsible for establishing compensation policies for directors and executives of the corporation. It is charged with making certain that their policies are both appropriate and supportable and that they are consistent with the mission and objectives of the entity.

Executive Oversight: Compensation

One of the most significant responsibilities of the BOD is the oversight of management. The board meets this responsibility through its management **compensation** policies and through **monitoring** of management.

Management compensation policies require the board to find a balance between different forms of compensation that may, on one hand, motivate management to strive to perform at the utmost level or may, on the other, cause management to find ways to maximize their own compensation at the detriment of, or at least without considering benefit to, the entity.

- If the compensation package includes too high a proportion of fixed compensation and too low a proportion of incentive compensation, management will not have incentives to take risks that may be appropriate and necessary for the achievement of the entity's objectives.
- If the opposite is true, it may provide management with the incentive to take risks that are not consistent with the entity's risk appetite. As a result, the combination of fixed and incentive compensation should be carefully evaluated.

Fixed compensation generally consists of the officer's salary and perquisites (perks). Perks may include such items as a company automobile or access to a company plane or limousine, health and life insurance, and retirement benefits.

Incentive compensation can be provided in a wide variety of forms, such as the following:

- **Bonuses** – In most cases, bonuses are based on some version of accounting profit. While this rewards management for good entity performance, it is often easy to manipulate profits in the short run by deferring or accelerating expenses or revenues, through capitalization and depreciation policies, and various other means.
- **Share-based compensation** – This includes such items as stock options, shared appreciation rights, restricted shares, and performance shares.
    - **Stock options** give the officer the ability to buy shares at a fixed price for a specific period of time. Although this clearly ties compensation to performance, it may cause management to focus too heavily on short-term stock price rather than long-term objectives. In addition, a decline in price may make it appear that the option will never be "in the money" (where the stock price exceeds the option price), negating any incentive.

- **Shared appreciation rights** operate similarly to stock options with the same advantages and disadvantages. The additional advantage to officers is that it provides them with cash payments resulting from increases in the stock price rather than the opportunity to buy shares at a potential bargain.
- **Restricted shares** are shares of stock that may not be disposed of for a specified period. This provides the advantage that the officer does not have to pay for shares and gives management an incentive to strive to increase the stock price, at least during the period of restriction. Clearly, the longer the restriction, the greater the potential for benefit to the entity.
- **Performance shares** are shares that are issued to management if specific performance objectives are met. These are potentially very effective to encourage management to concentrate on the meeting of specific performance objectives.

Executive Oversight: Monitoring Management

Internal Audit

One of the most common ways to monitor management, and often the most effective, is through internal audit. When internal auditors report directly to the audit committee of the BOD, they are more likely to be effective in helping the board monitor the performance of management, largely because the audit committee is made up exclusively of independent directors.

The IIA provides the following **definition of internal auditing**:

> Internal auditing is an independent, objective assurance and consulting activity designed to add value and improve an organization's operations. It helps an organization accomplish its objectives by bringing a systematic, disciplined approach to evaluate and improve the effectiveness of risk management, control, and government processes.

External Auditors

External auditors are also potentially effective in contributing to the monitoring of management. As part of their monitoring role, the independent external auditor is required **to communicate** with the **audit committee** regarding:

- Critical accounting policies and practices being used
- Alternative treatments, acceptable under GAAP, that have been discussed with management, including implications of such treatment and the public accounting firm's preference
- Any additional written communications with management, including any management letter or schedule of unadjusted differences

The Sarbanes-Oxley Act (SOX), which is discussed in more detail below, established the Public Company Accounting Oversight Board (**PCAOB**) to regulate auditors of public companies, subject to SEC oversight. SOX also establishes very strict rules as to the **independence** of external auditors, including a prohibition against the performance of many nonaudit services, a requirement that any nonattest services be preapproved by the audit committee, and audit partner rotation.

Other Monitoring Devices

There are several other means by which management is monitored:

- The company will be scrutinized by various members of the investment community, including **investment banks** and **securities analysts**, who use information about the company to make their decisions or recommendations as to the purchase or sale of its securities.

Corporate Governance, Internal Control & ERM

- **Creditors** and **credit agencies** make similar analyses and monitor compliance with debt covenants, although they largely depend on management and external auditors for the information on which they base their decisions.
- **Attorneys** also monitor management when they are involved in securities filings, legal conflicts, or are engaged to advise management.

Sarbanes-Oxley Act (SOX)

As a result of numerous incidents involving fraudulent financial reporting involving such companies as Enron, WorldCom, Global Crossing, and others, Congress passed the Sarbanes-Oxley Act (SOX). SOX was created to restore investors' confidence. The following SOX Titles and sections are testable in BEC with respect to corporate governance.

Title III – Corporate Responsibility

- **301** – Makes audit committee, which must be **independent**, responsible for appointment, compensation and **oversight** of any **audit work** performed by the audit firm. Allows the SEC to de-list any issuer not in compliance with Title III.
- **302** – Requires principal executive and principal financial officers (**CEO and CFO) to certify**, in each annual or quarterly report:
    - That they reviewed the report
    - The report does not contain any untrue statement of material fact or omission of a material fact
    - Financial position and results of operations are fairly presented

  Officers also certify that they:
    - Are responsible for establishing and maintaining effective internal control
    - Have evaluated the effectiveness of the controls within 90 days prior to the report
    - Have presented their conclusions as to the effectiveness of internal control
    - Signing officers required to disclose to auditors and audit committee:
    - Significant deficiencies in the design or operation of internal controls
    - Any fraud, regardless of materiality, that involves management or employees involved in internal controls
    - Report of signing officers also indicates changes in internal controls over financial reporting.
- **303** – Prohibits an officer or director of an issuer to fraudulently influence, coerce, manipulate, or mislead the auditor.
- **304** – Requires executives of an issuer to forfeit any bonus or incentive-based pay or profits from the sale of stock, received in the 12 months period after the date of issuance of financial statements subject to an earnings restatement (**Claw-back Policy**).
- **305** – The SEC may bar any person who has violated federal securities laws from serving as an officer or director of an issuer.
- **306** – Prohibits trading by officers and directors during blackout periods established between the end of a quarter and the earnings report date.

Title IV – Enhanced Financial Disclosures

- **401** – Requires all financial statements prepared in accordance with GAAP to reflect all material adjustments identified by the auditors.

- **402** – Prohibits personal loans to directors and executive officers.

- **403** – Requires directors, officers, and principal shareholders to disclose the amount of all equity securities in which they hold a beneficial interest and any changes in their interests since the previous filing.

- **404** – Requires that management acknowledge its responsibility for establishing and maintaining adequate internal control over financial reporting (ICFR) and that management assess the effectiveness of internal control as of the end of the period. Also requires the auditor to attest to (ie, give an opinion), and report on, management's assessment. This is the result of an examination of internal control that is **integrated** with the **audit** of the financial statements.

- **406** – Requires an issuer to disclose whether it has adopted a **code of ethics** for senior financial officers and, if not, the reasons for not having done so.

- **407** – Must **disclose** whether at least one member of its audit committee is a "**financial expert**."

- **408** – Provides for enhanced review of periodic disclosures by Board.

- **409** – Requires issuers to disclose material changes in the financial condition or operations on a rapid and current basis.

Title VIII – Corporate & Criminal Fraud Accountability

- **802** – It is a felony to **alter, destroy**, or make **false entries** in any document with the intent to obstruct or influence a legal investigation. Penalties include fines up to $15 million and/or imprisonment not to exceed 20 years.

- **804** – The statute of limitations on securities fraud claims is extended to five (5) years from the fraud, or two (2) years after the fraud was discovered.

- **806** – Employees are extended **whistleblower protection** that would prohibit the employer from taking certain actions against employees. Whistleblower employees are also granted a remedy of special damages and attorney's fees.

- **807** – **Securities fraud** is punishable of up to **25 years in prison**.

Title IX – White Collar Crime Penalty Enhancements

- **906** – Requires the **CEO and CFO** to **certify** that the reports filed with the SEC (10Q, 10K) comply with relevant securities laws and also fairly present the financial condition and results of operations of the company. If they are found criminally liable for certifying false and defective financial statements, they could be imprisoned for 10 to 20 years and fined from $1 million to $5 million.

Title XI – Corporate Fraud Accountability

- **1103** – Grants the SEC the authority to freeze the funds of a company that is suspected of securities violations.

- **1105** – Grants the SEC the authority to prohibit persons from serving as officers or directors.

Lecture 2.02 – Internal Controls

PCAOB Integrated Audit

AS 2201 requires the auditor to examine the design and operating effectiveness of internal control over financial reporting (ICFR) to provide a sufficient basis for an opinion on its effectiveness in preventing or detecting material misstatements in the financial statements (F/S). The results may be expressed in either separate reports or one combined report on the F/S and the ICFR. The F/S audit portion of the integrated audit is similar to any other F/S audit, but its "integrated" nature means that auditors rely much more on internal control (I/C) and less on substantive procedures.

Reporting on Internal Control

Section 404 of SOX (Title IV) requires each annual report to contain a report on I/C in which management acknowledges its responsibility for establishing and maintaining ICFR. It will include an assessment by management as to the effectiveness of ICFR as of the end of the most recent fiscal period. The registered accounting firm that audits the entity's F/S is also required to attest to the assessment made by management.

Management's report on ICFR should include:

- Management's acknowledgment of its responsibility for ICFR
- Management's assessment of ICFR as of the end of the most recent period
- An identification of the framework used to evaluate ICFR
- An indication that the auditor has issued an attestation report on management's assessment

COSO's Internal Control Framework

The most commonly used framework to benchmark internal controls in the U.S. is *Internal Control – Integrated Framework* developed by the Committee of Sponsoring Organizations of the Treadway Commission (COSO). COSO describes I/C as *"a process, effected by the entity's board of directors, management, and other personnel designed to provide reasonable assurance regarding the achievement of objectives relating to operations, reporting, and compliance."*

- Operational objectives relate to the effectiveness and efficiency of operations and incorporate the achievement of financial performance goals and the safeguarding of assets.
- Reporting objectives relate to the reliability, timeliness, and transparency of financial and nonfinancial reporting for both internal and external uses.
- Compliance objectives relate to complying with applicable laws and regulations.

Since I/C is a process that is affected by people, it can only provide reasonable assurance, as opposed to absolute assurance, that the entity's objectives will be met.

The COSO Board added the **17 I/C Principles** because they are presumed essential in assessing that the five components (**CRIME**) are present and functioning properly. Here are the 17 listed by I/C component:

CONTROL *E*NVIRONMENT

1. Demonstrates commitment to integrity and ethical values
2. Exercises oversight responsibility

3. Establishes structure, authority, and responsibility
4. Demonstrates commitment to competence
5. Enforces accountability

_R_ISK ASSESSMENT

6. Specifies suitable objectives
7. Identifies and analyzes risk
8. Assesses fraud risk
9. Identifies and analyzes significant change

CONTROL ACTIVITIES

10. Selects and develops control activities
11. Selects and develops general controls over technology
12. Deploys through policies and procedures

_I_NFORMATION & COMMUNICATION

13. Uses relevant information
14. Communicates internally
15. Communicates externally

_M_ONITORING

16. Conducts ongoing and/or separate evaluations
17. Evaluates and communicates deficiencies

> The mnemonic **CRIME** reminds management that it would be a crime not to consider all the internal control elements when designing the system.

The Control **E**nvironment

The control environment is the combination of standards, processes, and structures that enable I/C to be effective throughout the organization. Setting the tone of an organization by influencing the control consciousness of people, the control environment is the foundation of I/C. The control environment encompasses 5 principles.

a. Commitment to integrity and ethical values demonstrated through
   - The tone at the top established through the directives, actions, and behavior of management and governance
   - Standards of conduct understood by all members of the organization and others with which it interacts and against which behavior and performance is evaluated
   - Timely and consistent identification of and response to deviations from standards
   - COSO indicates that the control environment, or tone at the top, is the most significant I/C component when it comes to sending a message throughout the organization as to the entity's attitude about ethical behavior. It further indicates that this can best be demonstrated through the exemplary behavior of the leadership.

b. Governance's independence from management and oversight of I/C demonstrated through:
   - Identification and acceptance of oversight responsibilities
   - Inclusion of members with appropriate levels of skill and expertise to effectively oversee management with sufficient numbers independent of management and objective

- Involvement in and oversight of I/C

c. Management's establishment of an appropriate hierarchy and structure to achieve entity objectives demonstrated through:
    - Establishment of reporting lines considering all structures of the entity
    - Assignment of, and limitations on, authorities and responsibilities

d. Commitment to attracting, developing, and retaining individuals who are competent and in accord with entity objectives demonstrated through:
    - Setting expectations requiring appropriate levels of competence
    - Evaluating competence and addressing deficiencies
    - Providing mentoring and training to attract, develop, and retain competent personnel and business relationships
    - Establishing contingency and succession plans

e. Individuals are held accountable for their control responsibilities, demonstrated through:
    - Establishment of mechanisms that hold individuals accountable for performance of I/C responsibilities including performance measures, incentives, and rewards, which are to be evaluated for relevance on an ongoing basis
    - Evaluation and moderation of pressures associated with performance
    - Evaluation of performance including rewards or remedial action, as appropriate

Factors of the control environment include (**CHOPPER**):

- **C**ommitment to Competence – Employees must possess the skills and knowledge essential to performing their jobs, especially those responsible for performing important control functions.
- **H**uman resource policies and procedures – Effective policies and practices for hiring, training, evaluating, counseling, promoting, and compensating employees are vital to the environment.
- **O**rganizational structure – Provides a basis for planning, directing and controlling operations.
- **P**hilosophy and Operating style of Management – The manner in which management runs the organization can have a significant effect on the control environment. Unethical management can lead to unethical employees.
- **P**articipation of the BOD or audit committee – Both groups play a key role in establishing IC.
- **E**thical and Integrity values – Management should encourage appropriate behavior and lead by example. Values are established through a code of conduct, official policies, and by example. This includes codes of conduct, the attestation process, whistle-blower processes, investigation and resolution, training and reinforcement both internally and with third parties.
- **R**esponsibility and Authority Assignment – Communicated through documents such as job descriptions and organizational charts; personnel need a clear understanding of their responsibilities and the rules and regulations that govern their actions.

Risk Assessment

Risk assessment refers to an entity's recognition of the fact that events may occur that pose risks to the achievement of the entity's objectives and the process that is established to identify and evaluate those risks. Risk assessment encompasses 4 principles.

a. Objectives are sufficiently clear to allow for identification and evaluation of risks to their achievement, demonstrated through:
    - Consideration of operational objectives, internal and external reporting objectives, and compliance objectives
    - Reflects management's choices in relation to operational objectives, and internal reporting objectives

b. Risks are identified and analyzed to determine appropriate management, demonstrated through:
    - Consideration of internal entity level risks, such as related to infrastructure, management structure, personnel, access to assets, and technology; and external entity level risks, such as related to the economy, the environment, regulation, foreign operations, and the social and technological environment.
    - Consideration of risks at the transaction level.
    - Consideration of factors such as likelihood of occurrence and its effect if it does; the speed with which the effect will be incurred upon occurrence of the event representing the risk; and the length of time the effect will last after occurrence of the event.
    - Consideration as to whether the appropriate response is accepting the risk by taking no preventive action; avoiding the risk by changing the objective or discontinuing the activity that creates the risk; sharing the risk by entering into a relationship, such as a joint venture, or participating in hedging activities; or reducing the risk through a variety of decisions, including the establishment of control activities.

c. Risk assessment includes a consideration of the possibility of fraud, demonstrated through:
    - Consideration of the nature of fraud, including the types of fraud that may be perpetrated against the entity.
    - Assessment of the characteristics of fraud, including incentives or pressures that may be inherent in the entity's activities; opportunities to commit or conceal fraud; and attitudes and rationalizations that may allow management or others to commit fraud.

d. The potential impact of changes within the entity on the effectiveness of I/C is identified and assessed, as demonstrated through:
    - Identification and assessment of changes in the external environment.
    - Identification and assessment of changes in the business model or the entity's leadership.

      An entity's risk assessment for financial reporting purposes is its identification, analysis, and management of risks (risk response) relevant to the preparation of financial statements that are fairly presented in conformity with GAAP. Risk assessment includes risks that may affect an entity's ability to properly record, process, summarize, and report financial data. Risk assessment, for example, may address how the entity considers the possibility of unrecorded transactions or identifies and analyzes significant estimates recorded in the financial statements.

    - Risks relevant to financial reporting include *external and internal* **factors** such as the following:
        - Changes in operating environment (competition)
        - New technology or revamped information systems (internal factor)
        - Rapid growth

- New personnel or lines of business, products, or activities
- Corporate restructurings
- Foreign operations
- Accounting pronouncements

Control Activities

Control activities are the actions established by policies and procedures that help ensure that management's directives are carried out. Control activities encompass three principles.

a. Selection and development of control activities contribute to reducing risks to the achievement of the entity's objectives, as demonstrated through:
   - Integration with the entity's risk assessment and consideration of entity specific factors, including the various levels within the entity requiring control activities.
   - Identification of those processes and activities that require control activities.
   - Inclusion of a range of types of control activities, including manual and automated controls, preventive and detective controls, and appropriate segregation of duties.

b. General controls over technology are developed to support the achievement of the entity's objectives, as demonstrated through:
   - Management's understanding of the relationship between internal processes, automated controls, and general controls over technology.
   - The establishment of relevant control activities regarding technology infrastructure; security management; and acquisition, development, and maintenance.

c. Policies identify expectations and procedures convert policies into actions, as demonstrated through:
   - The incorporation of control activities into daily processes, designating responsibility and establishing accountability.
   - Tasks are performed in a timely manner, using competent personnel, with corrective action taken as appropriate.
   - The regular reassessment of control activities to verify their continued relevance.

Types of control activities include:

- **P**erformance reviews – actual vs. budget, P/Y, financial to nonfinancial
- **I**nformation processing – (IT) General vs. Application controls (ie, Input, Processing and Output controls)
- **P**hysical controls – Access to assets
- **S**egregation of duties includes assigning different people the responsibilities of **authorizing** transactions, **recording** transactions, maintaining **custody** of assets, and performing **comparisons**. It is intended to reduce the opportunities to allow any person to be in a position to both *perpetrate and conceal errors or irregularities* in the normal course of their duties (**ARCC**).
   - **A**uthorization of transactions
   - **R**ecording (posting) of transactions
   - **C**ustody of assets
   - **C**omparisons

Information & Communication

Information and communication refers to the processes by which management obtains or generates and uses information and how it is disseminated throughout the entity and to appropriate business relationships. Information and communication encompass three principles.

a. The functioning of all components of I/C is supported by relevant, quality information obtained or generated by the entity, as demonstrated through:
   - Identification of information requirements and the internal and external sources from which it is derived.
   - The transformation of data into information through processing throughout which quality is maintained.
   - Consideration of the cost of obtaining and disseminating information, weighed against the benefits.

b. The functioning of all components of I/C is supported by the internal communication of objectives and responsibilities, as demonstrated through:
   - Establishment of processes to communicate objectives and responsibilities to all appropriate personnel.
   - Communication between management and governance.
   - The provision of mechanisms, such as whistle-blower hotlines, that establish alternate channels of communication, allowing anonymous or confidential communication as needed.
   - Consideration of factors such as the nature and timing of information and its intended audience in establishing methods of communication.

c. External parties are informed as to matters affecting the effectiveness of appropriate components of I/C, as demonstrated through:
   - The establishment of channels and processes for communicating with external parties to provide relevant and timely information and obtain relevant and timely information from others.
   - The communication with governance of relevant information obtained from external parties.
   - The establishment of alternative communication channels and the selection of relevant methods of communication.

Managers must have access to timely, reliable, and relevant information in order to make effective decisions. Information systems should be implemented to capture information and process, summarize and report the information on an accurate and timely basis. Proper communication involves providing employees with an understanding of their roles and responsibilities. Open communication channels are essential to the proper functioning of I/C.

- **Info system** consists of the methods and records used to identify, record, measure, process, summarize, present, disclose and report the company's transactions and to maintain accountability for the related accounts.
- **Communication** involves establishing individual duties and responsibilities relating to I/C and making them known to involved personnel.

Corporate Governance, Internal Control & ERM

Monitoring Activities

Monitoring refers to the processes the entity uses to determine if all components of I/C, including the principles within each component, are in place and are functioning in the manner intended. Monitoring activities encompass 2 principles.

- Evaluations are conducted on an ongoing basis, on a separate periodic basis, or both to determine if controls are in place and are functioning effectively.
- I/C deficiencies are communicated to parties responsible for corrective action on a timely basis.

To assess the quality of I/C performance (are controls working?), controls are monitored by performing *ongoing evaluations* of activities (eg, reviewing customer complaints when they come in) or by *separate evaluations* (eg, periodic audits). Information systems can have embedded modules that look for unusual or suspicious transactions or relationships. Two main categories of monitoring activities include "ongoing evaluations" and "separate evaluations."

In 2009, COSO issued *Guidance on Monitoring Internal Control Systems,* which elaborates on the monitoring component of I/C. Individuals who monitor controls within an organization are referred to as evaluators. **Evaluators** should be both *competent and objective.*

I/C systems *fail* because the controls are not designed or implemented properly; the environment changes or their operation has changed. Within a corporation, I/C should be evaluated by the internal audit staff who report to the BOD.

Monitoring may be considered as consisting of the following **sequence of activities**:

- **Control baseline** – Development of an understanding of how the system of internal control was designed and implemented.
- **Change identification** – Use of ongoing and separate evaluations to identify and address changes in the effectiveness of I/C to initiate changes to controls.
- **Change management** – Determination of when changes to I/C are needed and the types of changes that are likely to be effective.
- **Control revalidation/update** – Development of a new baseline understanding of the revised system.

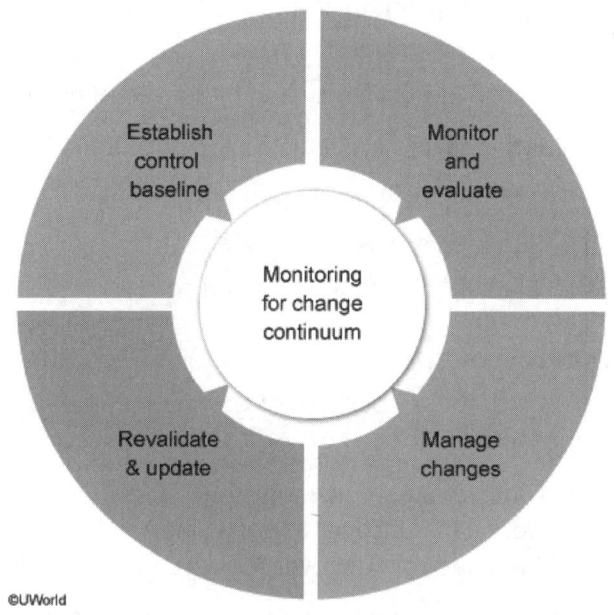

Limitations of Internal Control

A system of internal control can be designed to provide only reasonable assurance of achieving an entity's objectives. That is, even with an effective system of internal control, the following **inherent limitations (COP)** may result in failures (ie, fraud and error):

- **C**ollusion among employees to circumvent controls ⎫ Fraud
- **O**verride by management ⎭
- **P**oor human judgment and errors — Error

Fraud Risk Management Program

Fraud is any illegal act characterized by deceit, concealment, or violation of trust. It is generally considered to be intentional, and deals with the integrity of the perpetrator, as opposed to errors, which are considered unintentional and deal with the competency of the perpetrator. Typically, it can be divided into **asset misappropriation** (theft) or **misstatement of financial statements**.

Members of upper management are more likely to misstate financial statements. Nonmanagement employees are more likely to steal assets and then take steps to conceal the theft. By its very nature, fraud involves some sort of deceit. An entity is vulnerable to severe long-term impact from fraud without active measures to deter, detect and minimize it. Well-managed entities over a minimal size develop a fraud risk management program (FRMP) long before a probable fraud event occurs.

Purpose

Reasons for a FRMP span the spectrum from legal duty to entity survival.

- A FRMP helps the BOD satisfy:
    - Duty of care to stakeholders.
    - Statutory/regulatory requirements (Sarbanes-Oxley, SEC, PCAOB standards, etc.)
- A FRMP helps support stakeholder confidence (impact of fraud on profitability and available funding). Shareholders are unwilling to invest to support a fraudster; they invest to receive financial returns.
- A FRMP helps entity survival.
    - Greater profitability
    - Intact or enhanced image
    - Improved efficiency and increased ability to meet commitments and obtain financing
- A FRMP helps to prevent, detect, and deter fraud.
- A FRMP helps enhance employee morale.
    - Reduced stress
    - Greater job satisfaction and security

Fraud Discovery

According to the Association of Certified Fraud Examiners Report to the Nations on Occupational Fraud & Abuse:

- Tips and whistle-blowers uncover about 40 percent of fraud. Management review and internal auditors each uncover about 15 percent of fraud. Accidents uncover over 5 percent of fraud. External auditors uncover **less** than 5 percent of fraud.
- Fraud losses are estimated at 5 percent of revenues.
- "**Red flags**" are present in over 80 percent of cases:
    - Living beyond means or personal financial difficulties
    - Unusually close relationships with vendors or customers
    - Excessive control issues

Occupational fraud is the use of one's occupation for personal gain through the deliberate misuse or misapplication of the organization's resources or assets. Types of occupational fraud and abuse include misappropriations of assets, corruption, and financial statement fraud.

Corporate Governance, Internal Control & ERM

COSO's Five Steps in a FRMP

1. Establish governance policies
2. Conduct a comprehensive risk assessment
3. Plan and execute preventive and detective control processes
4. Perform timely and confidential investigations
5. Monitor and assess the program (periodically, on an ongoing basis, or both periodically and on an ongoing basis) reporting the results and improving the processes

An effective FRMP will deter, but not eliminate, fraud. An effective FRMP:

- Initiates a visible and rigorous fraud governance process
- Promotes a transparent and sound anti-fraud culture
- Entails a thorough periodic fraud risk assessment
- Plans, executes, and maintains preventive and detective fraud control processes
- Responds quickly to fraud allegations, including loss recovery actions and proceedings against perpetrators

Five Fraud Risk Management Principles (CRIME) under COSO

1. **Control *E*nvironment**: The organization establishes and communicates a FRMP that demonstrates the expectations of the BOD and senior management (**Tone at the Top**) and their commitment to high integrity and ethical values regarding management fraud risk (**CHOPPER**).

2. ***R*isk Assessment**: The organization performs comprehensive fraud risk assessments to identify specific fraud schemes and risks, assess their likelihood and significance, evaluate existing fraud control activities, and implement actions to mitigate residual fraud risks.

3. **Control Activities**: The organization selects, develops, and deploys preventive and detective fraud control activities to mitigate the risk of fraud events occurring or not being detected in a timely manner.

4. ***I*nformation & Communication**: The organization establishes a communication process to obtain information about potential fraud and deploys a coordinated approach to investigation and corrective action to address fraud appropriately and in a timely manner.

5. ***M*onitoring Activities**: The organization selects, develops, and performs ongoing evaluations to ascertain whether each of the five principles of fraud risk management is present and functioning and communications FRMP deficiencies in a timely manner to parties responsible for taking corrective action, including senior management and the BOD.

Roles of Key Parties in Managing Fraud Risk[1]

- **Those Charged with Governance (ideally, the Audit Committee)**
    - Consider the risk of management override of controls.
    - Monitor fraud risks throughout the entity (using internal auditor or other personnel).
    - Meet privately with appropriate individuals (eg, internal auditor, external auditors).
    - Consider reputation risk when reviewing work of management, internal auditors, and external auditors.
    - Remain cognizant of the external auditor's responsibilities pertaining to fraud.
    - Seek counsel when responding to allegations of fraud.

---

[1] As outlined by ACFE.

- **Board of Directors**
  - Understand fraud risks (both generally and those affecting the entity).
  - Establish and communicate an appropriate level of risk tolerance for the entity.
  - Maintain oversight of the fraud risk assessment.
  - Monitor management's reports on fraud risks, policies, and control activities.
  - Ensure that management provides effective fraud risk management documentation to encourage ethical behavior.
  - Retain outside experts as appropriate.
  - Remain cognizant of the external auditor's responsibilities pertaining to fraud.

- **Management (CEO, CFO, COO, etc.)**
  - Design, implement, maintain, and document the FRMP.
  - Maintain documentation of antifraud controls.
  - Evaluate design and operating effectiveness of antifraud controls.
  - Report to the BOD on actions that have been taken to manage fraud risks and the effectiveness of the FRMP.
  - Educate the entity on areas of potential compliance violations.
  - Enforce the entity's Code of Ethics.

- **Internal Auditors**
  - Report to those charged with governance.
  - Provide assurance to the BOD and management regarding existing controls' appropriateness given the risk tolerance established by the BOD.
  - Evaluate the design and operation of antifraud controls for comprehensiveness and adequacy, especially regarding management override risks.
  - Support the audit committee in performing detective activities around the risk of management override of controls.
  - Consider fraud risks when developing audit plans.
  - Support management's education of the entity regarding areas of potential fraud and compliance violations.

- **Employees (in all functions and at all levels)**
  - Have a basic awareness of fraud and "red flags."
  - Comprehend policies and procedures (eg, fraud policy, code of conduct, whistleblower policy, internal controls specific to position, etc.).
  - Contribute to a strong control environment.
  - Report suspicions or incidences of fraud and corruption.
  - Cooperate with audits and investigations.

Typical Shortcomings

A fraud risk assessment (part of an entity's broader risk assessment process) considers the ways that fraud and misconduct can occur by and against the entity. The ACFE finds that fraud risk assessment failures typically are due to one or more of the following:

- Assessment consists of an identification of risk factors, but omits an identification of schemes and scenarios.
- Lack of follow up after identification of fraud risks and linkage to mitigating controls.

- Potential perpetrators are not identified (which can lead to insufficient consideration of management override).
- Inadequate consideration of collusive fraud and management override of controls.
- Lack of appropriate involvement in assessment by internal auditors and other appropriate personnel.
- Lack of appropriate monitoring by the audit committee.

While a FRMP cannot guarantee the absence of fraud, it can deter fraud and minimize fraud loss much less expensively than other measures. Entities cannot rely complacently on an annual audit and a code of ethics to prevent fraud.

Lecture 2.03 – Enterprise Risk Management (ERM)

The business and economic environment is often unpredictable with significant technology evolution, rapidly shifting customer behavior, global influences, and fierce competition—all factors that stress strategic planning and the need to maximize operational capabilities to survive and thrive. All this creates uncertainty, which provides both risk and opportunity, and management must determine how to balance those risks and opportunities in alignment with the objectives of the entity. As you can imagine, this can be an extremely daunting task without an organized ERM approach to help keep up with the pace of change facing entities today.

To respond to the need for this organized approach, COSO developed an ERM **framework** in 2004 and updated it in 2017 to complement the I/C framework previously discussed. COSO's ERM framework is designed to be applied by all types and sizes of entities *to strategically identify events that may affect the entity and to manage those risks in accordance with the entity's risk appetite, to provide reasonable assurance of achieving the entity's objectives.*

As updated in 2017, due to the increasing complexity of business risks, the accelerated rate of emerging new risks, and the demand for better risk reporting, the framework, retitled *Enterprise Risk Management—Integrating with Strategy & Performance,* dives deeper to redefine risk in relation to strategy and performance and focuses on the need to embed ERM proactively throughout the entity.

Benefits

COSO touts several benefits to implementing its ERM framework:

- Promotes identification and *management of entity-wide risks*.
- *Increases identification of opportunities* by examining the pros and cons of possibilities.
- *Reduces costs* of negative surprises and *maximizes positive outcomes*.
- Manages performance risks to *reduce disruption and increase opportunity*.
- Prioritizes and *maximizes allocation of resources*.
- Enhances entity *resilience*—the ability to anticipate and respond to change.

Components & Principles Overview

COSO's new ERM framework has *5 components* **(COPe RR)** and *20* different associated *principles* as outlined below.

Governance & Culture

1. Exercises board risk oversight
2. Establishes operating structures
3. Defines desired culture
4. Demonstrates commitment to core values
5. Attracts, develops, and retains capable individuals

Strategy & Objective Setting

6. Analyzes business context
7. Defines risk appetite
8. Evaluates alternative strategies
9. Formulates business objectives

Corporate Governance, Internal Control & ERM

*P*erformance
10. Identifies risks
11. Assesses severity of risks
12. Prioritizes risks
13. Implements risk responses
14. Develops portfolio view

*R*eview & Revision
15. Assesses substantial change
16. Reviews risk and performance
17. Pursues improvement in ERM

Information, Communication & *R*eporting
18. Leverages information systems
19. Communicates risk information
20. Reports on risk, culture, and performance

Governance & Culture

The first of the five components of the COSO ERM Framework is *Governance and Culture*. It sets the overall tone for the organization, addressing such issues as mission, vision, and core values. Governance encompasses the establishment of oversight responsibilities for ERM and the entity's tone. Culture refers to the ethical mindset, standards of acceptable behavior, and understanding the entity's risk.

Principle 1: Exercises Board Risk Oversight
"The board of directors provides oversight of the strategy and carries out governance responsibilities to support management in achieving strategy and business objectives."

The board's oversight role supports the creation of value in an entity and prevents its decline. The framework catalogs risk oversight responsibilities for boards. These responsibilities include overseeing governance and culture; strategy and objective-setting; performance; information, communications and reporting; and the reevaluation and improvement of practices to enrich entity performance. The board's risk oversight role includes, but is not limited to:

- Cultivating investor and stakeholder relations
- Authorizing management pay and incentives
- Reevaluating, questioning, and agreeing with management on:
    - Suggested strategy and target risk appetite
    - Coordination of strategy and business objectives with the entity's mission, vision, and values
    - Major decisions including mergers, acquisitions, capital allocations, funding, and dividend-related decisions
    - Reactions to substantial fluctuations in entity performance or the risk portfolio
    - Treatment of instances of deviation from values

Management is responsible for managing risks to the entity. To evaluate management's performance, a board generally would determine the answers to the following questions, among others. The answers may illustrate the entity's actual mindset for risk taking as opposed to what appears in documentation.

- Can all levels of management—not just senior management—articulate how risk is considered in the selection of strategy or business decisions?
- Can all levels of management clearly articulate the entity's target risk appetite and how it might influence a specific decision?
- How does the culture promote or retard responsible risk taking?
- How does management monitor the risk culture and how it changes? What changes have occurred?
- As changes occur, how does management ensure a suitable and prompt response?

Principle 2: Establishes operating structures

"The organization establishes operating structures in the pursuit of strategy and business objectives."

Principle 3: Defines desired culture

"The organization defines the desired behaviors that characterize the entity's desired culture."

Principle 4: Demonstrates commitment to core values

"The organization demonstrates a commitment to the entity's' core values."

Principle 5: Attracts, develops, and retains capable individuals

"The organization is committed to building human capital in alignment with the strategy and business objectives."

Principles 2 through 5 represent the *internal environment*, which sets the tone for the organization. It establishes a basis for the analysis of risk, incorporating management's philosophy, the entity's risk appetite, and the values that are important to the entity, such as *integrity and ethical values*.

The internal environment is exhibited in a variety of ways, both formal and informal. Some of the more formal components will include the entity's mission statement and its code of conduct. These should be evident in all aspects of the entity and should be incorporated into the entity's culture. A well-designed **mission statement** may address some or all of the following:

- The moral or ethical position of the entity and its desired public image
- The key strategic influence for the entity's operations
- A description of the entity's products or services, target market, and geographical domain
- Expectations in relation to growth and profitability

The informal aspect of the internal environment is probably the most important. It is comprised of the actual behavior of members of management and others who might be seen as influential within the organization. Whenever the behavior of such individuals is in conflict with the entity's mission statement or core values, or its formal policies and procedures, individuals both inside the organization and outside of it will assign more significance to the behavior.

One significant aspect of management and executive behavior is the relationship established with employees. Management should exhibit a willingness to tolerate mistakes, listen, and learn.

Strategy & Objective Setting

The second component of the COSO ERM Framework is *Strategy & Objective Setting*. It represents the entity's process for strategic planning. The entity determines its risk appetite, aligns it with its strategy, and develops business objectives to execute the strategy. This process serves as a basis for recognizing, evaluating, and responding to risk.

Principle 6: Analyzes Business Context

"The organization considers potential effects of business context on risk profile."

Business context refers to the environment in which the business operates. ERM involves considering a full range of potential events, enabling management to identify and take advantage of opportunities. Also see principle 10.

Principle 7: Defines Risk Appetite

"The organization defines risk appetite in the context of creating, preserving, and realizing value."

It is important for management to consider what level of risk is acceptable when evaluating alternatives, establishing goals, and developing policies, procedures, and other mechanisms to manage risks. For example, an entity should consider its risk appetite when determining its policy regarding the amount of information that must be obtained about a potential customer and how much must be verified independently before extending credit in order to avoid selling to someone who is not likely to pay.

Principle 8: Evaluates Alternative Strategies

"The organization evaluates alternative strategies and potential impact on risk profile."

Strategy is about developing a plan of action to achieve the entity's objectives. In evaluating alternative strategies, the entity must first align potential business strategies with the entity's mission, vision, and core values, and then determine the impact of those strategies with respect to the entity's risk profile (ie, risk appetite). COSO's ERM framework provides 3 types of risks to consider in this process:

- **Risks *to* a chosen strategy** and the performance of that strategy—These are factors an entity should address when choosing a strategy, such as customer demand, supply, competition, and technology infrastructure.

- **Risks that the strategy chosen will *not align* with the mission, vision, and values**—Even if a strategy is successful, a misaligned strategy increases the risk that the entity will not achieve its mission and vision, or its values will be compromised. While some entities have been reluctant to truly embrace their mission, vision, and values, they have been shown to be extremely important to risk management and resilience in times of change.

- **Risks *of, or from*, the chosen strategy**—Every choice has some downsides. The risks of the strategy that is chosen should be considered and aligned with the risk appetite of the entity. The board and management should determine how the strategy will steer the entity in setting objectives and whether resources will be allocated efficiently.

Note: It's important to realize that ERM is as much about *understanding* all the risks as it is about managing them to enhance the performance of the entity.

Principle 9: Formulates Business Objectives

"The organization considers risk while establishing the business objectives at various levels that align and support strategy."

While an entity's mission describes what it would like to accomplish, it does not set out a specific plan for accomplishing the mission. Management translates the mission into goals or objectives that support the mission and take into account the entity's risk appetite. The *department manager* would be the best person to devise and execute the risk procedures for a particular department, as they are the most able to identify risky events within that department.

There are four types of business objectives to establish:

- Setting objectives begins at the top with **strategic objectives**, which establish a unifying theme for the entity and direct actions and decisions. While strategic objectives set the direction for the entity, objectives related to *operations, reporting, and compliance* provide the mechanisms for meeting those objectives. To be most effective, objectives should be set at each level and, when appropriate, in each of the three categories. A division manager, for example, should know what outputs their division is expected to provide, to whom, to what specifications, and on what timetable so that the manager can make the decisions that will accomplish those objectives.

- The strategic objectives may relate to the quality and other characteristics of the outputs and how the division will be operated. In order to achieve the strategic objective as to quality, the division manager will need the appropriate raw materials, qualified laborers, and the equipment or other resources necessary to convert those inputs into the desired outputs. **Operational objectives**, as a result, may be set to address the acquisition of raw materials, the screening and assignment of laborers, the acquisition and maintenance of equipment and support, and the process for completing the outputs.

- **Reporting objectives** would be established to determine how the division is progressing toward meeting the operational objectives and, ultimately, the strategic objectives. The manager will need to devise a means of determining if the needs of the customer are being met. This may involve obtaining feedback from a subsequent department as to the quality and amount of output that is being transferred. It may involve obtaining feedback from the work force as to the quality of the raw materials that are being provided or from supervision regarding the efficiency of the labor. Achievement of reporting objectives may require sophisticated reports that provide a large amount of information manipulated in a variety of ways. The most effective information is often limited in scope to one or very few parameters, does not require a great deal of effort to accumulate and report on a timely basis, and can be simply understood.

- **Compliance objectives** make certain that the division operates within appropriate guidelines, including both regulatory requirements and internal company policies. This includes making certain that employees are not working against the better interests of the employing entity. At the same time, they must be designed so that an employee does not violate requirements externally imposed in a misguided attempt to help the entity.

*Pe*rformance

The third component of COSO's ERM Framework is *Performance*. It represents the process of actually identifying, evaluating, and responding to risks. The risks should be prioritized by severity with regard to the entity's risk appetite. The entity then chooses the appropriate responses, while

Corporate Governance, Internal Control & ERM

keeping an overall view of the amount of risk assumed. Results are reported to the appropriate stakeholders.

Principle 10: Identifies Risks

"The organization identifies risk that impacts the performance of strategy and business objectives."

The occurrence or nonoccurrence of certain events (ie, risks) will determine whether or not the entity will achieve its objectives. Thus, risk identification involves determining what those events may be and how to distinguish between those events that representing opportunities, which should be encouraged and exploited, and those representing threats, which should be dealt with in accordance with the entity's risk appetite.

- **Opportunities must be exploited** in order to gain a competitive advantage, sustain one, or prevent a competitor from obtaining one. As such, opportunities should be considered in developing the strategic and other objectives of the entity. A plan might be established, and resources might be set aside, to take advantage of an opportunity in case it arises. Of course, the amount of effort going into the design of the plan and the resources set aside to take advantage of the opportunity will be a function of the likelihood that the event will occur, which is analogous to risk assessment, and the benefit that will be derived from it, which will be a factor in determining the appropriate response.

- Likewise, **risks must be prepared for** so that the entity does not lose a competitive advantage or allow a competitor to gain one. As a result, adverse events are considered in the entity's risk management process. The entity will consider the likelihood that an event will occur, the magnitude of the effect of the event, and the amount the effect will be influenced by actions of the entity in determining an appropriate response.

Event identification is primarily the identification and monitoring of the sources of information that pertain to areas of risk for the entity. Since resources are limited, the entity must be discreet in deciding which sources of information will be monitored. One approach, an aspect of risk assessment, is to determine the resources that are critical to achieving the objectives of the entity. The entity might then be able to identify the types of events that would affect that resource and might be able to seek out sources of information that would help the entity estimate the likelihood of the event and alert the entity of its occurrence, or imminent occurrence, on a timely basis. There are various techniques for identifying relevant events for ERM:

- **Event inventories** are detailed lists of the types of events the entity may be subject to due to the industry it is in, its geographic location, or other characteristics of its operations.

- **Internal analysis**, often done as part of routine business planning, may consist of discussions at meetings, or formal processes that are conducted on a routine basis. They utilize information that is developed internally as well as that obtained from external sources including customers, suppliers, and business relationships, as well as from the news, governmental reports, and other general sources.

- **Escalation or threshold triggers**, which involves the establishment of benchmarks or other criteria against which experiences can be compared to identify those that may require attention. These may be routine, such as reports on delinquent accounts receivable that will trigger collection procedures or monitoring devices that warn of factory temperatures exceeding certain limits.

- **Facilitated workshops or interviews** may be conducted for the specific purpose of learning of event indicators. They may involve staff, outside consultants, or experts in various fields. An auditor, for example, is required to conduct a brainstorming session with key staff to identify fraud risk factors. This enables the auditor to use the combined knowledge and experience of all participants to identify signs of fraud. Similarly, a meeting with factory staff may be useful in identifying signs of an unsafe condition, thereby preventing an undesirable event in the form of an accident.

- **Process flow analysis** involves the consideration of all components of a process including its inputs, tasks, responsibilities, and outputs. The factors affecting each aspect of the process can be considered to identify events that may be relevant, such as a potential scarcity of a resource used as a raw material in the process.

- **Leading event indicators** involves identifying data that is indicative of a pending event, such as an increase in consumer spending, which may correlate with possible increases in future interest rates.

- **Loss event data methodologies** are collections of information regarding past losses that may have been incurred by the entity or others to identify causes or trends. In anticipating allocating a new contract among different manufacturing plants, analyzing returned goods may identify that certain plants are delivering defective parts and the company can avoid a loss by not awarding the contract inappropriately. *Black swan analysis* involves evaluating the occurrence of events that had a negative effect and were unanticipated or viewed as highly unlikely.

ERM also identifies categories of events, including:

- **Internal** factors such as infrastructure, personnel, processes, and technology
- **External** factors such as economy, natural environment, politics, social factors, and technology

Three broad approaches might be employed to identify events that may have an adverse effect on an entity. These approaches are not mutually exclusive and an entity should apply all in its risk assessment at all levels of the organization. These three approaches can be described as a balance sheet approach, a process approach, and an event identification approach.

- Under the **balance sheet approach**, the entity should identify the resources within its control and determine which ones might be vulnerable and the degree of vulnerability. Most any assets might be misappropriated, for example, but the likelihood of misappropriation and the damage the entity would sustain upon misappropriation will be important factors in evaluating risk.

    o *Assets essential to the achievement of the entity's objectives*, such as raw materials; exclusive information, formulae, or processes; and customer lists, for example, might be so essential to the entity that they will require protection regardless of their cost or the likelihood of their misappropriation. Other assets might not be essential to the entity but might be used by employees or general consumers in their everyday lives. These might include cash, supplies, and other assets like certain inventories. The risk evaluation must take into account that these assets are particularly susceptible to misappropriation or other misuse.

    o When applying the balance sheet approach, it is important to consider *assets owned by the entity, its intellectual property, and its human resources*. It is also important to consider all of the individuals who are in position to create events that will affect the entity. This might include employees with access to, or custody of, assets. As discussed earlier, threats may come from internal sources, including employees, officers, and directors. They may also come from external sources, including competitors and potential competitors, customers, and con artists.

- The **process approach** involves evaluating the processes that are used to achieve the entity's objectives. At the entity level, this might include the process for establishing objectives and allocating resources. All processes, at all levels, should be considered. This will include the process for determining when a raw material or supply should be purchased, the process for providing a service or manufacturing a component of inventory, the process for obtaining supplies, and the process for recording a transaction. The evaluation of risk under this approach includes the consideration of various possibilities. For each possibility, the entity must consider the likelihood that the possibility will become a reality and its consequences. Examples might include the risk that a process will not be performed, that it will not be performed on a timely basis, or that it will not be performed correctly. Consequences may range from being negligible to very significant. Neglecting to perform a process properly may result in defective inventory, a work stoppage, or product liability.

- The **event identification approach** incorporates many of the principles already discussed. One of the most difficult aspects of this approach is limiting the number of areas in which sources for information are sought. This might be accomplished when viewing the entity from the standpoint of competition. In *Contemporary Strategy Analysis*, Robert Grant discusses Michael Porter's Five Forces of Competition. These include customers, suppliers, competitors, potential entrants into the market, and substitutes. The entity should seek to identify events that might affect any of these five forces.

    o In the case of *customers*, increases or decreases in the *demand* for their products or services may affect the demand for the entity's products or services. *Economic events* may make it easier or more difficult for customers to pay for the entity's products or services on a timely basis. *Changes in customers' needs* may make certain features of the entity's products or services more or less valuable to customers. Other types of events may create *new customers*, such as a change in an industry's manufacturing process that makes the entity's products or services valuable to entities that had no previous use for them.

    o When an entity is evaluating *events that may affect suppliers*, it must consider all of its suppliers, including *suppliers of human resources, financial resources, and physical resources*. Events including changes in school enrollments or *graduation rates, failing or emerging industries*, and *shifts in population* may affect the supply of human resources. *Economic and social events*, as well as events affecting other entities seeking the same human resources, may affect the compensation and benefits required to attract or retain the appropriate human resources.

    o *Economic events may affect the availability and the cost of capital.* The entity's access to financial resources will also be affected by the availability of investment alternatives. The availability of physical resources may be affected by events related to weather or other natural phenomena. In addition, increases or decreases in the *demand* for the goods and services of an entity's suppliers will affect the cost and availability of those goods and services to the entity.

    o *Events that affect competitors* also affect the entity. Innovations that result in changes to their processes may provide them with a competitive advantage or eliminate one held by the entity. When operating in a finite market, events that create an advantage to competitors generally result in a disadvantage to the entity. As competitors devote more resources to marketing, they may improve their access to customers and reduce the entity's market share. More resources devoted to recruiting may increase access to human resources, decreasing those available to the entity. When events affect competitors' sales volumes, it affects their demand for raw materials, which will affect the price and availability of those raw materials to the entity.

- o Events that change the cost of entry into the market will encourage or discourage potential competitors. Events might include those related to the cost of capital, access to customers or suppliers, or the ability to emulate or improve processes. Obviously, events that lower the cost of entry into the market will increase competition, while events that increase it may decrease competition and, at a minimum, will slow down increases in it.
- o Substitutes affect the entity in two ways. They are in competition for the attention of suppliers as well as for the attention of customers. Substitutes include those who might use the same resources that are used by the entity. Events that increase or decrease their need for common resources will affect the price and availability of those resources to the entity. In addition, the extent to which events will cause customers to see other products or services as substitutes for those of the entity will increase or decrease demand for the entity's products or services.

Principle 11: Assesses Severity of Risks

"The organization assesses the severity of risks."

Management must evaluate the extent of potential effects of identified events on the ability of the entity to achieve its objectives. The likelihood of the occurrence of each identified risk is measured as well as the potential effect on the entity if the event were to occur. Here's three approaches used to quantify risk:

- **Benchmarking**, which compares expected outcomes to common measures.
- **Probabilistic models**, which develop expected values using probabilities of possible outcomes (quantifying risk).
- **Nonprobabilistic models**, which use subjective assumptions to measure possible outcomes (qualitative, but not quantitative).

Principles 12. Prioritizes Risks

"The organization prioritizes risks as a basis for selecting responses to risks."

Once management has identified and assessed the severity of the risks that may affect the entity's ability to achieve its objectives, it can decide how to prioritize the risks so that management can effectively assess capital needs and allocate capital where it is most needed or will be most productive.

Principle 13. Risk Response

"The organization identifies and selects risk responses."

When deciding on an appropriate risk response, the entity must consider inherent risk and residual risk.

- **Inherent risk** is the risk to the entity *if no action is taken*.
- **Residual risk** is the risk to the entity that would remain *if action were taken* and controls are taken into account.

The *reduction in risk*—basically the difference between an event's inherent risk and its residual risk—*can be compared to the cost of taking action to determine if action is appropriate*. This type of analysis is also useful in deciding among alternative actions when more than one risk response is available.

Among the **alternative responses to risks** are the decisions to *avoid* a risk, *mitigate* the risk, *share* the risk, or simply *accept* the risk. For example, if there is not sufficient verifiable information about a potential customer, the company can avoid risk by not extending credit, reduce it by limiting the amount of credit extended, share it by entering into an agreement with a third party, such as a bonding company or a guarantor, or accept it by extending credit.

- **Acceptance** of a risk indicates that the entity would take no action and simply allow the event to occur. This would be appropriate when the entity believes that inherent risk is already at an acceptable level or that the cost of taking action would exceed the reduction in risk that would result from the action anticipated.

- If the inherent risk is above an acceptable level, an entity might next seek to share that risk. **Sharing** the risk might involve the use of insurance or fidelity bonds, entering into an arrangement with another entity to share the risk, or outsourcing an activity. Outsourcing may be considered an example of sharing risk or avoiding it. In addition, the risks being "avoided" by the outsourcing entity are taken into account and incorporated in the cost of the product or service being outsourced.

- An entity that cannot find a cost-efficient manner of sharing the risk may decide to reduce it. **Reducing** the risk may require a change in the internal environment or may be accomplished through control activities, which can often reduce risk to an acceptable level. An entity may reduce the risk of inventory misappropriation, for example, by keeping it in a more secure location. It may also minimize losses through early detection. This could be accomplished if the entity maintains a perpetual inventory system and conducts regular and frequent counts. Such a system may be costly, and the costs should be compared to the anticipated reduction in risk to determine whether such control activities would be cost effective.

- When risk cannot be reduced to an acceptable level, **avoidance** may be the best alternative. This may require an entity to change an internal process, eliminate a line of business or product, stop using a particular raw material or buying from a specific supplier, or discontinue selling to a particular customer. An entity may determine that it does not have the ability to monitor receivables efficiently and the cost of reducing losses to an acceptable level would be prohibitive. As a result, the entity may decide to make all sales for cash, checks, and debit or credit cards and discontinue accepting sales on open account.

Principle 14. Risk Portfolio
"The organization develops and evaluates a portfolio view of risk."

ERM is designed to help management evaluate the interrelated impacts of decisions and deal with multiple risks. One risk may combine with other risks or offset other risks. Management must be careful when developing policies and procedures that are designed to affect one issue as, due to the integrated nature of business, it increases a different risk. For example, if we decide not to sell to the customer on credit, we also risk losing the customer to a competitor and adversely affecting the enthusiasm of the salesperson who worked to bring the customer in.

*R*eview & Revision
The fourth component of the COSO ERM Framework is Review & Revision. It represents the process of evaluating how well ERM components perform over time and refining the components as conditions change, as necessary.

Principle 15: Assesses substantial change

"The organization identifies and assesses changes that may substantially affect strategy and business objectives."

Principle 16: Reviews risk and performance

"The organization reviews entity performance and considers risk."

Principle 17: Pursues improvement in ERM

"The organization pursues improvement of enterprise risk management."

Risk assessment is an ongoing process, not a "one-time" activity. The entire ERM system must be monitored so that changes can be made on a timely basis. Monitoring may be through ongoing management activities or as part of a separate evaluation of the entity's ERM process.

Information, Communication & Reporting

The last of the five COSO ERM Framework components is *Information, Communication & Reporting*. It represents the ongoing exchange of internal and external information up and down as well as across the entity.

Principle 18: Leverages information and technology

"The organization leverages the entity's information and technology systems to support enterprise risk management."

Principle 19: Communicates risk information

"The organization uses communication channels to support enterprise risk management."

Principle 20: Reports on risk, culture, and performance

"The organization reports on risk, culture, and performance at multiple levels and across the entity."

People must have relevant information to carry out their responsibilities. As a result, the entity must have a means of identifying what information is pertinent from all of its internal and external sources.

Relevant information may be financial or nonfinancial and may be quantitative or qualitative in nature. It may also be formal or informal, such as that derived from conversations with customers or suppliers. It can potentially come from such a wide range of sources that it becomes very important for an entity to determine what sources are reliable as well as what information is relevant.

Once identified, relevant information must be captured, processed, and communicated to those who can benefit from it. It must be put into a form that is usable and must be provided on a timely basis so that decisions can be made to prevent losses.

Communication must include parties to whom it is relevant. It is most effective when lines of communication move in all directions within and around an organization. There should be communication at all levels, including upward and downward communication. Likewise, relevant information should be communicated with customers or suppliers to enhance the entity's ability to meet the needs of customers and have its needs met by suppliers.

BEC 3 – Business Processes & Information Technology

Table of Contents

Lecture 3.01 – IT Role in Business — 1
- BUSINESS PROCESS CONTROLS — 1
- IT ENABLEMENT — 3
- BUSINESS SYSTEMS — 4
- IT ENVIRONMENT — 5
- IT DEPARTMENT — 6

Lecture 3.02 – IT Governance & Frameworks — 8
- OVERVIEW — 8
- CONTROL OBJECTIVES FOR INFORMATION AND RELATED TECHNOLOGY (COBIT) — 9
- NATIONAL INSTITUTE OF STANDARDS AND TECHNOLOGY CYBERSECURITY FRAMEWORK — 12
- SUMMARY — 12

Lecture 3.03 – IT Infrastructure — 13
- OVERVIEW — 13
- HARDWARE — 13
- SOFTWARE — 14
- CENTRALIZED VS. DISTRIBUTED PROCESSING — 15
- NETWORKS IN GENERAL — 15
- NETWORK CONFIGURATIONS — 16
- NETWORK TOPOLOGY — 17
- ENTERPRISE RESOURCE PLANNING (ERP) SYSTEMS — 17
- CLIENT-SERVER COMPUTING VS. CLOUD COMPUTING — 19

Lecture 3.04 – Electronic Commerce — 22
- OVERVIEW — 22
- ELECTRONIC DATA INTERCHANGE — 22
- E-COMMERCE RISK — 23
- E-COMMERCE IMPACT ON PRODUCT LIFE CYCLE — 24

Lecture 3.05 – IT General Controls — 26
- OVERVIEW — 26
- IT GOVERNANCE — 26
- LOGICAL ACCESS CONTROLS & CYBERSECURITY — 26
- CHANGE CONTROLS — 28
- PHYSICAL SECURITY — 28
- BUSINESS RESILIENCE PLANNING — 29
- SUMMARY — 33

Lecture 3.06 – Application Controls — 34
- OVERVIEW — 34
- INPUT CONTROLS — 34
- PROCESSING CONTROLS — 35
- OUTPUT CONTROLS — 36
- SUMMARY — 36

Lecture 3.07 – Change Controls & Systems Documentation — 37
- SYSTEMS DEVELOPMENT LIFE CYCLE (SDLC) — 37
- CHANGE MANAGEMENT – CHANGES TO PROCESSES & SYSTEMS — 38
- SYSTEMS DOCUMENTATION — 39

Lecture 3.08 – Business Processes: Revenue Cycle — 44
- EMPLOYEES & DUTIES — 44
- DOCUMENTS & RECORDS — 45
- REVENUE CYCLE CONTROL ACTIVITIES — 46

Lecture 3.09 – Business Processes: Spending Cycle — 47
- OVERVIEW — 47
- EMPLOYEES & DUTIES — 47
- DOCUMENTS & RECORDS — 47
- CONTROL ACTIVITIES — 48

Lecture 3.10 – Business Processes: Investing, Financing, Production & Conversion Cycles — 50
- INVESTING & FINANCING CYCLE — 50
- FIXED ASSETS — 50
- PRODUCTION & CONVERSION CYCLE — 51

Lecture 3.11 – Business Processes: Personnel & Payroll — 53
- OVERVIEW — 53
- EMPLOYEES, DUTIES, DOCUMENTS & RECORDS — 53
- CONTROL ACTIVITIES — 54

Lecture 3.12 – System & Organization Controls (SOC) Reports — 55
- OVERVIEW — 55
- SOC 1 – SOC FOR SERVICE ORGANIZATION: ICFR — 55
- TRUST SERVICES — 56
- SOC 2 – SOC FOR SERVICE ORGANIZATIONS: TRUST SERVICES CRITERIA — 57
- SOC 3 – SOC FOR SERVICE ORGANIZATIONS: TRUST SERVICES CRITERIA FOR GENERAL USE REPORT — 58
- SUMMARY — 58

Business Processes & Information Technology

Lecture 3.01 – IT Role in Business

Business Process Controls

When designing an internal control (I/C) structure, a systematic process should be applied that will provide assurance that:

- All types of transactions and activities are considered,
- Risks associated with each type are considered, and
- The systems have those elements that are conducive to more effective controls.

The foundation of the system will be developed around those repetitive transactions that affect the entity on a regular basis. This includes, for example, processes for sales, collections, purchasing, disbursements, and payroll. Depending on the industry in which the entity operates and the nature of its operations, it may include various other core systems.

A **business process** is a combination of procedures performed in a particular sequence for a desired result. For our discussion, we'll divide up the flow of transactions and business processes into the following six **operating cycles**.

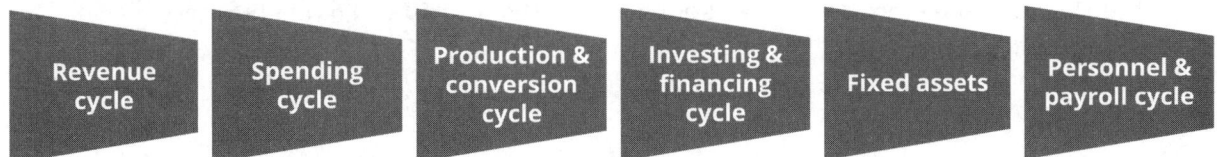

We'll take a closer look at the most common business processes within these operating cycles and their specific controls later. For now, let's see what they all have generally have in common.

The different **types of transactions/events** within business processes that occur on an ongoing basis affect an entity's operations and financial position. Each business process has certain components and controls:

- **Start** – At what point is a transaction **initiated**? In a sales transaction, for example, some transactions may be initiated when a customer contacts the entity, such as by arriving at a retail outlet, contacting the company by phone, or placing an order over the Internet. In others, sales personnel or other representatives of the entity call upon potential customers seeking orders.

- **Authorization** – What must occur before the entity is willing to commit resources to fulfilling its performance obligations in the transaction? Before committing resources, an entity will determine that the counterparty to the transaction is a legitimate party with the intent and ability to perform or that the event is real. For example, in a sales transaction, the credit department may need to determine that the customer is within its credit limit and is current on its account before a sale may be approved.

- **Completion (execution)** – What procedures will entity personnel perform, and what forms will be completed, as the entity meets its performance obligations associated with the transaction? Execution includes all procedures involved from the time a transaction is initiated until the time the entity's role in it has been fulfilled. The entity should have policies and procedures to make certain that its obligations in transactions and its responses to recurring events/circumstances are being performed in accordance with management's directives. This will include the flow of documents, services, goods, and other resources throughout the system. For example, in a sales transaction, the entity will identify and isolate the products sold, ship the merchandise, verify receipt, and prepare an invoice.

- **Recording** – The entity should have a system for making certain that all transactions, events, or circumstances that affect operations or financial position are properly captured and reflected in the entity's financial records.

- **Evaluate defenses** – What safeguards are built into the system to make certain that errors are not made and fraud is not committed? Verification occurs throughout the process. Each system should have checks and balances (ie, **verifications**) to make certain that each function is performed properly and in the appropriate sequence.
    - This may involve policies requiring the **matching of documents** (manually or automated). For example, requiring the shipping department to compare a customer's purchase order with an internal sales order and to a list of goods transferred from stores before shipping the goods.
    - It may also involve accounting for the sequence of **prenumbered documents**, checking for **authoritative signatures**, or periodically **reconciling recorded amounts** to physical assets. For example, in a sales transaction, this may involve completing a prenumbered sales order when an order is received. Someone in accounting will then verify that all forms within a sequence are accounted for.

> It should be easy to remember that a good system of I/C is **SACREd** to a business.

Documents

A well-designed system for a business process will include forms (whether paper or electronic) that are designed to require the process to:

- Be completed properly
- Make certain that all appropriate parties, and only appropriate parties, receive copies that have the information needed to fulfill their role in the process
- Provide for the segregation of incompatible duties

Segregation of Incompatible Duties

Incompatible functions, which should be kept separate, are (**ARCC**):

- **A**uthorization of transactions
- **R**ecording of the transactions
- **C**ustody of resources associated with those transactions
- **C**omparison and reconciliations of physical resources to recorded information

Segregation of duties is generally accomplished by having different parties or departments responsible for different aspects of a transaction. This is not necessarily achievable in a **small business environment**, in which there may be limited numbers of individuals among whom to allocate responsibilities.

It is also challenging in an environment that is **IT enabled**, in which the duties of authorization, reporting, and custody may be segregated with:

- **Authorization** associated with **inputs**
- **Reporting** associated with operations and **processing**
- **Custody** associated with **outputs** and the librarian function

Segregation can often be accomplished by using:

- **Physical Access Controls** – Limiting physical access to various components of the system to those who need access
- **Logical Access Controls** – Using **firewalls** and **passwords** to limit access from within the system

IT Enablement

IT enablement is the use of technology to increase the efficiency of processes while reducing costs and ensuring the accuracy of data. IT enablement is achieved through **business process reengineering (BPR)**. BPR is the redesigning of business processes to take advantage of newer technologies to automate manual tasks and capture important data. Such **digital transformations** improve competitive advantage.

The Internet and other technologies ushered in a paradigm shift from the computer as a number-crunching device to a communication tool. This shift was aided by significant declines in computing costs coupled with dramatic increases in computing power in the last several decades. Since the introduction of smartphones in 2007, technology has driven another shift from desktop computers to mobile devices (ie, **mobile computing**), integrating computers more fully into daily life.

Obviously, businesses are still using the number-crunching aspect of computers. Indeed, **automation** of many tasks once performed by humans is ubiquitous. The communications aspect's applicability to accounting might be less obvious. For example, employees use smartphones to take pictures of any paper receipts. Employees submit those pictures of receipts to a website that "reads" them and requests approval. Once approved, an electronic payment is issued to the employee's bank account.

Other examples of technologies employed to enhance business processes include:

- **Electronic business (e-business)** – This includes any business conducted over the internet (eg, paying taxes online).
    - **Electronic commerce (e-commerce)** – E-commerce is any activity that involves buying and selling products/services over the Internet.
        - **Electronic Data Interchange (EDI)** – A distributor's computer can communicate through EDI with manufacturers' and retailers' computers to order and ship products without human intervention.

    E-commerce and EDI are discussed in further detail in the next section.
- **Internet of Things (IoT)** – Nowadays, any electronic item can be embedded with computing devices that send and receive data from the Internet. IoT enables automation and delivers valuable data, among many other uses. For example, an electric company can install communicating meters on homes to receive readings on the meters without having a human physically go out to read them each month.

- **Blockchain** – Blockchains are expanding chains of blocks (or records) that are linked and secured using cryptography. Each block typically contains a timestamp, a link to a previous block, and the transaction data. Inherently, blockchains are nearly impossible to modify. Thus, blockchain promotes trust among e-business trading partners, among other uses.

- **Robotic Process Automation (RPA)** – RPA is a type of business automation software that repeats a set of tasks normally conducted by a human employee using a graphical user interface (GUI). For example, RPA can automate repetitive, rules-based tasks such as opening an email with a sales order, extracting the data, and then entering that sales order into a computer application.

- **Artificial intelligence** – Artificial intelligence is computer learning, planning, and solving problems, when the computer perceives its environment and executes actions designed to reach a goal. Examples include smart assistants (eg, Siri or Alexa) understanding human speech, and manufacturing robots.

- **Machine learning** – Machine Learning is a type of artificial intelligence that gives computers the ability to learn from data without being programmed to do so. Examples of machine learning include self-driving vehicles, Amazon recommendations based on past purchases, and automatic fraud detection.

- **Collaborative computing** – This allows users to connect, communicate and work on projects and documents together in real time. Examples include instant messaging (google chat), video conferencing, multicasting, email applications, groupware systems, just to name a few.

- **Geolocation** – This is information about your physical, real-world location that can be associated with an IP or MAC address. This information can be used by applications to show how nearby your friends or employees are, get directions to a restaurant or customer, or to **geotag** your photos.

- **Social media** – Social media enables individuals to create, share, and exchange information and ideas in virtual communities and networks. Social media has proven an effective tool for:
  - Market research
  - Communication
  - Sales promotions
  - Relationship development (match.com)
  - E-commerce

Business Systems

Transaction processing systems focus on relieving humans of the tedious work involved in general recordkeeping and reporting. **Management reporting systems** assist in the decision-making process within the organization. The most common business systems include:

- **Management information system (MIS)** – An organized assembly of resources and procedures required to collect, process, and distribute data for use in decision making.

- **Decision support system** – An interactive system that provides the user with easy access to decision models and data, to support semi-structured decision-making tasks.

- **Enterprise Resource Planning (ERP)** – A packaged business software system that allows an organization to automate and integrate the majority of its business processes (eg, sales, inventory management, planning and forecasting), share common data and practices across the entire organization, and produce and access information in a real-time environment.

- o These systems span both transaction processing systems and management reporting systems.
- o Examples of ERP include SAP, Oracle Financials, and J.D. Edwards.
- o ERP systems are discussed in further detail in a later section.

- **Customer Relationship Management (CRM)** – CRM is a system that manages an entity's customer relationship data. CRM is generally used by marketing, sales, and business development departments. It manages data regarding past, present, and potential customer to improve profitability and customer service. CRM can be part of an ERP system.

- **Supply Chain Management (SCM)** – SCM is a system that manages an entity's supply chain, which includes the purchasing, conversion, and logistics processes. The supply chain is the flow of goods from suppliers all the way to the customer. Thus, SCM is generally used by the purchasing, manufacturing, warehousing, and shipping departments. SCM can be part of an ERP system.

- **Executive support system** – These are systems designed specifically to support executive work (eg, nonroutine decisions, such as answering questions regarding competitors, identifying new acquisitions, and sales forecasting).

- **Analytical processing system** – Software technology that enables the user to query (ask) the system, retrieve data and conduct analysis.

- **Expert system** – This type of system uses artificial intelligence. An expert system has a built-in hierarchy of rules, which are acquired from human experts in the appropriate field. Once input is provided, the system should be able to define the nature of the problem and provide recommendations to solve the problem.

Transaction Processing

The processing of transactions can take place in one of two general ways:

- **Online Transaction Processing (OLTP), or online real-time (OLRT) processing** – OLTP means that the database is updated as soon as a transaction is received (**immediately**). This produces records that are as up-to-date as possible, but requires the system to be running continually. This is a good method to be used by retail businesses. This is generally the default processing method for most business activities.

- **Batch processing** – This involves gathering information and then entering transactions in a group **periodically**. This allows for greater control over the input process, including more possibility for verifying data entry with control totals and authorization before input. Due to the **delay** between the transactions and the input, accounting records may not accurately reflect the current situation at a particular point in time.

IT Environment

The Information Technology (IT) environment is largely dependent on the size of the company and the number of employees and type of computers involved. Historically, a few large computers were operated exclusively by IT personnel. With personal computers, tablets, and phones networked together, all employees use some type of electronic device daily. While the diversity of devices has proven to be extremely useful in the efficiency and effectiveness of business processes, the increase in access points creates more risk for an IT system.

Benefits of IT

Some of the benefits of IT include:

- **Consistency** – Computers process data the same way every time.
- **Timeliness** – Electronic processing and updating is normally more efficient.
- **Analysis** – Data can be accessed for analytical procedures more conveniently (with proper software).
- **Monitoring** – Electronic controls can be monitored by the computer system itself.
- **Circumvention** – Controls are difficult to circumvent when programmed properly, and exceptions are unlikely to be permitted.
- **Segregation of duties** – Security controls can prevent the performance of incompatible functions by the same individual or group through security controls in applications, databases, and operating systems.

Risks of IT

While there are many benefits of IT systems, there are also many risks that must be managed:

- **Overreliance** – Without clear output, IT systems are often assumed to be working when they are not.
- **Unauthorized Access** – Disclosure, destruction, and alteration of large amounts of data are possible if unauthorized access occurs.
- **Unauthorized changes in programs** – Severe consequences without detection are possible if unauthorized program changes occur.
- **Failure to change** – Programs or systems are sometimes not updated for new laws, rules, or activities.
- **Manual intervention** – Knowledgeable individuals can sometimes alter files by bypassing the appropriate programs.
- **Loss of data** – Catastrophic data loss is possible if appropriate controls aren't in place.

IT Department

To control these risks, it is important that IT systems are operating as designed. This is generally the responsibility of the IT department.

- Large companies will have a separate IT department.
- Others will have some IT functions outsourced or partially outsourced and partially performed by end users.
- An IT department will normally include systems development and maintenance, operations, and other technical services.
    - **Systems development and maintenance** might include the following roles:
        - A **systems analyst** designs the information system using systems flowcharts and other tools and prepares specifications for applications programmers, as well as acting as an intermediary between the users and programmers.

- An **application programmer** writes, tests, and debugs programs that will be used in the system. The programmer also develops instructions for operators to follow when running the programs.
- A **database administrator** is an individual or department responsible for the security and information classification of the shared data stored on a database system. This responsibility includes the design, definition, and maintenance of the database.

o **Operations** might include the following roles:
- The **data control department** is responsible for collecting data for input into a computer's batch processing operations as well as the dissemination of the finished reports. A **data control clerk** schedules jobs for the computer and manages the distribution of reports and other output. Data control clerks may be involved in coding activities, calculating, and checking batch totals, and related clerical tasks.
- **Data entry** includes keyboard entry, scanning, and voice recognition. When transactions are entered (batch data entry), they are just stacks of source documents to the keyboard operator. Deciphering poor handwriting from a source document is a judgment call that is often error prone. In online data operations, in which the operator takes information in person or by phone, there is interaction and involvement with the transaction and less chance for error.
- A **computer operator** operates a computer in a datacenter and performs such activities as commanding the operating system, mounting disks and tapes, and placing paper in the printer. Operators may also write the job control language (JCL), which schedules the daily work for the computer.
- **Librarians** are the individuals responsible for the safeguarding and maintenance of all program and data files.

o **Other technical services** might include the following roles:
- A **network administrator** is responsible for maintaining and enhancing computer networks and network connections.
- A **systems programmer** is responsible for updating and maintaining the operating systems (typically for mainframe computers).
- A **systems administrator** or **technical support** typically installs, upgrades, and monitors software and hardware.
- A **security administrator** is responsible for security of the system including control of access and maintenance of user passwords.

Lecture 3.02 – IT Governance & Frameworks

Overview

IT governance is a formal structure within an entity that is overseen by the board of directors (BOD) and executive management, and typically facilitated by using one or more governance frameworks, such as COBIT 2019 (see below). IT governance helps a business meet strategic goals and objectives through the management and control of IT acquisition, deployment, and use.

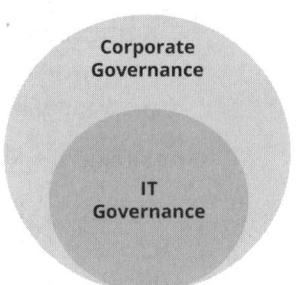

Overall Objectives of IT Governance

The IT Governance Institute outlines five overall objectives of IT governance, all of which are driven by an entity's primary goal of meeting the needs of business stakeholders. Together, these objectives represent the continuous life cycle of IT governance.

Stakeholder Needs

Strategic alignment – IT strategy must align with business strategy for efficient and effective operations.

Value delivery – IT investments and activities must provide value to the business and meet stakeholders' needs.

Performance measurement – A balanced scorecard approach is recommended to track projects and monitor IT services to maintain alignment with business strategy.

Risk management – To protect IT assets and the value they deliver, exposure to threats must be identified and managed, minimizing their impact on operations.

Resource management – Clear policies and oversight for the acquisition, deployment, and use of IT resources (eg, people, infrastructure, and applications) are key in balancing the cost of optimizing IT performance in meeting its objectives.

Frameworks

IT governance frameworks provide tools that assist an enterprise in translating governance objectives into strategies, policies, and processes that fit their needs. Governance frameworks do not address *how* IT management, compliance, or controls are implemented. Rather, they provide a methodology (ie, a set of best practices) for establishing responsibility, standards, and measurements that align IT strategy with enterprise strategy.

Tone at the Top

The tone at the top—the vision, strategy and ethical values of the BOD and executive management—dictates how IT governance is implemented and what governance components are prioritized. A variety of factors are considered when implementing and executing a system of IT governance, including, for example:

- The business's reliance on technology for growth and operations support
- The entity's ability to implement and support complex technology
- Industry and environmental factors
- The entity's risk appetite

- Laws and regulations (eg, SOX compliance requirements)

Committees and Oversight

In order to tailor IT governance to a business, the BOD and management rely on committees, particularly the IT Strategy and IT Steering Committees, to provide oversight, prioritize stakeholder requests, set policy, and monitor IT activities.

	IT Strategy Committee	**IT Steering Committee**
Description	A **board-level committee** made up of board members and specialists	A **management-level committee** made up of executives, key users and advisors from various departments
Typical Responsibilities	<ul><li>Assists BOD in overseeing IT matters</li><li>Sets high-level goals for IT governance practices</li><li>Provides IT strategy guidance to management</li></ul>	<ul><li>Prioritizes IT projects and allocates IT resources</li><li>Uses policies and standards to communicate control and risk information to the organization</li><li>Evaluates IT performance</li></ul>
Authority	Makes no final decisions and has no role in management	Oversees day-to-day management of IT operations

> 👉 Accountants help ensure good governance by reviewing budget expenditures, auditing performance measures, verifying policy and standards, and communicating independent opinions regarding the value and alignment of initiatives. Accountants also help manage systems development and ensure that controls are properly designed, implemented and functioning.

Control Objectives for Information and Related Technology (COBIT)

ISACA (formerly known as Information Systems Audit and Control Association) has developed a framework, referred to as **C**ontrol **Ob**jectives for **I**nformation and Related **T**echnology (COBIT), for the governance and management of enterprise IT. At the end of 2018, ISACA issued COBIT 2019, which provided substantial revisions and updates to the previous COBIT 5 framework.

The COBIT framework is business oriented in that it provides a systematic way of integrating IT with business strategy and business risk. COBIT 2019 is based on six principles that describe the core requirements of an enterprise information and technology governance system.

1. Providing Stakeholder Value

The objective of an entity is to bring value to stakeholders by addressing their needs and generating a financial return or public service. Stakeholder needs are met by transforming their requirements into actionable strategy. To accomplish this, ISACA suggests the use of a "goal cascade," consisting of four steps:

Stakeholder Drivers and Needs – First, factors influencing stakeholder needs are identified.

> **Enterprise Goals** – Second, stakeholder needs are translated into generic goals of the entity. COBIT 2019 suggests 13 enterprise goals that fall into categories that align with the four Balanced Scorecard Dimensions.

Enterprise Goals	
Financial - Portfolio of competitive products and services - Managed business risk - Compliance with external laws and regulations - Quality of financial information	**Internal** - Optimization of internal business process functionality - Optimization of business process costs - Staff skills, motivation and productivity - Compliance with internal policies
Customer - Customer-oriented service culture - Business service continuity and availability - Quality of management information	**Growth** - Managed digital transformation programs - Product and business innovation

> **Alignment Goals** – Third, all IT efforts of the business are aligned with enterprise goals. COBIT 2019 suggests using alignment goals that translate the enterprise goals to the IT Balanced Scorecard. For example, the enterprise goal of "managed *business* risk" becomes the alignment goal of "managed *IT-related* risk."

>> **Governance and Management Objectives** – Finally, the alignment goals are used to develop what COBIT 2019 refers to as **components of a governance system**. COBIT 2019 outlines seven categories of components that interact to produce a holistic governance system that supports governance and management objectives:

- Processes
- Organizational structures
- Principles, policies, and procedures
- Information
- Culture, ethics and behavior
- People, skills and competencies
- Services, infrastructure, and application

2. Enabling a Holistic Approach

COBIT 2019 is considered a single integrated framework because it aligns with other relevant standards and frameworks. Rather than having many isolated frameworks that address strategic components independently, COBIT 2019 ensures that the IT impact and initiatives generated by the use of other frameworks align with management goals across an organization. This holistic approach ensures business initiatives are clearly connected to an overarching strategy.

3. Ensuring the Governance System is Dynamic

COBIT 2019 uses "design factors" (eg, enterprise goals and strategy) to influence the design of an enterprise's governance system. When there is a change in a design factor, the impact of those changes should be considered and the governance system should be updated, as necessary.

4. Separating Governance from Management

COBIT 2019 distinguishes between governance and management objectives:

Governance (EDM)	Management (APO, BAI, DSS, MEA)
<ul><li>*Evaluates* strategic options based on stakeholders needs</li><li>*Directs* management on strategies chosen</li><li>*Monitors* management's achievement of strategies</li></ul>	To achieve strategy set by governing body, management:<ul><li>*Aligns, plans, and organizes* IT activities</li><li>*Builds, acquires, and implements* IT solutions</li><li>*Delivers, services, and supports* IT services</li><li>*Monitors, evaluates, and assesses* IT performance in accordance with internal targets, internal control objectives, and external requirements</li></ul>

5. Tailoring the Governance System

COBIT 2019 provides guidance to help businesses in different industries create a governance system that can meet their specific needs. The primary method of tailoring a governance system to a business is through the selection and use of **design factors**. Design factors are used to assess an enterprise's technology capabilities and growth objectives, select framework components that will meet those objectives, and identify **focus areas** that target specific governance needs.

Examples	
Design Factors	**Focus Areas**
<ul><li>Enterprise size, strategy and goals</li><li>Risk profile</li><li>Threat landscape</li><li>Compliance requirements</li><li>Role of IT and IT-related issues</li><li>Sourcing model for IT</li><li>IT implementation methods</li><li>Technology adoption strategy</li></ul>	<ul><li>Cybersecurity</li><li>Digital transformation</li><li>Cloud computing</li><li>Privacy</li><li>Software development operations</li><li>IT architecture</li><li>Centralization (or decentralization)</li><li>Project and resource management</li></ul>

6. End-to-End Application

COBIT 2019 is designed to enable a business to apply IT governance across the organization. Thus, systems put in place for the governance and management of IT should apply to all information processing components, not just the IT function.

National Institute of Standards and Technology Cybersecurity Framework

Cybersecurity breaches can result in severe consequences to an entity's reputation, finances, customers, and assets. The National Institute of Standards and Technology (NIST) cybersecurity framework offers a flexible way to address such cyber risk. The NIST framework is organized into three parts: the framework core (we'll be focusing our attention here), implementation tiers, and framework profiles.

- The **framework core** is made up of five functions that consist of various cybersecurity-focused activities designed to achieve specific outcomes. Together, they represent a high-level overview of the continuous life cycle of cybersecurity management:

Function	Description	Example Outcomes
1. Identify	Understand organization to manage cyber-risk to systems, people, assets, data, and capabilities	• Risk assessment • Risk management strategy • Asset management
2. Protect	Apply safeguards to ensure delivery of critical services	• Data security • Systems maintenance • Access control
3. Detect	Implement activities to identify the occurrence of a cybersecurity incident	• Continuous security monitoring • Access log and user permissions auditing
4. Respond	Implement activities to take action with respect to a detected cybersecurity incident	• Response planning • Continuous improvement plans • Incident analysis
5. Recover	Maintain plans for resilience and restoration of capabilities or services impaired by a cybersecurity incident	• Incident recovery plans • Stakeholder communication • Organizational learning

- The **implementation tiers** help organizations:
    - Identify and understand the characteristics of their cybersecurity risk
    - Prioritize and achieve cybersecurity objectives
- The **framework profiles** help an organization to align and prioritize its cybersecurity activities with its business and mission requirements, risk tolerances, and resources.

Summary

Keep in mind that various frameworks can be integrated to achieve IT governance objectives. For example, here, we've covered COBIT and NIST's Cybersecurity Framework (CSF), but COSO's Enterprise Risk Management (ERM) Framework (previously discussed) can also be applied to manage IT risk.

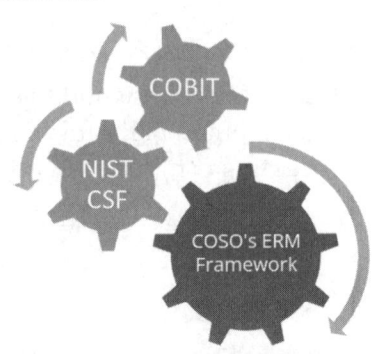

Lecture 3.03 – IT Infrastructure

Overview

IT infrastructure is the foundation of a business's IT system. It is made up of **hardware**, **software**, and **network** components that link everything together. However, these days, some of these components can be outsourced to cloud computing providers. Before we get to that though, let's cover the basics first.

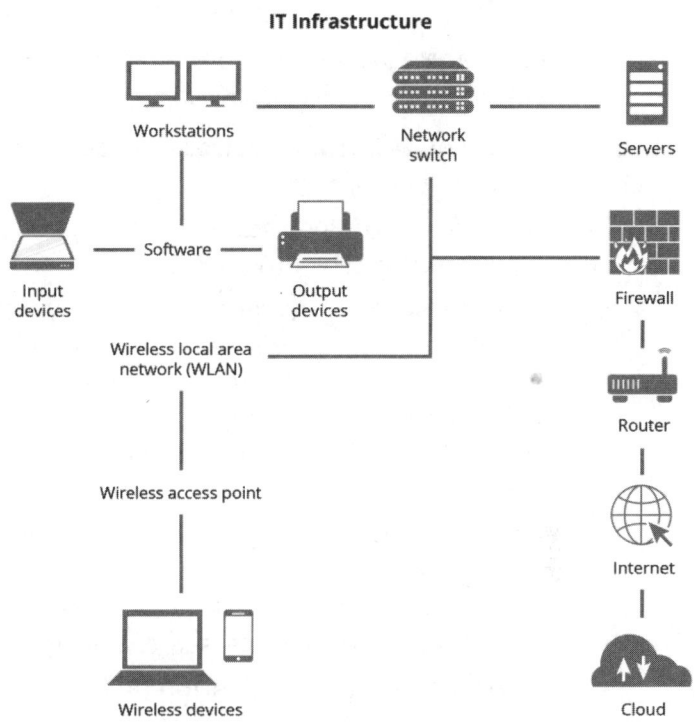

Hardware

Hardware is the physical electronic equipment. Common components include:

- **Network switch** – This device connects all the devices on an entity's computer network. It uses packet switching (ie, a way to group data) to move data between the devices.

- **Server** – A server is a computer with software that services other devices (ie, clients) on the network. There are several different kinds of servers, such as:
    - **Computing server** – This type of server provides central processing and memory to client computers (workstations) over a network. This type of **memory** is temporary internal storage space (aka, **random access memory** or RAM).
    - **File server** – A file server is a high-capacity disk storage device that stores data centrally for network users and manages access to that data.
    - **Database server** – A database server is similar to a file server, except it has more memory and processing capabilities to serve data over a network.
    - **Application server** – This type of server hosts programs that can be accessed and used by client computers.
    - **Mail server** – A mail server sends, receives, and stores emails.
    - **Web server** – This type of server hosts Webpages.

- **Internal Storage Hardware** – Persistent (not temporary) storage that can be accessed immediately by the **Central Processing Unit** (CPU)—the principal hardware component that processes programs.
    - **Magnetic disks or solid-state drives (SSD)** – Permanent storage devices inside a computer (including hard drives) that allow **random access** to data without the need to move forward or backward through all intervening data (like magnetic tape, discussed below).

- o Some systems use **redundant array of independent disks (RAID)**, which includes multiple disks in one system so that data can be stored redundantly and the failure of one of the disks won't cause the loss of any data.
- **External Storage Devices** – Devices used to store data or programs externally, including magnetic tape, flash drives (USB), digital video disks (DVDs), and compact disks (CDs).
  - o **Magnetic tape** – Inexpensive form of storage used primarily for backup, since only **sequential access** to data is possible.
- **Input (Data-entry) & Output Devices** – These are devices that allow for communication between the computer and users.
  - o Basic input devices include scanners, microphones, keyboard, light pen (ie, a stylus), etc. Some input devices can automate data entry and speed up business processes, such as:
    - **Point-of-sale (POS) system** – This is the most popular type of input device for retail and restaurants. POS systems in restaurants, like McDonalds, need an employee (or a customer) to key in the order on a **touch screen**. Stores generally use **barcode readers** (scanners) to send data from a UPC label directly to the register/computer. This process can also be completed by an employee or a customer (eg, self-checkout at Walmart).
    - **Optical Character Recognition (OCR)** – This technology is a used in conjunction with a camera or scanner to read text. It can be used for a myriad of purposes, such as reading documents for quick data-entry (eg, invoices, receipts), reading to the blind, converting PDFs to editable, searchable documents, etc.
    - **Radio Frequency Identification (RFID)** – This uses radio frequencies to track tagged objects and transfer data. It is most commonly used for inventory control purposes.
  - o Basic output devices include monitors, printers, speakers, etc.
- **Gateway** – This is a device (firewall, router) on a network that serves as an entrance to another network. In order for a home or business to connect to the Internet, for example, it must connect to a gateway computer at their Internet Service Provider (ISP), which is the first router in the process of connecting to the rest of the Internet.
  - o **Firewall** – A firewall prevents unauthorized users from accessing the system and data. A firewall can be in the form of a computer program (software) or a physical device that blocks the transmission media being used (hardware).
  - o **Router** – This is a specialized device that receives data packets from one computer and sends it toward its destination in the most efficient manner possible. The Internet primarily consists of a series of routers used to transmit information among all the computers connected to the Internet. Thus, when a computer in California connects to a website in Australia, there might be 10 computers between them acting as intermediary routers. When parts of the Internet go down, most people never notice because the routers find another way (route) to get the information to its destination.

Software

Software consists of programs and supporting documentation that enable and facilitate use of the computer. Software controls the operation of the hardware and the processing of data. Software is either system software or application software.

- **System software** is made up of the programs that run the system and direct its operations, comprised of the operating system and utility programs.

- o An **operating system (OS)** is a set of system software programs in a computer that regulate the ways application software programs use the computer hardware and the ways that users control the computer. Examples of commonly used operating systems are Windows and UNIX.
- o **Utility programs** are used for sorts, merges, and other routine functions to maintain and improve the efficiency of a computer system. There are many types of utility programs, such as backup software, anti-virus software, and firewall software used to control access to the computer or its files.
- o **A database management system (DBMS)** is system software for creating and managing databases. A DBMS makes it possible for end users to create, protect, read, update, and delete data in a database.
- **Application software** is designed to perform specific tasks for the company (eg, *Quickbooks*®).
- Software is created using a set of commands, instructions and other syntax called a **programming language**.
  - o **Source code** is a collection of commands and instructions written in a programming language.
  - o A **compiler** is a program that converts source code into object code, which are the instructions a machine understands (ie, 1s and 0s, or on-off).

Centralized vs. Distributed Processing

Centralized Processing

In the early days of computers, each device was so expensive that a company rarely had more than one and all activity had to take place on that single computer. Although different people could connect to that single computer using **remote terminals**, these were simply input and output devices (essentially equivalent to just the keyboard and monitor on a current desktop). All activity had to take place on the one computer, known as **centralized processing**.

Distributed Processing

Today, computers are so reasonably priced that, in many businesses, employees each are assigned their own computers. This allows the allocation of a large volume of tasks to different employees and computers at different locations, known as **distributed processing**. Since the data utilized by the company is no longer on a single computer, it is necessary for them to be able to connect to each other in some way to form a **network.**

Networks in General

In a computer network, computers are connected to one another to enable sharing of peripheral devices, data, and programs stored on a file server. The networking of different computers allows more than just the transfer of information from one to another. It also allows one computer to be used to operate the other.

Types of Networks

Networks may involve any size group from two (as in the case of many home networks) to the entire world.

- The **Internet** is a worldwide network that allows virtually any computer system to link to it by way of an electronic gateway. The Internet facilitates data communication services, such as remote login, file transfer, email, and newsgroups. To make use of the Internet more user-friendly, a framework for accessing documents was developed known as the **World Wide Web**. Here are some associated terms you should know:

- **Hypertext Transfer Protocol (HTTP)** – The language commonly understood by different computers to communicate via the Internet.

> **Protocol** – Rules determining the required format and methods for transmission of data.

- **Transmission Control Protocol and Internet Protocol (TCP/IP)** – An IP is a unique computer address and a TCP/IP is a communications protocol designed to network dissimilar systems, such as viewing a webpage.
- **User Datagram Protocol (UDP)** – A communication protocol which contrasts TCP, and is designed for speed at the expense of minor data loss and no guarantee of reception by the destination system. UDP is commonly used for Voice-over IP (VoIP) and real-time video traffic.
- **Uniform Resource Locator (URL)** – The "address" of a particular page on the Internet.
- **HTML** (HyperText Markup Language) and **XML** (Extensible Markup Language) are specialized languages used to create websites.
- **eXtensible Business Reporting Language (XBRL)** is an open, market driven computer language that allows for the free electronic exchange of business and financial data. Instead of treating financial information as a block of text (eg, standard Internet page or Word document), it provides a computer-readable identifying tag for each individual item of data.

  For example, "net income" has its own unique tag and a computer could immediately generate a comparison of net income for multiple companies or periods. XBRL eliminates the costly process of manual data comparison as computers can select, analyze, store, and exchange data in XBRL documents. Another benefit to XBRL is that it reduces the chance of errors when generating reports.
    - XBRL can handle data in different languages and accounting standards.
    - XBRL is built upon XML (Extensible Mark-up Language).
    - The SEC **mandated** that all public companies file financial statements in XBRL.

- An **Intranet** is a network that is limited to the computers of a single company.
- An **Extranet** is similar to an Intranet, since it is primarily for users within a single company, but select customers and vendors are able to participate as well.

Network Configurations

- **Local area networks (LANs)** – A LAN is a communications network that serves several users within a specified geographical area. A personal computer LAN functions as distributed processing in which each computer in the network does its own processing and manages some of its data. Shared data are stored in a file server that acts as a remote disk drive for all users in the network.
- **Wide area networks (WANs)** – A WAN is a computer network that connects different remote locations that may range from short distances (eg, a building) to extremely long transmissions that encompass a large region or several countries.
- **Value-added network (VAN)** – A VAN links computer files of different companies together.

- **Virtual Private Network (VPN)** – A VPN allows users to access network resources from remote locations. A VPN may or may not be incorporated as part of a larger cloud computing strategy.

The need for solid physical transmission media in LANs has been overcome through the development of **wireless local area networks (WLANs).** Short-range radio transmission allows different computers to communicate with each other and share printers, Internet connections, and other devices. The two prominent standards for WLANs are **Wi-Fi** and **Bluetooth**. Any devices (eg, cell phones) that are in the vicinity of each other and which follow the same standard can communicate.

Network Topology

Networking would get very complicated if every computer in a network had to be able to directly connect to every other computer in the network. Even in the case of a wireless network, a computer would have to be able to distinguish all the different signals coming from different computers.

Topology refers to the shape of a network, or the network's layout. How different nodes in a network are connected to each other and how they communicate are determined by the network's topology. To simplify the process, the communication is normally organized (and can be visualized) in one of the following ways:

- **Bus** – Computers (ie, nodes) are each connected to a common cable between hardware devices.
- **Star** – There is one computer (central hub) to which all other computers connect; all data is first received and then sent from that one computer.
- **Ring** – Each computer is connected to its two closest neighbors in a closed loop, and information is transferred through each intermediate computer to get to the intended destination. Notice there will be two directions that can be used, so an interruption of a single connection won't bring down the network.
- **Tree** – Groups of star-configured networks are organized in branches with one computer at the base. Computers on the same branch can connect to each other without going through the root computer; however, computers on different branches may have to go through the root computer.
- **Mesh** - Devices are connected with many redundant interconnections between network nodes. In a pure mesh topology, every node has a connection to every other node in the network.

Enterprise Resource Planning (ERP) Systems

ERPs can be broadly defined as information system packages that integrate information and information-based processes within and across functional areas of an organization. An ERP system is a packaged* business software system that enables a company to manage resources (material, human, financial, etc.) more efficiently and effectively by providing an integrated solution for the organization's information processing needs.

Packaged applications broadly refer to any pre-packaged or "off-the-shelf" software application.

Advantages

- **Timely information analysis** – ERP systems collect and distribute information in a timelier fashion; thus, they help managers improve their ability to process and analyze information.

- **Unified systems** - ERPs usually replace multiple systems, each of which was designed and managed for support of a much more discrete grouping of business functions. The consolidation of these functions allows for the implementation of unified application controls within a single system with a single database.
- **Interactivity** – ERP systems can interact with IT systems of customers and vendors.

Risks

- **Implementation & operation risks** – Due to the size and complexity of an ERP system, the implementation of a new system is likely to disrupt operations. Likewise, any failure in the system has the potential to halt operations throughout the organization.
- **Reduced segregation of duties** – A unified ERP system that consolidates business functions can lead to reduced segregation of duties and increase security risk.
- **Data access** - Complex data structures (eg, database tables, data flows) used within an ERP can inhibit access to data.
- **Business process risks** - An organization that utilizes packaged ERP software may need to change business processes to accommodate system data flows and functions. This can increase process interdependence risk, where one business process becomes a single point of failure for the whole system.

Custom vs. Packaged Applications

The alternative to packaged software is the development of custom applications. Custom applications are developed by, or at the behest of, an enterprise to meet specific business needs. These applications may serve similar business functions as those provided by packaged applications, or fulfill a business need where no suitable packaged application is available.

Custom applications tend to be more **expensive** overall than their packaged counterparts; however, they offer more **flexibility** along with the ability to better conform with established business processes and best practices.

	Packaged Applications	Custom Applications
Purpose	Mass produced for general use	Custom produced for specific use
Costs	Lower upfront costs	Higher upfront costs
Ownership	Licensed	Wholly owned
Features	May not meet all business requirements	Should meet all business requirements
Features	Difficult to customize	Can alter as required
Business Processes	General business processes that conform to best practices	Customized business processes
Maturity Model	Mature	Varies
Maturity Model	Tested in a variety of settings	Tested in a development setting

Applications Maturity Model

A maturity model is useful for evaluating risk and creating a metric to be used in risk calculations. Both packaged and custom applications create risks associated with business interruption, system security, database security, and process interdependency. The degree to which those risks have been addressed generally correlate to where an application is on the maturity model. The maturity model has the five phases. See the table below.

Phase	People	Processes	Programs
Initial	Uncoordinated activities; no set staff	No formal security or access processes	No security or controls
Developing	Leadership established; informal communication	Basic governance & risk management processes	Basic controls with limited or no documentation
Defined	Roles & responsibilities established	Security & access processes in place; minimal verification	Controls implemented & documented; controls reliant on individual IT staff
Managed	Roles & responsibilities clearly defined; increased focus on resources	Formal security processes established; verification & measurement processes established	Controls monitored & measured; compliance levels established; some controls are automated
Optimized	Continuous improvement culture; established staff focus on security, processes, & technology	Comprehensive surety & risk management processes in place; risks are understood & quantitatively evaluated	Controls fully implemented, automated, & continuously monitored; controls subject to continuous improvement processes

(Risk increases down the phases)

Client-Server Computing vs. Cloud Computing

Client-Server Computing

In client-server computing, the users of **client** computers will be able to access a **server** computer. Users can be given access to add, edit, or delete data on the server; operate programs running on the server; and download and/or transfer files to the server. The physical device used to access the server is called a **workstation**. The server doesn't have a particular user and doesn't need a monitor or keyboard, except for initial set up.

Virtualization is a method used to create multiple virtual machines for clients to access on a single physical server.

Cloud Computing

Cloud computing is a model that allows organizations to use the Internet to access and use services and applications that run on remote third-party technology infrastructure.

- Cloud computing is the integration of virtual machines, remote services for hardware and software, and Web access.

- Working in the cloud can mean simply using a remote server for data storage or using a browser to access Web-based applications.

- Because cloud computing utilizes third-party hardware and software, it usually has lower upfront costs for equipment and maintenance.

- Cloud computing is generally not the best way to secure sensitive corporate information, as there are security risks to transmitting information over the Internet.

- Common implementations of cloud computing involve off-the-shelf software that is not developed or modified in-house, with generally limited configuration and program modification options.

- Both packaged and custom applications require IT hardware infrastructure to host application code, house databases, and provide functionality to the enterprise. Cloud computing and application hosting arrangements (aka, cloud-based service arrangements) can offload some or all the back-end hardware requirements. This can reduce the need for on-site IT resources.

Common Cloud-Based Service Arrangements

- **Software as a Service (SaaS)**
  - SaaS is a method of **software** (application) **delivery** that allows a person to use the program over the internet without having the software on their device. In this web-based model, external service providers host and maintain the servers, databases, and code for an application or suite of applications.
  - SaaS is primarily concerned with third-party owned and maintained software that is delivered over a network. Users purchase licenses to use the vendor-hosted software on a subscription basis and access the software from remote devices using the Internet. This arrangement requires little to no technical staff on the part of the SaaS user.
  - Access controls are maintained by the SaaS user, while controls related to availability, data storage, and IT hardware are the responsibility of the SaaS provider.

- **Platform as a Service (PaaS)**
  - PaaS provides access to **hardware, storage, and operating systems** to a business **over a network**. PaaS facilitates deployment of applications by unifying and standardizing a system across an organization. This reduces complexity and costs associated with both software and hardware management.
  - In a PaaS arrangement, all software applications and controls are the responsibility of the PaaS user. Additionally, the development and deployment of applications is overseen by the PaaS user, requiring some IT staff.
  - PaaS providers are generally responsible for availability and all operational activities, maintenance, and management of the provided hardware, storage, and operating systems.

- **Infrastructure as a Service (IaaS)**
  - IaaS provides **physical resources and equipment**, such as network hardware, to a business. This helps reduce or eliminate direct upkeep and maintenance of IT equipment by the business.
  - Providers of IaaS generally undertake responsibilities related to physical security, environmental control, and monitoring services for the IT infrastructure.
  - This model allows the IaaS user freedom to deploy their systems in a manner consistent with their needs, but also requires a larger technical staff to maintain all software and systems.

Cloud-based service arrangements can use two or more of the above models in conjunction with each other. For example, consider a company that offers a payroll system as a service (SaaS) who in turn relies on Amazon's Web Services (AWS) to provide their infrastructure (IaaS).

Management does not have direct access to the systems and subsystems used by the SaaS and IaaS providers; thus, they must rely on **SOC 1** and **SOC 2 reports** to review the controls and the results of control testing for these **service organizations**. SOC reports and service organizations are discussed in further detail in a later section.

Cloud Deployment Models

Cloud computing technology is deployed in four general types, based on the level of internal or external ownership and technical architectures:

- **Public Cloud** – Cloud computing services from vendors can be accessed across the Internet or a private network. This uses systems in one or more data centers, shared among multiple customers, with varying degrees of data privacy control.
- **Private Cloud** – Computing architectures are modeled after Public Clouds, yet built, managed, and used internally by an enterprise. This uses a shared services model with variable usage of a common pool of virtualized computing resources. Data is controlled within the enterprise.
- **Hybrid Cloud** – A mix of vendor Cloud services, internal Cloud computing architectures, and classic IT infrastructure form a hybrid model that uses the best-of-breed technologies to meet specific needs.
- **Community Cloud** – The cloud infrastructure is shared by several organizations and supports a specific community that has shared concerns (eg, mission, objectives, security requirements, policy, and compliance considerations). It may be managed by the organization or a third party, and may exist on-premises or off-premises.

Advantages & Risks of Cloud-Based Service Arrangements

- **Advantages**
    - **Global accessibility** – Services are available to any location, including remote or home offices.
    - **Uniform deployment** – Users have a uniform experience and have the same version of all cloud-hosted applications.
    - **Centralized administration** – Administration, verification, and access can be controlled from a central location for all users and cloud-hosted applications.
- **Risks**
    - **Security risks** – Cloud services are designed to be globally accessible and introduce unique identity and access management risks. Cyber threats, such as distributed denial-of-service attacks (DDoS), are also increased.
    - **Deployment risk** – In any cloud services arrangement, there are applications or hardware that the subscriber does not control. Updates and upgrades are controlled by the cloud services vendor.
    - **Service delivery risk** – Reliance on third parties for business processes introduces risks associated with the disruption of those services, which cannot be controlled by the cloud services subscriber.

Lecture 3.04 – Electronic Commerce

Overview

Electronic business (e-business) includes any business conducted over the internet (eg, paying taxes online). **Electronic commerce (e-commerce)** is one of the most popular e-business implementations. It is any activity that involves buying and selling products/services over the Internet. **Electronic Data Interchange (EDI)** is a type of e-commerce that involves a distributor's computer communicating with manufacturers' and retailers' computers to order and ship products without human intervention. We'll be focusing most of our attention on e-commerce and EDI.

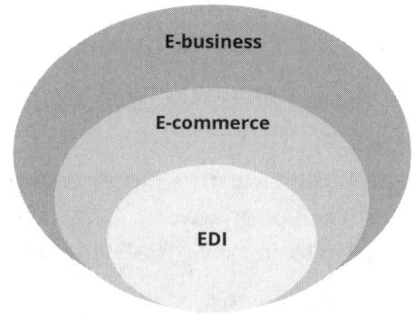

Electronic Commerce

Typically, a website will advertise goods/services, and the buyer will fill in a form on the website to select the items to be purchased and provide delivery and payment details. A website may gather details about customers and offer other items that may be of interest. The cost of physical store locations ("brick-and-mortar") is avoided; the savings are often a benefit to the customers, sometimes leading to spectacular growth.

E-commerce uses technology to enhance the processes of transactions among a company, its customers, and business partners. The technology used can include the Internet, multimedia, web browsers, proprietary networks, ATMs, home banking, and the traditional approach to EDI. However, the primary area of growth in e-commerce is through the use of the Internet as an enabling technology.

Electronic Data Interchange

Whenever a network allows one computer to initiate an action that will have an effect on the other, it is known as a **Value-Added Network (VAN)**. Extranets have been established as VANs to enable a process of communication between suppliers and customers (ie, trading partners) known as EDI. This allows a company, for example, to have its inventory program automatically send an order to a supplier when quantities in stock of an item drop below a certain level.

Note that It is also possible to use the Internet rather than a traditional VAN for EDI. The advantage is that this would permit suppliers and customers to use the system without having previously established an extranet with each other.

Electronic Funds Transfer & EDI Considerations

E-Commerce often involves electronic funds transfers (EFT), which can significantly reduce transaction costs. There are several special considerations related to EDI:

- **Strict standards** are needed for the form of data, so that it will be understood by the computers at both ends and to ensure **completeness** and **accuracy**. The critical nature of many EDI transactions, such as orders and payments, requires that there be positive assurances that the transmissions were complete.

- **Translation software** is needed by each computer so that it can convert data between the standard used for EDI and the form needed for processing internally. The process of identifying which field on the transmitted form corresponds to each field on the internal form is known as **mapping**.

- **Unauthorized access** to company computers and interception of transmissions are great dangers to EDI and EFT. Thus, EDI and EFT require the following **application controls**:
    - **Encryption** programs that make stolen data unreadable to someone without knowledge of the coding method
    - **Firewall** programs that prevent access to the network without the explicit permission originating from the company computer

In EDI **cryptography**, a public key certificate (aka, **digital certificate** or **identity certificate**) is an electronic document that uses a **digital signature** to bind together a public key with an identity. Such information may include the name of a person or an organization, their address, and so forth. The certificate can be used to verify that a public key belongs to an individual.

Advantages of EDI

There are numerous advantages associated with the use of EDI.

- It eliminates the need for human intervention, which **reduces errors** and **increases efficiency**.
- When inventory is ordered automatically at the point that the reorder point is reached, it eliminates gaps and **shortens the business cycle**.
- Payments are made and received automatically, which **reduces accounts receivable**.
- EDI enables:
    - Communication without the use of paper
    - EFT and sales over the Internet
    - Simplification of the recording process using scanning devices
    - Sending information to trading partners as transactions occur

E-Commerce Risk

E-commerce, as is true of any other form of commerce, depends on a level of trust between two parties. Some of the most important **risks** are:

- **Confidentiality** – Potential consumers are concerned about confidentiality of their personal information when providing it to unknown vendors.
- **Data integrity** – Data, both in transit and in storage, could be susceptible to unauthorized alteration or deletion (ie, through hacking or design/configuration problems in the system).
- **Availability** – Business may be conducted 24/7; hence, high availability is important with any system failure becoming immediately apparent to customers and/or business partners.
- **Authentication** – Parties should be in a known and trusted business relationship. This requires that they prove their respective identities before executing the transaction. There is a danger that orders and confirmations might be sent by an imposter (ie, **spoofing**), or transmitted files may be intercepted and altered maliciously by third parties before being sent to their destination. Controls might include:
    - Echoing of transmitted documents back to the claimed sender so they know what the recipient has received in their name

- - o **Digital signatures** on files and emails to prove the identity of the sender and to provide assurance that the information was unaltered in transmission
  - **Nonrepudiation** – After the transaction is executed, authentication of the transacting parties ensures that neither can deny the validity or terms of the transaction.
  - **Power shift to customers** – The Internet gives consumers unparalleled access to market information and generally makes it easier to shift between suppliers.
  - **Misuse of information** – E-commerce increases the risk of improper use of information. Controls might include:
    - Security mechanisms and procedures that, taken together, constitute a security architecture for e-commerce
    - Firewall mechanisms that are in place to mediate between the public network (the Internet) and an organization's private network
    - A process whereby participants in an e-commerce transaction can be identified uniquely and positively
  - **Improper distribution of information** – There is also the risk of *improper distribution* of transactions with information being electronically transmitted to an inappropriate company. Controls might include:
    - Routing verification procedures
    - Message acknowledgement procedures

Cryptocurrency is a digital asset exchanged over the Internet outside of traditional banking and government institutions (eg, Bitcoin).

- Rather than governments controlling the supply of currency by printing more money or changing banking reserve requirements—resulting in inflation (or rarely, deflation)—cryptocurrency is decentralized and has built-in restraints on how much may be created.
- Cryptocurrency uses **blockchains** to secure the transactions, maintain **integrity,** and control the creation of additional units of the currency. Blockchains are expanding chains of blocks (records) that are linked and secured using **cryptography**. Each block typically contains a timestamp, a link to a previous block, and the transaction data. Inherently, blockchains resist data modification.
- The safety, integrity, and balance of ledgers within cryptocurrency systems is maintained by a community of mutually distrustful parties, referred to as **miners**. Miners are members of the general public using their computers to help validate and timestamp transactions. Miners add transactions to the ledger in accordance with an algorithm. Collectively, miners provide **security** to the system, each having financial incentive to maintain accurate ledgers.
- Compared with cash or other traditional currencies held by banks, cryptocurrencies are more anonymous and less susceptible to seizure by law enforcement. Different currencies have different degrees of anonymity. Due to this anonymity, there is a risk that cryptocurrencies may become tools for cyber criminals, or will facilitate money laundering, tax evasion, or black markets (eg, illegal drug trade or other illegal activity).

E-Commerce Impact on Product Life Cycle

The Internet removes the physical constraints inherent in former economic models, giving rise to new paradigms. The **sales cycle** of a successful consumer item will grow to a peak. As its popularity declines, its physical shelf space will be assigned to a more popular item. Availability (and, hence, sales) will decrease to zero quickly.

On the other hand, if the item is available online, demand will peter into a small, but sustainable, niche market. Conceivably, a small but ongoing demand will result in more cumulative sales over time than that of the initial peak.

In other words, a physical retail environment has limited space; it is logical to replace less popular items with more popular ones. In the physical world, sales would likely end abruptly, as demand for the item moves to the declining, almost-horizontal portion of the life-cycle curve—the tail end.

In contrast, an electronic retail environment can hold less popular items indefinitely because warehouse storage space constraints are not a major concern. Also, the global reach of the Internet increases the likelihood that an extended sustainable niche market continues for less popular items.

Search engines enable a large audience to find items in the "niche market" portion of the graph. The digital business model allows the tail end of the product life cycle to be long. For some products, the units sold in the long tail can be larger in total than in the mainstream period, especially for electronic products like movies or games.

The graph below illustrates how demand for consumer items (clothing, books, music, etc.) changes over time. It shows an upward curve in the introduction period, a large peak when the item is popular, and a period when demand peters out.

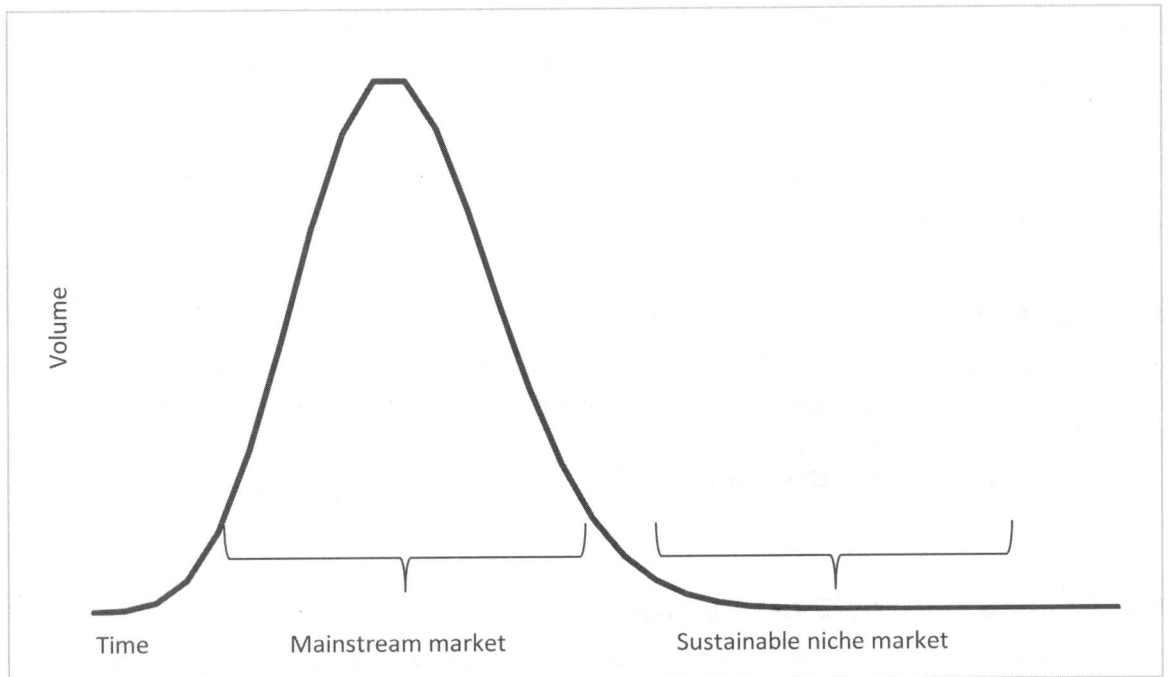

Lecture 3.05 – IT General Controls

Overview

One characteristic of an IT environment is a reduction in the segregation of duties. Although this might appear to create a potential problem:

- A computer has no incentive to conceal its errors.
- Functions often can be combined in an IT environment without weakening internal control.

In the operation of computer systems, management must focus on two broad types of controls:

- **General controls** – These relate to the **overall integrity of the system**. Controls include IT governance policies, procedures, and practices (tasks and activities) established by management to provide reasonable assurance that specific objectives will be achieved.

- **Application controls** – Application controls are those applied to specific business processes within a computerized processing system to achieve financial reporting objectives. They are designed to provide reasonable assurance that objectives relevant to a given **automated solution (application)** are achieved. That is, they ensure that a program performs properly, accepting authorized input, processing it correctly, and generating appropriate output. Application controls are discussed in more detail in the next section.

General Controls
- IT governance
- Logical access controls
- Change controls
- Physical security
- Business resiliency planning

Application Controls
- Input controls
- Processing controls
- Output controls

These controls may be:
- **Preventive** – Designed to prevent errors and fraud.
- **Detective** – Designed to detect errors and fraud.
- **Corrective** – Designed for following up on detected errors and fraud.

IT Governance

IT governance (as previously discussed) is a formal structure within an entity that is overseen by the board of directors (BOD) and executive management. IT governance helps a business meet strategic goals and objectives through the management and control of IT acquisition, deployment, and use. IT governance provides the **strategies**, **policies**, and **procedures** that are needed to meet IT objectives.

Logical Access Controls & Cybersecurity

Limiting access to an entity's computers and the data they hold is becoming an increasingly challenging problem. Clearly, general controls over **unauthorized access** to computers and files are of great significance in evaluating I/C in an IT environment. **Firewalls** and **user authentication** are particularly important in **networks** since the data is distributed widely; the more points of access there are, the greater the risk.

Furthermore, sensitive data should be **encrypted** to minimize the possible damage (ie, theft, alteration, or destruction of data) should the user authentication process fail. Such controls designed to protect against **cyberattacks** are referred to as **cybersecurity**.

- **Firewalls** – Another tool for establishing security is a **firewall**, which prevents unauthorized users from accessing the system and data. A firewall can be in the form of a computer program (software) or a physical device that blocks the transmission media being used (hardware).
  - A **network firewall** is designed to prevent unauthorized access to the company computers. Network firewalls are easier and cheaper to implement, but if penetrated, leave the computers at severe risk.
  - **Application firewalls** protect individual programs and data. They need to be installed for each program the company wishes to protect, but they allow additional user authentication procedures, making access more difficult.
- **User authentication – User IDs** and **passwords** are used to authenticate users (ie, they are who they say they are) and prevent others from accessing the system. Other methods of authentication might include biometrics, smartcards, security tokens, multifactor identification, and multimodal authentication.
  - Passwords should be changed regularly (eg, every 90 days) to make unauthorized access more difficult.
  - Protocols for passwords should encourage the use of random letters, numbers, and symbols, making it more difficult for someone to guess.
  - It is also considered good practice to require that individual users change assigned passwords when new accounts are created.
  - Failure to remove user accounts when an employee leaves a client is a major security risk.
  - A user should be locked out after three failed attempts to access the system.
- **Encryption of data** – There are two types of encryption:
  - **Private key encryption** – Data is encrypted and decrypted using the *same private key*.
  - **Public key encryption** – Data is *encrypted with a public key* and decrypted using a private key.
- **Vulnerability testing** – Systems should be tested periodically for vulnerabilities (ie, weaknesses). This process may be manual or an automated scan.
- **Penetration testing** – This involves IT personnel or an independent consultant attempting to hack the system intentionally.
- **Intrusion detection** – An intrusion-detection program monitors the system to detect network break-ins.

A network should also have **authorization controls.** These controls **limit access** to certain files to authorized employees and the **rights** that those individuals should have with respect to the files.

- **Role-based access controls** – This type of access control varies based on an individual's role in the organization. For example, just as in a manual system, one of the general controls in an IT environment involves segregation of the **incompatible duties**:
  - **Authorization** – The development of new programs and changes to existing programs should be performed by **systems analysts** and **programmers**. These personnel should not be involved in the supervision of computer operations or the control and review of output.
  - **Recording** – **Data input clerks** and **computer operators** have the role of entering information into the computer and running the programs. These personnel should not

have access to program code that would enable them to modify programs nor should they control the output.

- **Custody** – **Control clerks** and **librarians** review the output from computers to review exception reports indicating incorrect functioning of the computer, send outputs to the proper destinations, and maintain storage of data. These personnel should not have the ability to create or alter programs or to operate the computers that generate the information.

- **Rule-based access controls** – This type of access control can vary based on any set rule. Rules should be set so that:
  - Certain individuals have **read only access** rights to files.
  - Authorized individuals have the rights to **read, write, or edit** the data in the files.

There are various types of **malicious code** (malware) that could infect a system. **Antivirus software** is designed to detect and potentially eliminate malicious code before damage is done and repair or quarantine files that have already been infected. It should be deployed at multiple points in an IT architecture.

Social engineering is the development of a deceptive scenario that tricks an individual into disclosing confidential information for fraudulent purposes (eg, phishing). The best defenses against social engineering are employee **training** and **security policies**.

Change Controls

Change control measures should be implemented to ensure that changes to processing programs and business processes have minimal impact.

- **Systems Development Life Cycle (SDLC)** – SDLC consists of the phases deployed in the development or acquisition of a software system. It is used to plan, design, develop, test, and implement an application system or a major modification to an application system.
- **Change management** – After implementation, a formal change control process manages ad-hoc system changes.
- **Systems documentation** of new programs and alterations to existing programs ensures that IT personnel are aware of the availability and proper use of programs. Also, changes in programming personnel during projects will not interfere with the ability of other employees to understand what has been done previously. Such documentation may also assist the auditor in learning about the system.

Change controls and systems documentation are discussed in greater detail in a later section.

Physical Security

Physical security consists of **physical access controls** and **environmental controls**.

- Physical access controls can include locks, cameras, badges, biometrics, etc.
- Environmental controls include temperature and humidity control, fire protection without the use of sprinklers, uninterruptable power supply, etc.

Business Resilience Planning

The purpose of business resilience planning is to enable a business to quickly adapt and continue operations while safeguarding assets in the event of a disruption. The following general controls will contribute to a business's ability to return to normalcy as quickly as possible.

Identify the Business Processes of Strategic Importance

These are the key processes that are responsible for both the permanent growth of the business and for the fulfillment of the business goals. Based on the key processes, the risk management process should begin with a risk assessment. The risk is directly proportional to the impact on the organization and the probability of occurrence of the perceived threat.

Backup Controls

Copies of files and programs should be maintained to allow reconstruction of destroyed or altered files. This may include copies on the same computer, backups to removable storage media, such as disks, and off-premises backups to computers and locations outside the company. Copies may be identical, or the client may use the **grandfather-father-son** retention system. This involves the periodic saving of data versions to allow the reconstruction of records by starting with an older file and reentering lost data since that time.

The three basic backup strategies, which are commonly used together, are:

- **Full** – Makes a full backup of the system's data. This complete backup takes the longest and utilizes the most backup media. Usually performed over longer time periods, such as once a week.
- **Differential** – Copies *only* data that has changed since the last **full** backup. These backups are cumulative until the next full backup is complete and are typically done daily. Differential backups sacrifice completeness for speed, although as the week progresses, they, along with any required data restoration procedures, will take longer.
- **Incremental** – Copies *only* data that has changed since the last backup of any kind, usually in increments of hours or minutes. These small increments can be restored relatively quickly, but rely on the presence of a full backup. Any restoration must start with the last full backup, then load each incremental backup sequentially.

Planned Downtime Controls

Since some downtime is inevitable, planned downtime allows maintenance so that unplanned downtime doesn't interrupt system operations.

Checkpoints

This is similar to grandfather-father-son, but at certain "checkpoints," the system makes a copy of the database and this "checkpoint" file is stored on a separate disk or tape. If a problem occurs, the system is restarted at the last checkpoint.

Business Continuity & Disaster Recovery

The company should have plans in place that will allow operations to be restored and continued in the event of physical destruction or disabling of the site of computer operations. The configuration that represents the most complete disaster recovery plan should provide for an alternative processing site, backup and off-site storage procedures, identification of critical applications, and testing of the plan. This can be done by maintaining a(n):

- **Hot site** – This is an alternate site that has computers and data ready to begin operations immediately in the event of the disaster.
- **Cold site** – This is an alternate site that has space available for operations but will require setup of computers and loading of data before operations can begin.
- **Off-site mirrored server** – This is an off-site server that is replicated from a production server in real-time, and can take over operations in a matter of seconds in the event of an outage. This is used to ensure continuous delivery of mission-critical data or services, such as those needed by government and medical applications.

Incident Response Planning

An important part of business continuity planning is the detection and response to IT security threats. An **incident response plan** is the IT-focused counterpart to the **disaster recovery plan**, which primarily addresses physical disrupters. Incident response plans address a wide variety of IT-specific threats, including service outages, data loss, and intellectual property theft. Robust incident response plans help IT staff detect technology-related threats, and offer a course of action for all significant incidents.

Incident plans and their implementation are handled by the incident recovery team, which is made up of IT management and staff who are responsible for collecting preserving, and analyzing indecent-related data. Because incidents may impact legal obligations involving service delivery and data protection, the team may include legal and communications experts. The following five steps outline the incident plan creation process:

1. **Determine the critical IT services and components** – This includes a description of the risks to hardware, software, and data. Locations (either physical or virtual) and backups should also be identified and prioritized.

2. **Identify single points of failure** – When a single point of failure is identified, plans for redundancy should be made and implemented.

3. **Create a workforce continuity plan** – During an incident, employee safety is paramount and some physical locations or processes may be inaccessible. Alternative arrangements, such as remote worksites, virtual private networks (VPNs) and secure web gateways, should be used to enable continuity.

4. **Create an incident response plan** – The basic components of a formal plan designed to address a particular threat include:
   - A list of roles and responsibilities for the incident response team members
   - A summary of the tools, technologies, and physical resources that must be in place
   - Response procedures – There are four basic phases for incident response.
     - **Detection** – This includes controls and processes that raise an alert which can be assessed and escalated for review by an Information Security Officer or IT manager.
     - **Analysis** – Impact analysis is conducted to determine and prioritize evidence collection and response activities.
     - **Recovery** – This includes incident mitigation and elimination activities (eg, malware removal, remote data destruction on a cell phone), in addition to data restoration activities. Severe incidents may repeat the detection-analysis-recovery cycle several times.
     - **Review** – Once the incident has been handled, a post-incident review is conducted to determine root causes, system impacts, costs, and areas of improvement.

o Required internal and external communications (eg, senior management, employees, news outlets, social media)

5. **Test & Train** – IT staff must fully understand each component of the incident response plan, and test its effectiveness prior to an incident. It is also important to communicate the importance of the incident response plans to the overall organization, to ensure full employee cooperation during a significant IT breach or service disruption.

IT Risk Assessment & Mitigation

Cybersecurity risks directly involve critical business assets, including employees, intellectual property, and equipment. Accordingly, enterprises place a high value on managing, controlling, and mitigating that risk. IT risk assessment seeks to identify relationships between threats, IT vulnerability, and business assets to determine the impact, or cost and severity, associated with a security incident.

A **business impact analysis** (BIA) helps businesses identify and prioritize risks that affect IT systems. Similar to a business continuity plan, a BIA considers the resulting business impact of a system or IT-related process disruption, and helps management determine the likelihood, costs, and responses for those risks. Steps for conducting a BIA include:

- **Identify critical assets** – Critical assets include staff, software, hardware, and IT processes. In cases of overlap (eg, a server that hosts critical software), the penultimate resource (the server) is identified.

- **Identify impact** – Impact calculations include factors such as cost, time, criticality (eg, downstream system/process impact), legal requirements (eg, service contracts, regulations), ethical considerations, and negative publicity. Impact of a critical asset failure is assessed as low, medium, or high, depending on the severity of the above factors.

- **Assign likelihood** – Evaluates the likelihood of a critical asset being impacted in terms of low, moderate/medium, or high, based on the threat. For example, the likelihood of a server being impacted by an electricity disruption may be evaluated as moderate, while an attack from a virus or malware may be evaluated as high.

- **Define risk management strategy** – The asset, impact, and risk likelihood are used to formulate a risk management strategy, discussed in more detail below. Risk management is an important component of IT and business governance.

- **Prioritize risk management actions** – Corrective risk management actions are prioritized based on the identified threat and corresponding risk management strategy. High impact and high likelihood threats will require immediate action, while low impact or low likelihood threats may not require any action, based on management's risk appetite.

Management ultimately determines risk appetite and can choose one of the following **risk management strategies** to handle business risk:

- **Accept** – Accepting risk involves no action.
- **Avoid** – Risk avoidance involves using a strategy that circumvents the risk entirely.
- **Transfer** - Risk transference transfers the risk outside the company so that it becomes someone else's responsibility. Risk transference can be an appealing factor in cloud-based or service organization arrangements.

- **Mitigate** - Risk mitigation is the practice of using a strategy that reduces the likelihood of a threat or minimizes the impact of the threat.

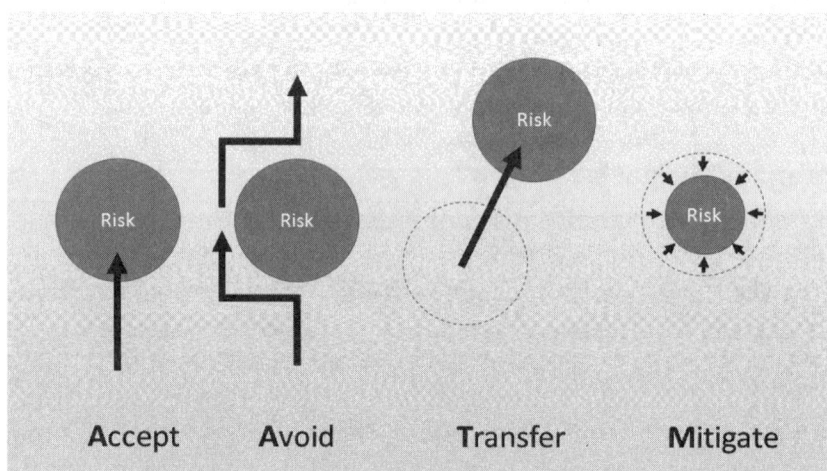

Business Impact Analysis Matrix				
Threat:		High Impact	Medium Impact	Low Impact
High Likelihood	Priority	High	High	Medium
	Action	Immediate	ASAP	Within reasonable timeframe
Medium Likelihood	Priority	High	Medium	Low
	Action	ASAP	Within reasonable timeframe	Within reasonable timeframe *or* None
Low Likelihood	Priority	Medium	Low	Lowest
	Action	Within reasonable timeframe	Within reasonable timeframe *or* None	None

Summary

Risks/Threats* – Overall Computer Environment	IT General Controls
Not Meeting IT Objectives	**IT Governance**
<ul><li>Misalignment of IT strategy with business strategy</li><li>IT doesn't deliver the value it should</li></ul>	<ul><li>Strategic guidance</li><li>Direction (setting policies & procedures)</li><li>Monitoring</li></ul>
Unauthorized Access	**Logical Access Controls & Cybersecurity**
<ul><li>Cyberattacks</li><li>Theft, alteration, or destruction of data</li><li>Malicious code</li><li>Social engineering</li><li>Misuse of data by employees</li><li>Incompatible functions (fraud/error)</li></ul>	<ul><li>Firewalls & user authentication (lock out after 3 unsuccessful attempts)</li><li>Encryption of sensitive data</li><li>Antivirus software</li><li>Employee training</li><li>Authorization controls</li></ul>
Computer Facility Vulnerabilities	**Physical Security**
<ul><li>Unauthorized access</li><li>Theft, physical destruction of IT assets</li><li>Environmental hazards</li><li>Fire, heat, humidity, electrical outages</li></ul>	<ul><li>Locks, ID badges, cameras etc.</li><li>Fire protection (no sprinklers)</li><li>Uninteruptable power supply (ie, battery backup) and emergency power supply (ie, generators)</li></ul>
Change Risk	**Change Controls**
<ul><li>Disruption of operations</li><li>Unauthorized system alterations</li><li>Uninformed IT staff</li></ul>	<ul><li>Systems Development Life Cycle (SDLC)</li><li>Change management</li><li>Systems documentation</li></ul>
Disruption of Operations	**Business Resilience Planning**
<ul><li>Accidental/intentional destruction or unauthorized alteration</li><li>Natural disasters</li></ul>	<ul><li>Back up controls</li><li>Disaster recovery planning</li><li>Incident response planning</li><li>IT risk assesment & mitigation</li></ul>

*This is not meant to be an all-inclusive list.

Lecture 3.06 – Application Controls

Overview

As previously mentioned, application controls are those applied to specific business processes within a computerized processing system to achieve financial reporting objectives. They are designed to provide reasonable assurance that objectives relevant to a given automated solution (application) are achieved. That is, they ensure that a program performs properly, accepting authorized input, processing it correctly, and generating appropriate output.

Input Controls

Input controls are designed to provide reasonable assurance that data received for processing have been **properly authorized** and **accurately entered** or converted for processing. These controls also provide the opportunity for entity personnel to correct and resubmit data initially rejected as erroneous. Errors can be avoided through:

- Observational controls
- Use of point-of-sale devices, such as scanners, to gather and record data automatically
- The use of preprinted recording forms
- Data transcription controls, such as preformatted screens, when converting data to machine-readable form
- Automated log-off of inactive users to prevent unauthorized access to sensitive data

 Historically, many of the controls discussed on the exam involve verifying data that has been input to ensure the program doesn't accept inappropriate information.

As data is being entered, it should be subject to various **forms of verification** (ie, **logic tests**):

- **Field checks** – Data is validated as to the correct length and format. For example, an entry of a license plate might be verified for type (alphanumeric, so that only letters and numbers are acceptable) and length (not longer than 7).

- **Validity checks** – Data is compared with a list of acceptable entries to be sure it matches one of them. For example, a field to accept the two-letter state abbreviation will be checked against a file that lists all the acceptable choices, so that an entry of OG for the state will be rejected as invalid.

- **Limit tests** – Numbers are compared to limits that have been set for acceptability. For example, the entry of a pay rate may be compared to the current minimum wage on the lower side and $50 per hour on the upper side to be sure the number entered makes sense. This is sometimes called a reasonableness test, and is the closest computer equivalent to human judgment in reviewing information.

- **Check digits** – Numbers with no obvious meaning, such as identification numbers, are often designed so that one of the digits is determined by a formula applied to the rest of the number. The computer applies the formula when a number is entered to determine if it is an acceptable one.

    This control makes it difficult for someone to invent a fake number if they don't know the formula; the program will recognize a number that isn't designed so that the check digit is correct. The check digit can be either a number or letter, and can be placed in any consistent position in the overall identification.

For example, many states have driver licenses that start with a letter which is derived from a formula applied to the numbers which follow it, and a person trying to create a fictional license will only have a 1 in 26 chance of correctly guessing the letter that should be in the first position based on the numbers.

When using batch processing of data, the data input clerk will often prepare manual **control totals** to be compared with computer-generated totals of entered information to ensure accuracy of inputs. These totals include:

- **Record count** – The total number of records entered into the program at that time.
- **Financial total** – The total dollar amount of entries that are financial in nature.
- **Hash total** – The total of values which cannot be meaningfully added together, but which serve as a way to verify the correct entry of these values.
- **Other quantitative total** – The total of some column of numbers, such as check numbers or invoice numbers, that can be used to determine that all transactions have been entered as well as that a sequence has not been broken.

> Assume that the checks written during a particular day are being entered into a checkbook program, and that the data input clerk is working from the following sheet to make the entries:
>
> | Check Number | Payee | Amount | Account Code |
> |---|---|---|---|
> | 1001 | Philipp Corporation | $500.00 | 307 |
> | 1002 | Rog Enterprises | $3,000.00 | 602 |
> | 1003 | Ruiz Company | $600.00 | 302 |
> | 3006 | | $4,100.00 | 1211 |
>
> After the data input clerk enters each of the checks, the computer will then indicate:
> Checks Entered = 3 (record count)
> Check Number total = 3006 (quantitative total)
> Amount total = $4,100.00 (financial total)
> Account Code total = 1211 (hash total)
>
> The data input clerk would have also determined these numbers by computing them from the input sheet; the agreement of the clerk's totals with those of the program will indicate all lines must have been entered correctly.

A program may also perform **edit checks** on batch-processed data to verify that each individual entry is appropriate; it will then generate a list of rejected transactions for review by the control clerk.

Processing Controls

Once data is input, processing controls are designed to provide reasonable assurance that data processing has been performed accurately without any omission or duplicate processing of transactions. Many processing controls are similar in nature to input controls, but they are used in the processing phases, rather than at the time input is verified.

- **Run-to-run totals** use values in the batch control record to monitor records as they move from one batch process to another batch process. They are calculated at the end of each batch process and compared to the batch control record.

- **Transaction logs** track whether transactions were successfully processed or not.
- **Prenumbered documents** ensure that there are no duplicate or missing records in a batch.
- **Sequence checks** ensure that records in a batch are processed in correct sequential order.
- A **concurrent update control** (concurrency control) helps to address conflicts in a multi-user system. For example, when two people are trying to purchase tickets at the same time, it will lock one user out, so as not to oversell the tickets.
- The most fundamental processing control a client can implement is **periodic system testing and evaluation** of the processing accuracy of its programs. This testing helps ensure that data is being handled or rejected appropriately, and that logical functions are correct and working.
    - Computer programs can be tested using **error testing compilers** to ensure that they do not contain programming language errors.
    - **Test data** exposes the program to one sample of each type of exception condition (ie, an unusual condition) likely to occur during its use.
    - **Systems and software documentation** allows system analysts to verify that processing programs are complete and thorough.

Output Controls

Output controls represent the final check on the results of computerized processing. Output controls are concerned with **detecting errors** rather than preventing errors. These controls should be designed to provide reasonable assurance that only authorized persons receive output or have access to files produced by the system.

Summary

Risks/Threats* – Specific Programs	Application Controls	
Inappropriate Inputs	**Input Controls**	
<ul><li>Invalid data</li><li>Poor data quality</li><li>Incomplete data</li><li>Inaccurate data</li></ul>	<ul><li>Check digit</li><li>Validity check</li><li>Edit test</li><li>Limit test</li></ul>	<ul><li>Financial total</li><li>Record counts</li><li>Hash total</li><li>Nonfinancial totals</li></ul>
Compromised Processing Integrity	**Processing Controls**	
<ul><li>Invalid data</li><li>Incomplete data</li><li>Inaccurate data</li><li>Redundant data</li></ul>	<ul><li>Run-to-run totals</li><li>Transaction logs</li><li>Prenumbered documents</li></ul>	<ul><li>Sequence checks</li><li>Concurrency control</li><li>Periodic system testing</li></ul>
Ineffective Outputs	**Output Controls**	
<ul><li>Inaccurate and/or incomplete data</li><li>Improper disposal</li><li>Improper distribution of information</li></ul>	<ul><li>System testing</li><li>Shredders</li><li>Distribution lists</li></ul>	

*This is not meant to be an all-inclusive list.

Lecture 3.07 – Change Controls & Systems Documentation

As previously mentioned, change control measures, such the Systems Development Life Cycle (SDLC), change management, and adequate systems documentation, should be implemented to ensure that changes to processing programs and business processes have minimal impact.

Systems Development Life Cycle (SDLC)

A traditional SDLC approach is made up of a number of distinct phases, each with a defined set of activities and outcomes. Designing and implementing a new information and control system provides an opportunity to reexamine business processes, making them more efficient and effective.

When designing an information and control system, the designers should heed the need for sustainability. The system should meet the entity's current needs while keeping in mind needs that may evolve in the future. Other considerations may include environmental, social, economic, governance, and resource factors.

SDLC Steps

1. **Analysis**
    - Determine the strategic benefits of implementing the system either in productivity gains or in future cost avoidance.
    - Identify and quantify the cost savings of a new system.
    - Estimate a payback schedule for costs incurred in implementing the system.
    - Intangible factors, such as readiness of the business users and maturity of the business processes, will also be considered and assessed.

    Define the problem or need that requires resolution and define the functional and qualitative requirements of the solution system. This can be either a customized approach or vendor-supplied software package, which would entail following a defined and documented acquisition process. In either case, the user needs to be actively involved.

2. **Design**
    - **Systems developed in-house** – Based on the requirements defined, establish a baseline of system and subsystem specifications that describe the parts of the system, how they interface, and how the system will be implemented. Generally, the design also includes program and database specifications, and will address any security considerations. Additionally, a formal change control process is established to prevent uncontrolled entry of new requirements into the development process.
    - **Purchased systems** – Based on the requirements defined, prepare a request for proposal (RFP) from suppliers of purchased systems. In addition to the functionality requirements, there will be operational, support, and technical requirements. These, together with considerations of the suppliers' financial viability and provision for escrow, will be used to select the purchased system that best meets the organization's total requirements (eg, Salesforce).

3. **Development**
    - **Systems developed in-house** – Use the design specifications to begin programming and formalizing supporting operational processes of the system. Various levels of testing also occur in this phase to verify and validate what has been developed. This would generally

include all unit and system testing, as well as several iterations of user acceptance testing. **Scope creep** refers to uncontrolled changes or continuous growth in a project's scope; this can occur when the scope of a project is not properly defined, documented, or controlled.

- o **Purchased systems** – If it is a packaged system, configure the system, to tailor it to the organization's requirements. This is best done through the configuration of system control parameters, rather than changing program code. Modern software packages are extremely flexible, making it possible for one package to suit many organizations simply by switching functionality on or off and setting the parameters in tables. There may be a need to build interface programs that will connect the acquired system with existing programs and databases.

4. **Testing**

    The final iteration of user acceptance testing and user sign-off is conducted in this phase. User acceptance testing is considered more important in an object-oriented development process than in a traditional environment. This is because of the implications of the inheritance of properties in hierarchies.

5. **Implementation**

    Establish the actual operation of the new information system. The system may also go through a certification and accreditation process. This process assesses the effectiveness of the business application in mitigating risks to an appropriate level. It also provides management accountability over the effectiveness of the system in meeting its intended objectives and in establishing an appropriate level of internal control.

6. **Maintenance**

    This phase includes monitoring and support of the new system. This includes ongoing training, help-desk resources, and a system for making authorized and tested changes to the system.

Change Management – Changes to Processes & Systems

Entities are always evolving. Change occurs as systems become obsolete or as resources become available to enhance systems. In other cases, change may occur as entities:

- Re-evaluate their missions
- Get involved in new types of transactions
- Expand into new geographical areas
- Establish relationships with new customers or suppliers
- Get involved in activities that were performed by others within the entity's supply chain

To make certain that change does not have any adverse effects, management will need to develop a process for controlling change. The basic **change control processes components** will include:

- **Change Requests** – Identifying when change is needed or desired. This may result for a variety of reasons, such as from:
    - o Change requests from parties within the existing system
    - o The failure of some aspect of the system, including a piece of equipment reaching the end of its useful life
    - o Experimentation to determine if processes can be made more efficient or effective

- **Change Analysis** – Evaluating the change. Various factors will be considered in determining whether a change is justified. The analysis basically involves comparing the costs to the benefits. Costs to be considered will include:
    - Economic costs
    - Costs associated with a potential disruption in the system
    - Training
    - Costs of potential mistakes (especially when the process is new)
- **Change Decisions** – Deciding on the change. Based on the evaluation, management will determine if a change is justified and if the benefits outweigh the costs.
- **Planning & Implementing the Change*** – This involves developing a plan that includes:
    - The new processes or components
    - An indication of all aspects of the existing process and all personnel within the entity that will be affected
    - Design or modification of forms or development of new management reports
    - Training of those who are part of the system

    Care must be taken to avoid scope creep during implementation.
- **Monitoring & Tracking the Change** – Once a change is made, it will be monitored with two objectives in mind.
    - First, management will want to make certain that the change is being properly executed.
    - In addition, management will want to determine if the change is having the intended effects.

Systems Documentation

There are several different techniques that are commonly used for documenting an entity's IT systems. The **form and extent** of documentation needed are influenced by the **size and complexity** of the entity.

Flowcharts & Diagrams

Flowcharts and diagrams are visual depictions of the I/C structure and the IT system. There are several different types of flowcharts and diagrams that are commonly used to show the different aspects and levels of detail in a system. You'll see some examples below.

- **System flowchart** – This is generally a high-level depiction of the client's entire system. It typically shows:
    - Inputs (eg, documents, data entry)
    - The overall flow of manual and automated processes
    - Outputs (eg, documents, reports,)
    - Electronic data stores and any physical storage of documents
- **Process diagram** –This shows:
    - A business process from beginning to end
    - Which departments or groups of employees are responsible for each function
    - The interaction among departments or groups of employees
- **Document flowchart** – This shows only the documents that are used in a business process and how they are distributed and disposed of.

- **Data flow diagram (DFD)** – Depending on the level of detail, a DFD shows how data flows within a system or a specific business process.
- **Entity-relationship (ER) diagram** – ER diagrams are typically used to describe details related to data structures, such as tables in a database, and how those structures relate to each other. An ER model uses three basic components to diagram data structures:
  - **Entities** – Any object, event, or business process that requires data storage (ie, a table)
  - **Relationships** – How entities are related (ie, one-to-one, one-to-many, and many-to-many)
  - **Attributes** – The characteristics of the entities (ie, fields in a table)
- **Decision table/tree** – Parts of an I/C structure may require an employee to choose from several alternative actions, depending on the conditions faced, and document such activities. This may best be accomplished by preparing a decision table that lists each possible condition and the actions that will result from each (ie, it depicts the logic of an operation or process).
- **System Interface Diagram** – This shows how a system, such as an ERP system, integrates with separate internal and external systems. This diagram may show the overall dataflow between discrete system modules and outside systems, display the business units or stakeholders that interface with a system, or show the specific interfaces where data is collected or entered into the system from external sources.

Flowcharts & Business Process Diagrams			
Symbol	Description	Symbol	Description
(trapezoid)	Manual operation (Prepare, compare or match)	(slanted rectangle)	Manual input (keyboard)
(rectangle)	Computer operation or Process (Print PO)	(parallelogram)	Input or output (general ledger)
(document shape)	Document (Invoice, PO, error listing)	(circle with tail)	Magnetic tape (Sequential access storage)
(circle)	On page connector (to connect to another location without a connecting line)	(pentagon)	Off page connector (eg, from customer)
(diamond)	A decision (granting credit, If, then, else)	(inverted triangle)	Off-line storage (file by name, date, order number)
(cylinder)	Magnetic disc storage (Database)	(curved rectangle)	On-line storage (disc, drum)
(oval)	Start/finish	(cylinder)	Direct access storage

Data Flow Diagrams

Symbol	Description	Symbol	Description
▭	Origin/destination of data	◯	Process
═══	Data storage	→	Data flow

Entity-Relationship Diagrams

Symbol	Description	Cardinality	Description
▭	Entity	——	One to one
◇	Relationship	—<	One to many
⬭	Attribute	>—<	Many to many

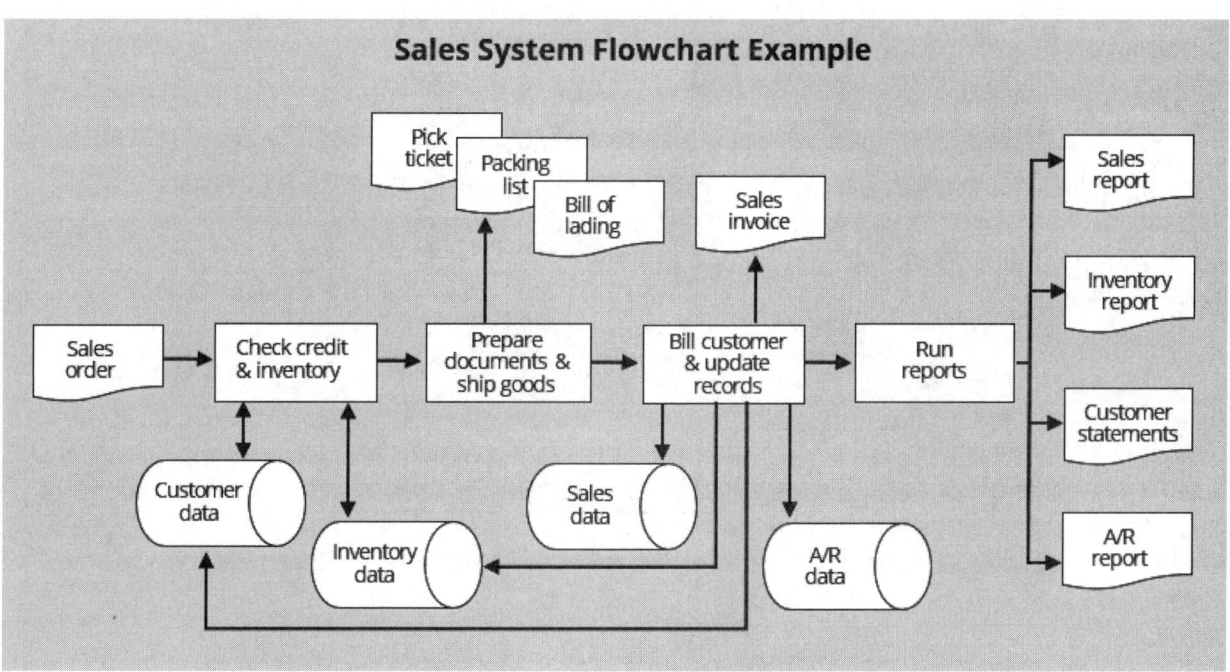

Sales System Flowchart Example

Collections Process Diagram Example
Mailroom
Cashier
Cash Receipts
A/R
Controller
G/L
Payments
Prepare deposit slip
Posts collections to customer accounts
Reconcile bank statements
Prepare remittance listing
Deposits funds
Yes
Discrepancy?
No
Posts to cash receipts journal
Prepare & send customer statements
Post journal entries

Document Flowchart for Sales Process Example
Sales
Credit
Warehouse
Shipping
Billing
A/R
G/L
A
B
C
Customer
Check inventory & prepare pick ticket
Sales order
Sales order
Sales invoice
Customer PO
Credit check
Pick ticket
Match goods to pick ticket & packing slip
Match bill of lading & sales order
Update customer data
Prepare sales order
Approved Cust. PO
Pick goods
Prepare bill of lading & shipping log
Sales journal
A/R subsidiary ledger
Sales order
Prepare Packing slip
Shipping log
Prepare invoice & update sales data
Reconcile reports
B
A
Customer
Packing slip
Bill of lading
Sales invoice
Customer statement
G/L
C
Update inventory data
Courier
Customer
Customer
Inventory subsidiary ledger

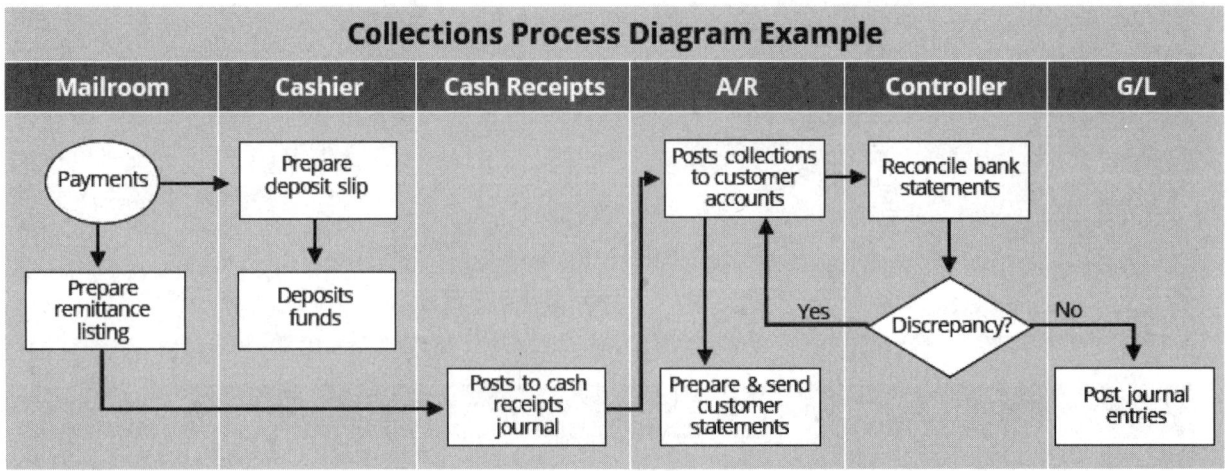

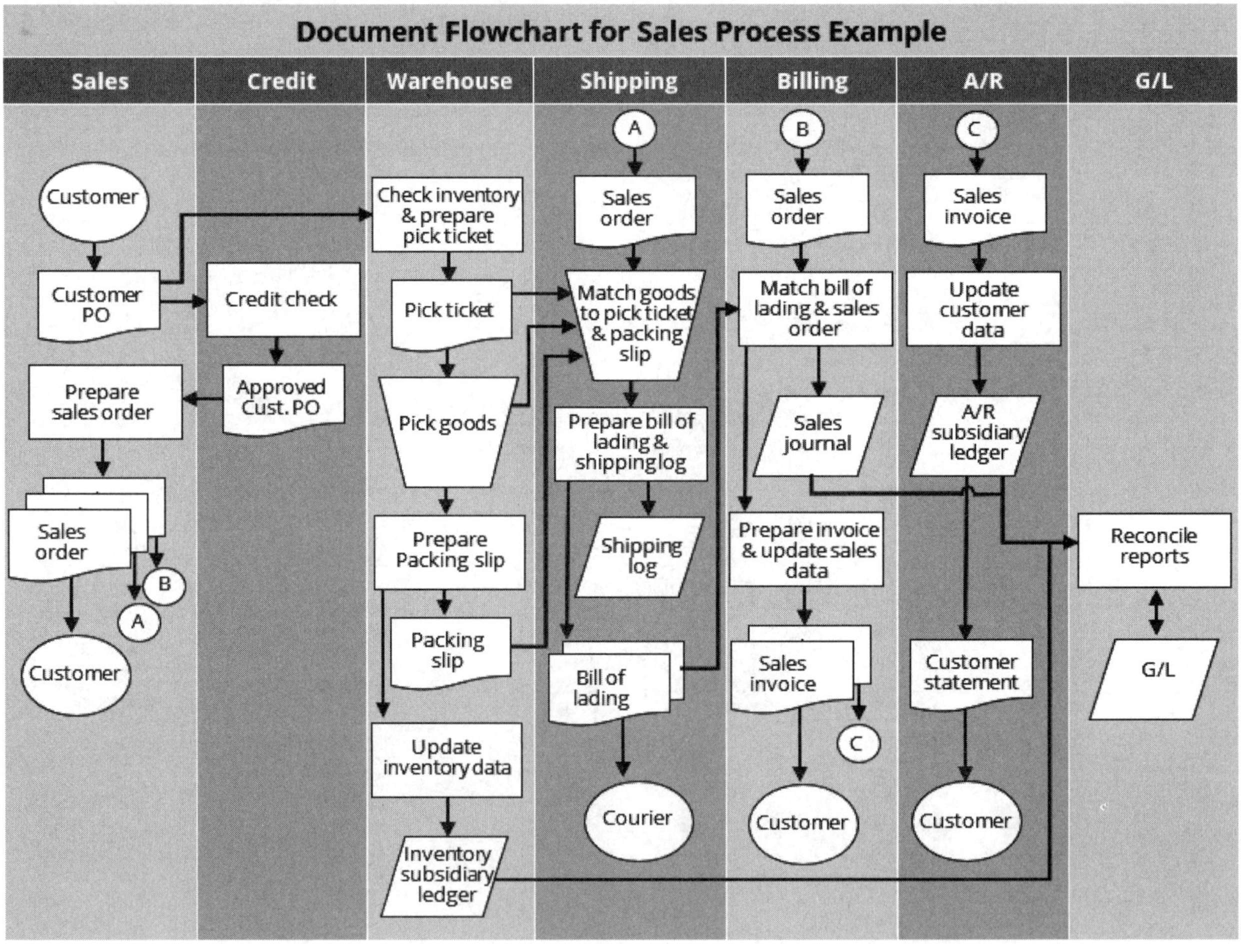

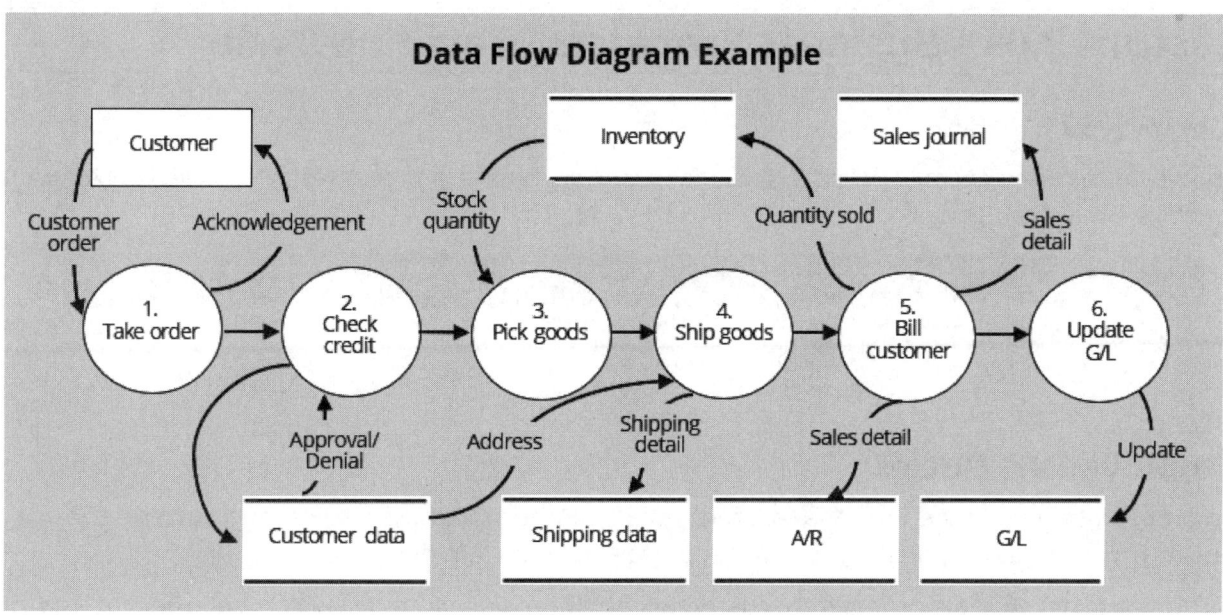

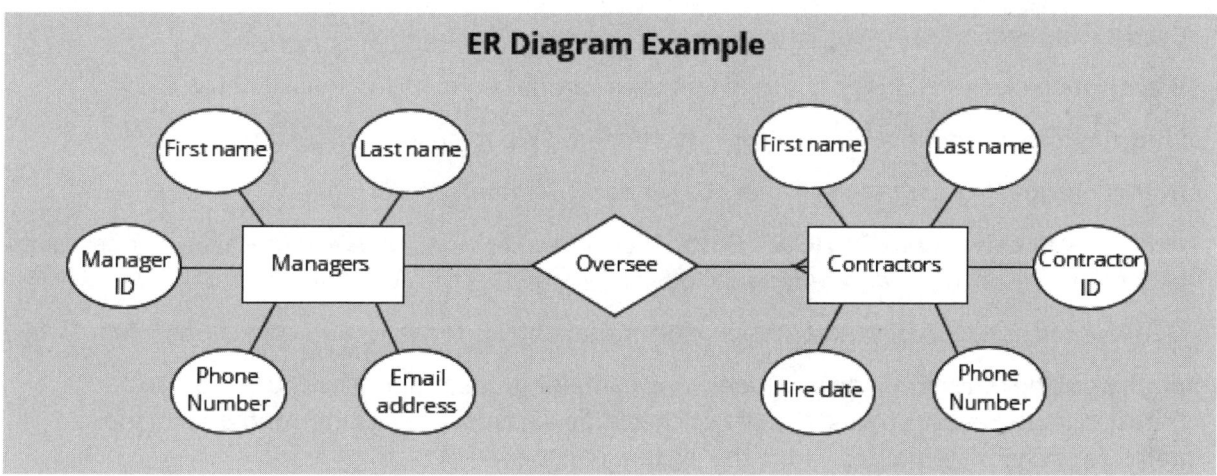

Narratives

A **narrative or memorandum** is in the form of a detailed written description of the I/C structure. It generally describes the system in a manner similar to how it is depicted in a flowchart or diagram but with words rather than symbols.

Flowcharts, diagrams, and narratives perform essentially the same function in that they generally:
- Describe each step in a cycle in sequence
- Identify the party or department responsible for performing the procedure
- Indicate what forms enter the cycle (eg, a customer's purchase order) or are created in the cycle (eg, material requisition form), how many copies are created, and how those copies are distributed; and most other aspects of the cycle

An *advantage of the narrative* is that it is easy to understand and often provides users a clearer view of the flow of a system and the interaction among the participants than other forms of documentation. *Disadvantages*, however, are that it is often difficult to identify whether responsibilities are properly segregated, and it may be difficult to trace the flow of documents.

Lecture 3.08 – Business Processes: Revenue Cycle

Overview

The revenue cycle generally consists of the following six business processes, which can be grouped into three main categories:

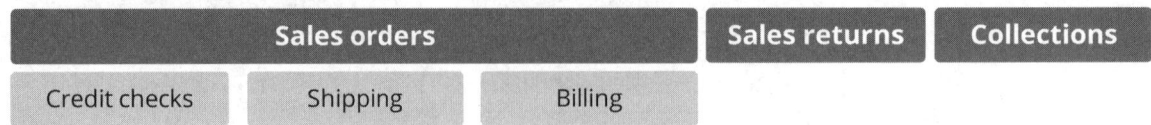

Employees & Duties

To properly segregate the incompatible functions of authorization, recording, and custody, the business processes may include specific employees with certain duties:

- **Salesclerk** – Accepts orders from customers and prepares written sales orders using internal prenumbered, preprinted forms (PPN) (recording).
- **Credit manager** – Approves customer credit on orders (authorization).
- **Warehouse clerk** – Holds goods in inventory awaiting requests for shipment (custody).
- **Shipping clerk** – Removes items from inventory to ship to customer (custody).
- **Billing clerk** – Prepares sales invoices to send to customers (recording).
- **Accounts Receivable (A/R) clerk** – Posts sales and collections to individual customer accounts based on sales invoices and remittance advices, respectively (recording).
- **General ledger (G/L) bookkeeper** – Posts journal entries for sales and collections (recording).
- **Mailroom clerk/receptionist** – Opens mail containing customer checks (or cash) and remittance advices, prepares a prelist of checks (ie, a remittance listing), and directs these items to appropriate parties within the system (custody).
- **Cashier** – Receives checks, prepares deposit slip, and deposits funds at the bank (custody).
- **Cash receipts clerk** – Receives remittance listing and posts to cash receipts journal (recording).
- **Receiving clerk** – Receives all goods that are being returned and returns them to inventory (custody).
- **Treasurer** – Approves credit memos for returns and write-offs of uncollectible accounts (authorization).
- **Controller/Internal Audit** – Bank reconciliations and analyses of past-due accounts receivable should be performed by individuals independent of cash receipts and disbursements (comparison).

A system may not necessarily include all the above employees.

- Sometimes a function may be performed by another employee or one of the above employees identified by a different title. For example, all the clerks involved in **recording** may simply be called **bookkeepers**. Also, periodic reconciliations may be performed by any employee who is not involved in the preparation of either of the two types of records being compared and does not have custody of resources being compared to recorded amounts.

- **Automation** can also affect these processes. It can reduce expenses, increase efficiency, and decrease the incidence of errors in the process. However, when errors do occur in an automated system, there is a risk that they will affect many transactions before being discovered and corrected.
  - For example, if the sales process is automated through the use of **e-commerce** or **electronic data interchange (EDI),** as previously discussed, several of the positions involved in the sales, billing, and collections processes could be eliminated.
  - Alternatively, if the entity uses a **point-of-sale (POS) system** with **barcode scanners**, a salesclerk would not need to manually take/input an order, reducing the possibility of error.
  - Furthermore, **Robotic Process Automation (RPA)** can repeat a set of tasks normally conducted by an employee using a graphical user interface (GUI). For example, RPA could automate repetitive, rules-based tasks, such as opening an email with a sales order, extracting the data, and then entering that sales order into a computer application.

Documents & Records

Some of the documents and records (paper or electronic) that may be used to capture, distribute, and summarize information within the revenue cycle include the following:

- **Sales order** – The list of goods ordered by the customer along with the prices (from a **price list**) to be charged. Even if a customer has submitted their own purchase order, a sales order will be prepared, since these are prenumbered, making it possible to periodically verify that orders were processed.
- **Pick ticket** – The list used by the warehouse clerk to gather the items ordered for shipping.
- **Packing slip** – The list of all items included in a particular shipment.
- **Bill of lading** – The shipping document that is signed by the courier, often a trucker, accepting goods from the shipping clerk.
- **Shipping log** – List of shipments that can be used to track the status of orders.
- **Sales invoice** – The bill that is prepared and sent to the customer after shipment to request payment. Before preparing a sales invoice, the billing clerk should compare the sales order and bill of lading to ensure they agree.
- **Sales journal** – A special journal in which sales on account are posted.
- **Subsidiary receivables ledger** – A ledger that lists the outstanding receivables with a separate record for each customer.
- **Receiving log** – List of goods returned in the order they were returned.
- **Receiving report** – Form completed by receiving personnel that indicates the quantity and condition of items returned.
- **Credit memo** – Documents the return of goods and adjusts the customer's account and credit limit.
- **Remittance advice** – The document included in an envelope with the check or other form of payment to indicate the purpose of the check.
- **Remittance listing** – A summary of the money received that day. This may be called a prelist in some cases, and is prepared by the employee first receiving the cash, which is usually the mailroom clerk.

- **Cash receipts journal** – A special journal in which the remittance listings are posted.
- **Deposit slip** – The document signed or stamped by the bank to acknowledge receipt of checks and that is periodically reconciled to postings into the cash receipts journal by an independent employee.
- **Bank reconciliation** – Comparison of the cash balance according to the entity's records to the amount indicated by the bank that it is holding on behalf of the entity.

Revenue Cycle Control Activities

Control activities may vary from entity to entity, even within the same industry. The following list includes some of the most common controls in the revenue cycle; however, it is not intended to be all-inclusive.

- **Performance reviews** – Management compares actual sales performance with forecasted sales and prior year sales to check for unexplained variances.
- **Information processing**
  - The sequence of **prenumbered documents** can be checked for omitted transactions.
  - **Matching documents** avoids invalid/duplicate transactions, inaccuracies, and period cutoff issues.
- **Physical controls** – Physical access to inventory, cash, and records should be controlled through the use of locks, cameras, passwords, etc.
- **Segregation of duties** – The following incompatible functions should be separated:
  - **Authorizing** sales, issuing (**recording**) credit memos and bad debt write-offs, and **custody** of cash
  - **Authorizing** sales, **recording** accounts receivable, and having **custody** of inventory
  - **Custody** of cash, **recording** of cash receipts, and preparing the bank reconciliations (**comparison**)
- **Authorization** – Sales on account should be authorized prior to executing the transaction to avoid fictitious customers and approve credit limits to avoid possible credit losses. Price lists and price concessions should also be authorized. Similarly, sales returns should be authorized prior to issuing credit.
- **Recording** – Recording of transactions should not occur until obligations have been fulfilled (eg, goods have been shipped). Recorded information should be compared to source documents and all source documents should be retained. Sending customers statements of their account helps detect and correct errors.
- **Custody** – Only certain individuals should have custody of assets (ie, cash and inventory) or access to programs and data to avoid theft or unauthorized alteration/destruction of programs/data. Obtaining **bonds** (insurance and background searches) for employees who handle large amounts of cash is an effective deterrent to theft and fraud since bonding companies often prosecute those accused of dishonest acts.
- **Comparisons – Periodic reconciliations**
  - Periodic reconciliations of inventory on hand to inventory records can indicate whether inventory has been lost or stolen.
  - Similarly, monthly reconciliations of deposits to the accounting records should be performed.

Lecture 3.09 – Business Processes: Spending Cycle

Overview

The spending cycle of a business can generally be broken down into the following six business processes and grouped into three main categories:

Employees & Duties

To properly segregate the incompatible functions of authorization, recording, and custody, the activities may include specific employees with each of the following duties:

- **Purchasing manager** – Approves purchase requests before they are processed and negotiates terms with vendors (authorization).
- **Purchasing clerk** – Places orders with vendors (recording).
- **Receiving clerk** – Receives delivery of goods from vendors (custody).
- **Payables clerk** – Prepares payment voucher, which is the basis for authorizing the issuance of a check to the vendor after verifying the accuracy of the vendor invoice and comparing supporting documents (recording).
- **Payables manager** – Oversees the posting of vouchers to appropriate purchase records (recording).
- **Treasurer** – Signs and mails check for payment (custody).
- **Shipping department** – Sends goods back to vendors when goods are nonconforming or a right to cancel an order is being exercised by the company (custody).

Since the spending cycle is essentially the opposite of the revenue cycle, **automation** may affect these processes similarly. For example, if the purchasing process is automated using **e-commerce** or **electronic data interchange (EDI)**, several of the positions involved in purchasing, accounts payable, and cash disbursement processes could be eliminated. Such automation can reduce expenses, increase efficiency, and decrease the incidence of errors in the process.

Documents & Records

The documents and records involved in the spending cycle generally include:

- **Purchase requisition** – The internal request by the department in need for goods to be ordered by the purchasing department.
- **Purchase order** – The external form mailed to the vendor to request that goods be delivered to the company. When the **purchase order** is prepared by the purchasing clerk to send to the vendor, additional copies are sent to the receiving department and the payables department.
  - The receiving department copy is a **blind copy**; that is, it does not include price or quantities to ensure that the receiving department will perform an **independent count** of the goods delivered.
  - The payables clerk compares the purchase order and receiving report with the vendor invoice to ensure they agree before preparing the payment voucher.

- **Packing slip** – The list of all items included in a shipment.
- **Bill of lading** – A shipping document that is signed by the receiving clerk, accepting goods from the courier.
- **Receiving report** – The document prepared in the receiving department to note the quantity and condition of the items received. and signed by the courier to acknowledge the goods that have been delivered to the company.
- **Receiving log** – A list of all receipts in the order they were received.
- **Purchase (vendor) invoice** – The document received from the vendor indicating the goods the vendor claims to have shipped. This is the same document that is known as the sales invoice when considered from the vendor's side of the transaction.
- **Invoice register** – A listing of all invoices received from vendors.
- **Payment voucher** – The document prepared by the payables clerk to request that a check be issued for payment to a vendor.
    - The check for payment is usually prepared by a clerk in the treasury department who doesn't have signature authority. They will provide the **unsigned check** along with the **payment voucher** and **supporting document** to the treasurer for signature. The treasurer makes sure the check **agrees** with the voucher and other documents before signing.
    - Immediately after signing, the treasurer **cancels** the **supporting documents** (so that they won't accidentally be processed again), places the check in the envelope, seals it, and arranges for mailing.
- **Purchase journal (or voucher register)** – A listing of all payment vouchers generated by the company.

Control Activities

The following list includes some of the most common control activities (**PIPS-ARCC**) in the spending cycle; however, it is not intended to be all-inclusive.

- **Performance reviews** – Management can compare actual purchases to the budget to check for unexplained variances.
- **Information processing**
    - The sequence of **prenumbered documents** can be checked for omitted transactions.
    - **Matching documents** avoids invalid/duplicate transactions, inaccuracies, and period cutoff issues.
- **Physical controls** – Physical access to inventory, cash, and records should be controlled using locks, cameras, passwords, etc.
- **Segregation of duties** – The following incompatible functions should be separated:
    - **Authorizing** purchases, receiving goods purchased (**custody**), and **recording** the purchase
    - **Authorizing** payment for purchases, **recording** payments, access to checks (**custody**), and reconciliation of the bank account (**comparison**)
    - **Authority** to approve vouchers for payment and access to unused purchase orders

- **Authorization** – Vendors and purchases should be authorized prior to executing the transaction to avoid fictitious vendors, excess purchases, and pricing issues. Similarly, purchase returns and debit memos should be authorized prior to returning items.
- **Recording**– Receiving reports should be prepared for all goods received and that credit memos are prepared for all goods that are returned.
- **Custody**– All goods should be received by the receiving department and returns should be shipped by the shipping department.
- **Comparisons** – Periodic reconciliations of inventory on hand to inventory records can provide evidence of lost or stolen inventory, fictitious purchases, unrecorded purchases, or period cutoff issues.

Lecture 3.10 – Business Processes: Investing, Financing, Production & Conversion Cycles

Investing & Financing Cycle

The investing and financing cycle deals with transactions involving acquisition and disposal of assets other than inventory and transactions with creditors and shareholders.

Control Activities

Many of the following control activities will typically be applied by management or other employees at a very high level, reflecting the extremely large value and great danger of fraud in connection with marketable securities. Examples of such control activities generally include:

- **Performance reviews** – Controls should be regularly reviewed by senior management or some independent body. Securities on hand are examined by senior management to ensure that they are registered in the name of the company or confirms such with custodians of the investments.

- **Physical controls** – The entity maintains physical custody of investments in a secure physical location. Requiring two officers to be involved in access is common

- **Segregation of duties** – As usual, the incompatible functions of authorization, recording, custody, and comparisons should be separated.
    - **Authorization** – Definitions, limits and constraints on investment activities should be reviewed regularly. Senior management should authorize investment transactions.
    - **Custody** – It is generally best to have an independent trustee maintain possession of securities so that they are safeguarded from all misappropriation by company employees.
    - **Comparisons**
        - Regular reconciliations to control account balances should be performed.
        - The internal auditor makes a list of securities in bank safe deposit boxes and compares them with the securities listed in the records.
        - The treasurer vouches the agreement of broker advices on purchases with cancelled checks.
        - The controller determines that debt securities are classified in the records correctly as trading securities, available-for-sale securities, or held-to-maturity securities, based on management decisions as to the intent of holding them.
        - The recorded values of investments are periodically compared to current market prices.
        - The investments on hand and held by custodians are periodically reconciled to their recorded amounts.

Fixed Assets

In a good I/C structure, the internal audit staff will periodically inspect physical assets. This cycle includes acquisitions, disposals, and depreciation expense. Among the **objectives** are:

- Verifying the *existence* of recorded assets by vouching from records to the physical assets. This can assist in identifying unrecorded disposals.

- Verifying the completeness of acquisitions by tracing from the physical assets to the records. This can assist in identifying unrecorded acquisitions.

A common problem involves the recording of equipment purchases in expense accounts, especially for repairs and maintenance. Besides the tracing of physical assets to records mentioned above, the internal audit staff may also examine the relevant accounts and compare them with budgeted amounts, since large variances may indicate the expensing of costs that should have been capitalized.

Production & Conversion Cycle

The production and conversion cycle deals primarily with manufacturing operations. It generally consists of the following business processes, which can be grouped into three main categories for our purposes:

Employees, Duties, Documents & Records

The results of **production planning** will determine what, how, when and the quantity of products to be produced in addition to the resources that will be needed to do so. This can be broken down into the following four processes:

- **Engineering** – In this process, engineers will provide the designs and specifications of products as well as the methods for producing the products. The following documents will also be prepared:
  - **Bill of materials** – A list of materials and parts needed for production of a product.
  - **Operations list** – A list of the processes to perform to produce a product.
- **Capital budgeting** – This process will determine the budget for resources (generally fixed assets) needed for production.
- **Scheduling** – This process determines when production activities will occur while trying to meet customer demand, coordinate with the availability of materials and resources, and minimize down time. The following documents will be prepared:
  - **Production order** (or work order) – This document authorizes the production of a product, which may be initiated by a sales forecast or a sales order.
  - **Production schedule** – This document specifies the timing of a production run.

Production is the process of converting raw materials into finished goods.
- **Materials requisition** (or routing slip) – This documents the quantity and type of raw materials moved into work-in-progress inventory at the beginning of the production process.
- **Inventory status** (or move ticket) – This documents the work completed at each stage of production, moving it to the next stage of production.

Inventory control – Acquisition of, and accounting for, raw materials purchased in a manufacturing process is similar to merchandise inventory in a nonmanufacturing entity. Thus, we won't cover inventory control again here since it is so similar to that which has already been covered in the spending cycle.

Control Activities

Examples of controls related to the management assertions for manufactured inventory include:

- **Performance reviews**
    - Management can compare actual production costs to the budgeted production costs to check for unexplained variances.
    - Allocations of salaries and wages to inventory are reviewed to make certain appropriate amounts are included.

- **Information processing**
    - The sequence of **prenumbered documents** can be checked for omitted transactions (eg, acquisition of raw materials).
    - **Matching documents** avoids invalid/duplicate transactions, inaccuracies, and period cutoff issues.

- **Physical controls** – Physical access to inventory and records should be controlled using locks, cameras, passwords, etc.

- **Segregation of duties** – As usual, the incompatible functions of **Authorization**, **Recording**, and **Custody** should be separated.

- **Comparisons**
    - Perpetual inventory records are regularly **reconciled** to goods in inventory to make certain that recorded amounts are still on hand.
    - Direct labor charged to individual time tickets is compared to the total direct labor charged to work-in-process to ensure direct labor costs have not been charged to manufacturing overhead.

Lecture 3.11 – Business Processes: Personnel & Payroll

Overview

The personnel & payroll cycle can be broken down in three basic categories of business processes:

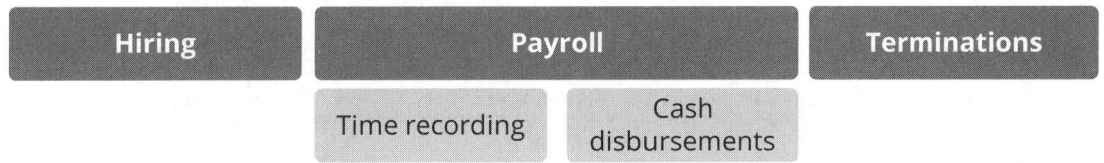

These processes, however, are normally spread across four different departments to segregate the duties properly.

	Authorize	Recording	Custody	Comparison
Department	**Personnel**	**Accounting**	**Treasurer**	**Controller**
Duties	Hire & fire	Calculate pay	Signs & distributes checks	Bank reconciliations
	Salary rates		Custody of cash	

Employees, Duties, Documents & Records

- **Personnel (Human Resources)** – HR is responsible for **authorization.**
    - HR is involved with personnel **records** and all **hiring forms**, including **forms** for payroll **deductions.**
    - HR approves changes in **pay rates**.
    - HR is also involved in the termination process. It is essential that they promptly send employees' **termination notices** to the payroll department.
- **Employee** – The employee prepares a **timecard**, and submits it to the supervisor for authorization. The timecard is then sent to the payroll department.
- **Payroll accountant** – Payroll accountants are responsible for **recording**.
    - They examine and then **update records** based on authorization forms for hiring, firing, and pay rates received from personnel.
    - They **calculate payroll** based on timecards and other reports approved by appropriate supervisors. They enter all timecard and wage rate information into the **payroll register.**
    - They also prepare a **payroll cost allocation** based on the timecard information. The payroll cost allocation is used to distribute payroll costs over the various accounts affected.
    - They **prepare vouchers** for payment.

- o They may also be involved in the preparation of **paychecks** if they do not have the ability to sign them and do not receive custody of signed but unclaimed paychecks.
- **Treasurer** – The treasurer is responsible **custody.**
  - o Paychecks are submitted to the treasurer for signature and distribution to employees.
  - o Unclaimed checks should *not* be returned to the payroll department. Unclaimed paychecks should be retained until they are either distributed or voided.
  - o If payment of wages is in cash, employees should be required to sign a receipt for the amount received.
- **Controller** – As an overall verification of custody controls over cash, the controller should prepare monthly **bank reconciliations (comparison)** to verify that there were no errors made.

Key Documents
- Personnel records
- Hiring & deduction authorization forms (W-4)
- Timecards
- Payroll register
- Paychecks
- Payroll cost allocation
- Bank reconciliations

Control Activities

- **Performance reviews** – Management should review payroll documents for unusual information.
- **Information processing**
  - The sequence of **prenumbered checks** can be checked for omitted transactions (ie, paychecks that were unrecorded).
  - **Matching** the payroll register with established payrates avoids inaccuracies.
  - **Batch processing – Control totals** and **hash totals** can be used to verify the appropriate payroll amounts.
- **Physical controls** – Physical access to cash, blank checks, as well as personnel and payroll records should be controlled using locks, cameras, passwords, etc.
- **Segregation of duties** – The following incompatible functions should be separated:
  - o **Authorizing** the hiring of personnel, payroll processing (**recording**) and distributing payroll checks (**custody**)
  - o **Authorizing** payroll rate changes and payroll processing (**recording**)
  - o Preparation of payroll checks (**recording**) and the signing of the checks (**custody**)
- **Authorization** – Supervisors should review and approve timecards.
- **Comparison** – Periodic bank reconciliations should be performed. Also, having a separate bank account for payroll will make this process easier.

Lecture 3.12 – System & Organization Controls (SOC) Reports

Overview

Service organizations are entities that provide services—such as payroll or web-hosting—to other entities (ie, **user entities**). **System and Organization Control (SOC) reporting** establishes a reputation of trust for these organizations, and gives management of user entities better insight into the systems and controls such venders are using to provide their services. From a *user-entity perspective*, SOC reports:

- Provide information that can be used to **assess operational effectiveness** and ability of a vendor to fulfill their contractual obligations and service level agreements (SLAs).

- Assist the business by allowing it to proactively identify and **address risks** associated with using a service organization.

- Increase **transparency** and **trust** from their own stakeholders.

- May help **reduce** compliance **costs** and audit time by providing key vendor information.

There are three types of SOC for service organization examinations:
- SOC 1® – SOC for Service Organizations: **ICFR**
- SOC 2® – SOC for Service Organizations: **Trust Services Criteria**
- SOC 3® – SOC for Service Organizations: **Trust Services Criteria for General Use Report**

SOC 1 – SOC for Service Organization: ICFR

Report on Controls at a Service Organization Relevant to User Entities' Internal Control over Financial Reporting

When an entity under audit uses a service organization, AU-C 402[1] provides guidance to the auditors of user entities (ie, **user auditors**) as to the *impact on an audit*. It defines a service organization as "an organization or segment of an organization that provides **services** to user entities that are **relevant to** those user entities' **internal control over financial reporting [ICFR]**."

SOC 1 reports are useful for service organizations who provide, for example, payroll, collection, claims, and credit card processing. This is because controls over these activities, or the lack thereof, could affect a user entity's F/S.

User entities and their auditors cannot always examine the control activities of a service organization themselves to determine their impact on the user entities' financial statements (F/S). Thus, SOC 1 reports describe the **service auditor's** procedures and the services of the organization that are covered by the report. This enables the user auditor to understand the overall impact of the service organization's work on the user entity's I/C structure.

Since SOC 1 reports (AT-C 320[2]) are intended to meet such specific needs, they are **restricted** to the use of user entities, their auditors, and management of the service organization itself.

---

[1] *Audit Considerations Relating to an Entity Using a Service Organization*
[2] *Reporting on an Examination of Controls at a Service Organization Relevant to User Entities' Internal Control Over Financial Reporting*

Two Types of SOC 1 Reports

There are two types of SOC 1 reports that the service auditor may issue.

- A **type 1 report** is a report on management's description of the service organization's system of controls and the suitability of the **design** of the controls. It consists of:
    - Management's description of the system
    - Management's written assertion that, in all material respects, based on appropriate criteria:
        - The description of the system fairly presents the system that was designed and **implemented** as of a specified date.
        - Controls related to objectives stated in management's description were **suitably designed** to achieve those objectives.
    - A report from the service auditor, expressing an opinion in relation to management's written assertions

- A **type 2 report** is a report on management's description of the service organization's system of controls and the suitability of the **design and** the **operating effectiveness** of the controls. It consists of:
    - Management's description of the system
    - Management's written assertion that, in all material respects, based on appropriate criteria:
        - The description of the system fairly presents the system that was designed and **implemented** as of a specified date.
        - Controls related to objectives stated in management's description were **suitably designed** to achieve those objectives.
        - The controls related to the specified objectives were **operating effectively** throughout the specified period.
    - A report from the service auditor expressing an opinion in relation to management's written assertions and describing the **tests of controls** performed and the **results** of those tests

Relying on SOC 1 Reports

To rely on a SOC 1 report (type 1 or type 2), the user auditor should:

- Determine that the **date** of a type 1 report, or the **period covered** by a type 2 report, is **appropriate** for the auditor's needs.

- Evaluate whether the **evidence** provided by the report is **appropriate** and **sufficient** for the purpose of obtaining an understanding of the user's I/C.

- Determine if the user entity has developed **complementary controls** that address risks of material misstatement relating to relevant assertions in the user's F/S. For example, the user should authorize transactions before they are processed by the service organization.

Trust Services

In addition to internal IT systems, it is common for an enterprise to rely on external IT systems or services that are beyond their direct control. These services can range from providing basic communication or documentation handling, to services that encompass a large portion of an enterprise's IT operations. It is *also* possible for external entities to rely on services provided by the enterprise's systems.

Trust Services, which are governed by SSAE (Statements on Standards for Attestation engagements), provide a method for businesses to communicate and assess IT risks and controls, and to evaluate the suitability of the design and operating effectiveness of a service organization's controls. Trust Services provide advisory or attestation services to evaluate controls within an entity's cyber risk management program, as well as for SOC 2 and SOC 3 engagements.

The evaluated trust criteria and their related points of focus come from the COSO framework, and are grouped in to the following five Trust Services Criteria (TSC) **principles:**

- **Security –** Information and systems are protected against unauthorized access and disclosure. Additionally, appropriate controls and risk management strategies exist to prevent or limit damage to systems that could compromise the availability, integrity, confidentiality, and privacy of information or systems.
- **Availability –** Information and systems demonstrate appropriate availability and reliability for operations. This would include an assessment of a service organization's ability to meet their contractual obligations.
- **Processing integrity –** Data controls ensure system processing is complete, valid, accurate, timely, and authorized.
- **Confidentiality –** Information designated as confidential is protected to meet business objectives.
- **Privacy –** All personal information is collected, used, retained, disclosed, and disposed in accordance with the business's objectives.

SOC 2 – SOC for Service Organizations: Trust Services Criteria

Report on Controls at a Service Organization Relevant to Security, Availability, Processing Integrity, Confidentiality or Privacy

These reports are designed to provide **detailed** information and assurance about controls over security, availability, and processing integrity of service organization IT systems, and the confidentiality and privacy of user data. That is, the emphasis of SOC 2 reports is on the operational fitness of IT systems, not ICFR. These reports can play an important role in:

- Oversight of the organization
- Vendor management programs
- Internal corporate governance and risk management processes
- Regulatory oversight

A SOC 2 report is required when a business is reliant on a service organization for the processing and storage of **sensitive** or **confidential** data. A SOC 2 report is written for a **technical audience** in internal audit, risk management, operations, IT, as well as regulators. Thus, use of these reports are also **restricted**.

Two Types of SOC 2 Reports

Similar to a SOC 1 report, there are two types of reports:

- A **type 1** report is on management's description of a service organization's system and the suitability of the **design of controls**.
- A **type 2** report is on management's description of a service organization's system and the suitability of the **design and operating effectiveness of controls**.

SOC 3 – SOC for Service Organizations: Trust Services Criteria for General Use Report

SOC 3 reports are also intended to meet the needs of users who seek assurance about controls over security, availability, and processing integrity of IT systems, as well as the confidentiality and privacy of data. These reports, however, are designed for a **nontechnical audience**. Thus, SOC 3 reports are **general-use reports**, and can be freely distributed. The most common examples of a SOC 3 report are WebTrust and SysTrust.

- **WebTrust** – An assurance function designed to reduce the concerns of Internet users regarding the existence of a company and the reliability of key business information placed on its website.

- **SysTrust** – An assurance function that reviews an entity's computer system to provide confidence to business partners and customers concerning the security, privacy, and confidentiality of information in addition to system availability and processing integrity.

Both WebTrust and SysTrust are designed to incorporate a seal management process by which a seal (logo) may be included on a client's website as an electronic representation of the practitioner's unqualified report. If the client wishes to use the seal (logo), the engagement must be updated at least annually. Also, the initial reporting period must include at least two months.

Summary

Examination	Report on internal controls over:	Type	Control Coverage	Users
SOC 1	Financial reporting	1	Design	User entities User auditors
SOC 1	Financial reporting	2	Design & operating effectiveness	User entities User auditors
SOC 2	Security Availability Processing Integrity Confidentiality Privacy	1	Design	Management Regulators
SOC 2	Security Availability Processing Integrity Confidentiality Privacy	2	Design & operating effectiveness	Management Regulators
SOC 3	Security Availability Processing Integrity Confidentiality Privacy	N/A	In general	Anyone

BEC 4 – Data

Table of Contents

Lecture 4.01 – Data Basics 1
    Data Structure 1
    Descriptions of Data 2
    Relational Databases 3
    Database Management Systems 4

Lecture 4.02 – Big Data & Business Intelligence 6
    Big Data Overview 6
    Business Intelligence (BI) 7
    Data Analytics 8
    Examples of Data Analytic Techniques & Visualizations 9

Lecture 4.03 – Data Governance & Management 14
    Data Governance: Overview 14
    Data Governance: Evaluation 14
    Data Governance: Directing Management 16
    Data Governance: Monitoring/Measurement 17
    Data Management 18
    Data Lifecycle Phase 1: Plan & Design 19
    Data Lifecycle Phase 2: Build & Acquire 20
    Data Lifecycle Phase 3: Store 21
    Data Lifecycle Phase 4: Use 22
    Data Lifecycle Phase 5: Share 22
    Data Lifecycle Phase 6: Archive & Destroy 23
    Summary 23

Lecture 4.04 – Working with Data (ETL) 24
    Overview 24
    Extract 25
    Transform 26
    Load 28
    Data Integrity 29
    ETL Tools 29
    Summary 31

Data

Lecture 4.01 – Data Basics

Data Structure

Data structure refers to the relationships among files in a database and among data items within each file. Since computers do not actually think and visualize, but are simply electronic machines, the storage of data is in the form of switches. **Switches** have only two possible positions (ie, they are *binary*); thus, computers can only think in terms of bits (binary digits) of information that are *on or off ("1" or "0")*.

The following terms are important in understanding the basics of data structure:

- **Bit** – A single switch in a computer that is either in the on (1) or off (0) position.
- **Byte** – A group of 8 bits representing a character.
- **Character** – A letter, number, punctuation mark, or special character.
    - **Alphanumeric** – A character that is either a letter or number.
- **Field** – Represents an **attribute** (**characteristic**) of an entity, person, event, etc., such as a name or phone number (ie, a group of related characters representing a unit of data). A field may also be referred to as an **element** of data or a **column** in a table.
- **Record** – A collection (**row**) of attributes (fields) related to an entity, person, event, etc. in a file/table/dataset. A record is sometimes referred to as a *tuple* in a database. It can also be referred to as a **member** of a dataset.
- **File** – A group of logically related records (eg, contact info for all employees).
    - **Master file** – A permanent source that is used as an ongoing reference and that is periodically updated.
    - **Detail file** – A file listing a group of transactions which may be used to update a master file. This is also frequently called a *transaction file*.
- **Dataset** – A collection of data (eg, a file or a table in a file) that share common characteristics or relationships.
- **Database** – A stored collection of related files.
- **Data repository** – A broad term that may refer to a **population** of data, as well as the supporting infrastructure that stores the data, makes the data available for use, and organizes the data. Data held within a data repository can be used for further analysis and reporting. Specific types of data repositories include **data warehouses**, **data lakes**, and **data marts**. We'll take a closer look at the different types of data repositories in the next section.
- **Data dictionary** – Hidden data that describes the logical structure of a database, including information such as titles, descriptions, and format of fields (ie, data types) as well as the relationships that exist between the data. It will also tell you who has access to what data. This type of data is called **metadata** (ie, "data about data").
- **Data type** – Refers to the specific *format* and *size* of data that can be stored in a field. It also limits the kind of data that can be stored (eg, numbers, text, dates, images). Identifying the data type for each field is important when designing a database. It helps users to search and

sort records, perform calculations, and compare the value of fields. Every database has its own specific data types. Here are some of the most common:

- **Integer** – Used for whole numbers that can have a positive, negative or zero value (ie, no decimals).
- **Decimal** – Used for numbers with decimals (eg, currency).
- **String (or Text)** – Used for a set of alphanumeric characters, which may include letters, numbers, spaces, or special characters (eg, "/" or "&"). The value of a string is often enclosed in quotation marks to identify the data as text. String data types are often designated as fixed length or variable length.
- **Boolean** – Used for storing the binary values of true/false (or, for example, yes/no in a field labeled "CREDIT_APPROVED").
- **Date/Time** – Used for storing dates and times.
- **BLOB** – Used for storing **b**inary **l**arge **ob**jects, such as videos, audio files, or images.

Descriptions of Data

A data description is metadata that defines the data within a dataset or data repository. This description allows users to **understand** the **nature** of the data, its **purpose**, what determines **membership** (ie, whether a data point is included or excluded), and the **limitations** of the data. To be sure that a description is not misleading, it should meet certain criteria[1]:

- It includes the **purpose** of the data. This helps users of the data to understand whether the data are **relevant** to their intended use.
- It is **complete and accurate,** and includes:
  - The **population** of events or instances – Users of the data need to understand the factors that determined the inclusion or exclusion of certain data points (ie, members or records of data).
  - The **nature** of elements – Each data element (aka, attribute, field) is a characteristic of an event or instance that should be carefully defined to avoid misunderstanding. For example, data on "course attendance" might include a count of students physically present, but it might also include students who are virtually present. Hence, the data would differ depending on how course attendance is defined and measured.
  - The **sources** of the data – Understanding the source of data helps users evaluate the credibility of the source. For instance, data from free online sources may be more biased than data obtained from commercial data providers.
  - The **units of measurement** (eg, dollars, gallons, meters) – This provides context when analyzing the data and helps users understand whether they need to convert or standardize data elements.
  - The accuracy, correctness, or **precision of measurement** – To properly use the data, the user needs to understand the precision of measurement of the data. For example, monetary units expressed in millions may lack the precision needed to accurately forecast inventory purchases.

---

[1] As defined by the Assurance Services Executive Committee of the AICPA in *Criteria for Describing a Set of Data and Evaluating Its Integrity*, 2020.

- The **uncertainty** inherent in the data – Some data may be based on estimates or other uncertainty (eg, a weather forecast states there is a 75% chance of rain). In such cases, information regarding the measure of uncertainty, such as the credibility of those who calculated estimates, should be provided. Other indicators may include standard deviation, historical variations, margin of error, and range of possible values.
    - **Date or period of occurrence** – Addressing the time or period of data collection helps users understand whether the data are relevant and current.
    - **Other factors or characteristics** – Any other factors that help a user understand the data should be identified. Examples include data classification (ie, sensitive, confidential, internal, or public), who can access the data, who owns the data, and retention requirements.
- It identifies or **references other information** that has not been included, but is necessary to understand the data. For example, GAAP rules would not be included in a description, but a reference should be made to GAAP for financial data based on such rules.

Relational Databases

While there are different types of databases (eg, *network* and *hierarchical*), we will focus on the **relational database** since most companies use systems that employ the relational database approach (eg, ERP systems) to structure their data.

- **Table** – Each table (aka, *relation*) represents an *object* that generally fits into one of 3 categories: *Resources* (eg, Inventory), *Events* (eg, Sales), or *Agents* (eg, Employees)—REA. A table has a specified number of columns (fields/attributes), but can have any number of rows (records). A file may consist of one or more tables.
- **Primary key** – The field in a record that *uniquely* identifies a record (eg, Social Security number, invoice number, customer ID, employee ID). This field must have a value for every record.
    - **Composite key** – Two or more fields together make up the primary key.
- **Foreign key** – A field in one table that is a primary key in another table, creating an association between the tables.
- **Associations** – Tables/objects in a relational database are linked (via embedded keys) in one of 3 ways. See table below.

Relationship	Example
One to one (1:1)	For every department, there is only one manager.
One to many (1:M)	For every manager, there are many employees.
Many to many (M:M)	Employees may provide services to many clients and clients may receive services from many employees.

Data normalization is the process of organizing a database into smaller tables for minimum repetition and redundancy. Data is fully normalized once all attributes in a table are dependent on the primary key. This enhances efficiency and removes the danger of information being stored inconsistently in different places. See example below.

Normalized tables

Customers

Customer ID	Name	Address	City	State	Zip
4526	Bob Lee	14 Main St.	Eek	AK	99578

Invoices

Invoice number	Invoice date	Ship date	Invoice amount	Customer ID
558496	2/1/XX	2/5/XX	145	4526

Line items

Invoice number	Item number	Quantity	Price	Extended price
558496	125A	5	20	100
558496	254B	3	15	45

Denormalized table

Cust. ID	Name	Address	City	State	Zip	Inv no.	Inv date	Ship date	Inv amt	Item no.	Qty	Price	Ext. price
4526	Bob Lee	14 Main St.	Eek	AK	99578	558496	2/1/XX	2/5/XX	145	125A	5	20	100
4526	Bob Lee	14 Main St.	Eek	AK	99578	558496	2/1/XX	2/5/XX	145	254B	3	15	45

Database Management Systems

A database management system (DBMS) is a program that controls the creation, modification, organization, storage, access, and retrieval of data in a database. A relational DBMS commonly uses SQL, or *Structured Query Language,* to accomplish these tasks. SQL has five main sub-languages that handle different types of database commands:

- **Data Definition Language (DDL)** – Defines the database (eg, names of tables, fields, and relationships) to the DBMS. There are three levels referred to as *views*:
  - *Internal view* – A single view generally for programmers that shows the *physical* arrangement of records and access paths.
  - *Conceptual view (Schema)* – A single view that shows a logical description of the database in one big table (even though the data is broken down into smaller tables).
  - *User views (Subschema)* – The set of data a user needs. Different users have different levels of access; thus, their view of a database would omit files, tables, fields, or records that they are not permitted to access (eg, Social Security numbers may be hidden from a project manager but not payroll personnel).
- **Data Manipulation Language (DML)** – Used to create, modify, and remove records.
  - *Forms* may be used to enter and modify data in the database.
- **Data Query Language (DQL)** – Used to retrieve data from the database.
  - Users making database queries often need to combine (ie, *join*) more than one table to get the desired information.
  - DQL is also used to select or filter out specific data from a larger set of records.
  - Custom *reports* can be created to provide useful information to decision makers.

- **Data Control Language (DCL)** – Used to control access to data.
- **Transaction Control Language (TCL)** – Used to commit (write) or rollback (undo) a data transaction.
    - TCL commands are used to apply DML commands (create, modify, and remove) to the database.
    - TCL commands also group DML commands together into logical transactions to ensure that data changes are applied in the correct order.

SQL Commands*				
DDL	**DML**	**DQL**	**DCL**	**TCL**
CREATE	INSERT	SELECT	GRANT	COMMIT
ALTER	UPDATE		REVOKE	ROLLBACK
DROP	DELETE			

Not intended to be an all-inclusive list.

The following table provides some examples of these commands. Note that:

- The WHERE condition applies to SELECT, UPDATE, and DELETE commands and limits SQL statements to certain records.
- All SQL commands are terminated with a semi-colon.

Command	Description	Example
ALTER	Used to add, delete, or modify columns in an existing table.	ALTER TABLE Employee_table DROP COLUMN Email;
DROP	Used to remove an existing table in a relational database.	DROP TABLE Employee_table;
INSERT	Used to add new records to a table in a relational database	INSERT INTO Employee_table (EmpID, EmpFname, EmpLname) Values (1, 'Test First Name', 'Test Last Name');
UPDATE	Used to update existing records in a table in a relational database	UPDATE Customer_table SET ContactName = 'Test Name', City = 'Test City' WHERE CustomerID = 1;
DELETE	Used to remove existing records from a table in a relational database	DELETE FROM Customer_table WHERE CustomerID=1;
SELECT	Used to retrieve records from a table in a relational database	SELECT CustomerName, City FROM Customer_table;
GRANT	Used to allow certain users to perform certain tasks	GRANT SELECT ON Customer_Database TO user2;
REVOKE	Used to remove access from certain users	REVOKE DELETE ON Customer_Database FROM user2;

Lecture 4.02 – Big Data & Business Intelligence

Big Data Overview

Big data is typically described as data in such high volumes that it is difficult for traditional information processing to collect and analyze. It is generated by the large volume of IT processing, such as social media use, website-tracking data, e-commerce transactions, and the internet of things, or "IoT"—ie, everyday objects embedded with computing devices that send and receive data from the Internet.

Instead of merely storing information for contractual, operational, reporting, and compliance purposes, big data is viewed as an asset that can be mined and analyzed to identify trends, enhance insight, and support decision making.

Characteristics of Big Data

While we've seen many different V-words associated with big data to describe its characteristics, we'll narrow it down to the four most important to remember and consider when working with such data:

- **Volume** – *How big is big data?* The answer is a moving target and depends on the capabilities of the user's system, but it is generally considered to start somewhere in the terabytes zone.

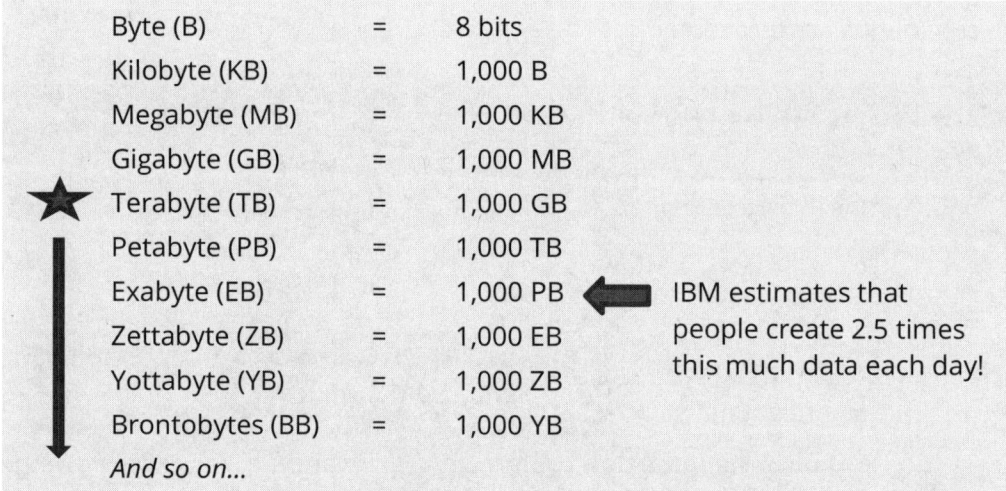

- **Velocity** – *How fast is the data being generated?* For example, it is estimated that over 300 hours of video are posted on YouTube every minute.

- **Variety** – *What is the structure and format of the data?* There are three types of data structures: structured, unstructured, and semi-structured. The vast majority of big data is unstructured or semi-structured, so it makes the data a little trickier to work with than structured data.

    o **Structured** – Data contained in fields within records or files (eg, databases and spreadsheets).

    o **Unstructured** – Raw data not contained within a database/spreadsheet. (eg, text, video, audio, photos).

    o **Semi-structured** – Data that has information associated (ie, metadata or tags) that makes it easier to process than unstructured data (eg, email, EDI, sensor data, web server logs, and HTML, XML, and XBRL tagged text).

- **Veracity** – *Is the data accurate, precise, and trusted?* Can it be *relied* on to make decisions? Often, this is the biggest challenge with big data. As the volume, velocity, or variety of the data increases, the veracity, or accuracy, of the data tends to suffer due to bias, noise (ie, meaningless or corrupt data) and other inconsistencies.

Business Intelligence (BI)

The explosion of big data combined with the technology that enables its storage and software to model and visualize the data have ushered data analytics to a whole new level of utilization in recent years. Data is being extracted, both *internally* and *externally*, for every facet of operations to gain insights that are then used to strategize and drive an organization's decisions to solve its problems and stay competitive in today's challenging business environment.

The term **business intelligence** can be thought of as the intersection of big data, technology, data analytics, and human intelligence to create information out of existing data for management.

Some of the technologies that support data analytics and business intelligence include the following:

- **Data lakes** use a flat architecture to store massive amounts of data in its original format (very useful for *unstructured data*) until it is needed.

- **Data warehouses** are databases designed to provide a place to collect and store large amounts of historical data from different sources (*usually structured data*) for quick retrieval when needed.
    - Note that data in a data warehouse is typically not normalized (ie, broken down into smaller tables) like in a relational database since historical data is static. Therefore, data that is loaded into a data warehouse from a relational database would first be denormalized into one large table for efficient processing.

- **Data marts** are essentially just smaller versions of a data warehouse, usually intended for a specific purpose.

- **Cloud computing,** as previously discussed, allows organizations to use the Internet to access/use services and applications that run on remote third-party technology infrastructure, rather than relying on in-house platform solutions. Working in the cloud can simply mean using a remote server for data storage or using a browser to access Web-based applications.

- **Data analytics and data visualization tools** include software, such as Excel, Power BI, Tableau, and Qlikview.

- **Dashboards** are data visualization tools that provide a single webpage of statistics, charts, and other visuals that describe the current status of business intelligence metrics, such as *key performance indicators (KPIs)* or other important data points for the user.
    - *Data visualization* is the process of presenting data in a visual format, typically a diagram, chart, or table. These presentations are limited only by the preparers' imaginations. More on data visualization later.
    - KPIs measure the effectiveness of an organization's most important business objectives. There are many different KPIs, the appropriateness of which depend on the type of organization/team and its goals. Some examples of commonly used KPIs include sales revenue, gross profit margin, return on assets (ROA), return on investment (ROI), return on equity (ROE), etc. We talked about performance measures in a previous section, so we won't carry on about these here again.

- **Machine Learning** is a type of artificial intelligence that gives computers the ability to learn from data without being programmed to do so. Examples of machine learning include self-driving vehicles, Amazon recommendations based on past purchases, and automatic fraud detection.

Data Analytics

What is the Difference between Data Analytics and Data Mining?

Data analytics is the process of examining, cleaning, organizing, and modeling data with the goal of making conclusions to support decision making (ie, turning raw data into useful information).

While it is generally agreed that there are only four types of data analytics (see table below), **data mining** is sometimes seen as a type of data analytic all on its own. However, it is essentially the foundation of the data analytic process itself. It involves looking for patterns, trends, relationships (associations) or anomalies without advance knowledge of the meaning of the data. Some refer to data mining as *data discovery*, *knowledge discovery*, or *discovery analysis*.

Type	What do they tell you?
Descriptive Analytics	*What has happened?*
Diagnostic Analytics	*Why did something happen?*
Predictive Analytics	*What should happen* based on past patterns and trends?
Prescriptive Analytics	*What should be done* to get to the results desired? (based on the first three types of analytics)

Asking the Right Questions

Data analytics can be used to create valuable insight and foster innovation in many ways. It all starts with asking the right questions.

- What is the *purpose* of the data analytics? Some examples include to:
    - Solve a problem
    - Manage risk
    - Increase market share
    - Increase internal audit efficiency or effectiveness
    - Increase other operational efficiencies/effectiveness
    - Analyze changing trends and consumer behavior

    > Data analytics are also very useful for external auditing, of course, but audit data analytics (ADAs) and the auditor's perspective are tested in AUD. In BEC, the focus of data analytics testing is from management's point of view.

- What does the entity *need to know* to accomplish the purpose of the data analytic? What data does the entity already have, and where can the data that is needed be obtained? Examples of *data sources* include:

Internal/Primary Data	External/Secondary Data
Data collected by the organization itself	Data collected by others for various purposes
Accounting data	Industry data
Customer data	Government data
Employee data	Census data
Marketing data	Social media
Supplier data	
Shipping data	

Access & Data Preparation

Sometimes referred to as **Extract, Transform** and **Load (ETL)***, accessing, integrating, and preparing the data to be analyzed can be the most complicated and time-consuming part of data analytics.

- *Data preparation* includes "cleaning" or "scrubbing" the data. This is the process of validating the veracity (accuracy) of the data and removing errors and noise in the data (eg, duplicates, empty fields, numeric fields that contain text, etc.) so that it can be analyzed properly.

- Data preparation may also require standardizing the data, such as merging the format of a field from different systems into one. For example, the format of dates could be different—MM/DD/YYYY vs. DD/MM/YYYY.

ETL will be discussed in more detail in a later section.

Examples of Data Analytic Techniques & Visualizations

While there are four main approaches to data analytics, there are many different techniques and visualization options to choose from.

Techniques

- **Sentiment analysis** – Using *natural language processing (NLP)* and *text analysis* to identify and categorize opinions and emotions in text (eg, social media), determining whether the writer's attitude is positive, negative, or neutral.

- **Decision tree (aka, classification analysis)** – Dividing up a dataset in a way that shows the sequential/hierarchical relationship between events, decisions, or objects.

- **Affinity grouping analysis** – Identifying the nature and frequency of relationships (associations) between variables.
  - **Market basket analysis** – Analyzing sales combinations to identify past customer behaviors to predict future customer behavior.

- **Estimation analysis** – Making predictions (ie, estimations) based on historical data.

- **Cluster analysis (aka, segmentation analysis)** – Grouping data by similarities (ie, attributes) in a way that shows the structure/relationships/differences between the data (eg, customers can be segmented by location, demographics, or common interests to facilitate target marketing).

- **Comparative analysis** – Comparing the relationships between variables over two or more periods.
  - **Trend analysis** – Analyzing changes in data over time to look for trends (a type of comparative analysis).
- **Ratio analysis** – Calculating ratios to discover relationships among financial and nonfinancial data.
- **Regression analysis** – Using statistical analysis to examine the relationship between one or more independent variables (ie, predictors) and a dependent variable.
  - **Time-series regression analysis** – A regression analysis that uses data from more than one past periods to make predictions for future periods.
  - **Cross-sectional regression analysis** – A regression analysis that uses data from *one period of time or a point in time* to make predictions.

Visualizations

Data visualization boils down to four basic presentation types: *comparison, composition, distribution, and relationship*. Some techniques, such as regression analysis, are generally associated with certain visualizations, like a scatterplot, which shows both distribution and relationship. Most visualizations, however, are a matter of judgment as to which options to combine to best communicate the results of a data analytic. The user should not need to read too much to understand the visualization.

Sentiment Analysis

Word clouds are one simple way to visualize the sentiment in textual data by making words that reappear the most bigger and bolder. This word cloud was created from Roger CPA Review student testimonials.

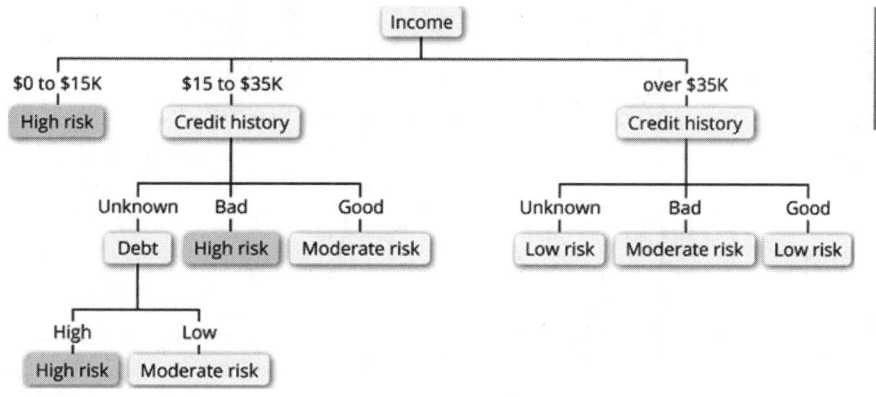

Decision Tree Analysis

Decision trees can be used to classify data, find the solution to a problem, support decisions, analyze processes, and make predictions based on relationships in the data.

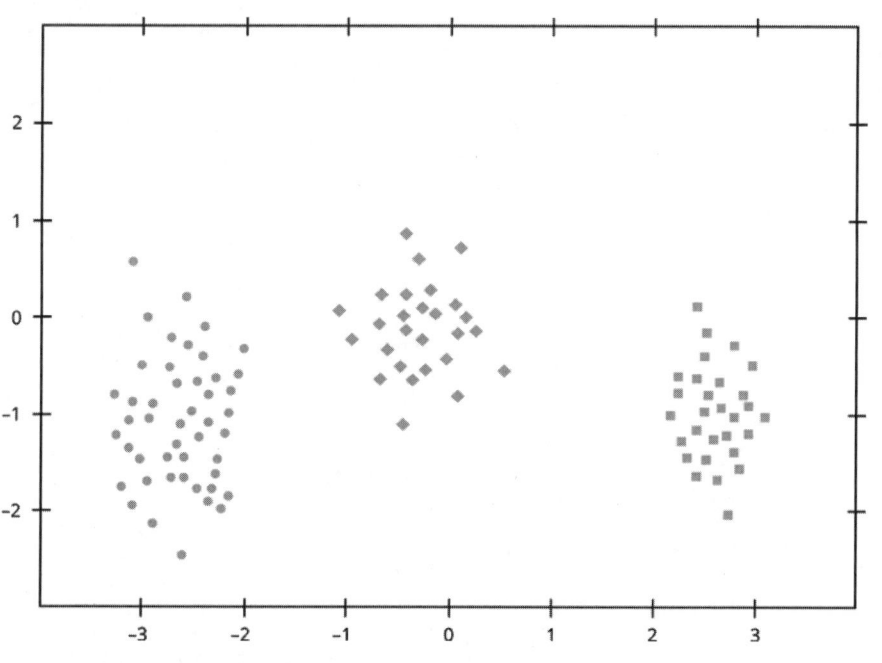

Cluster Analysis

A *scatterplot* is the most basic visualization for a cluster analysis.

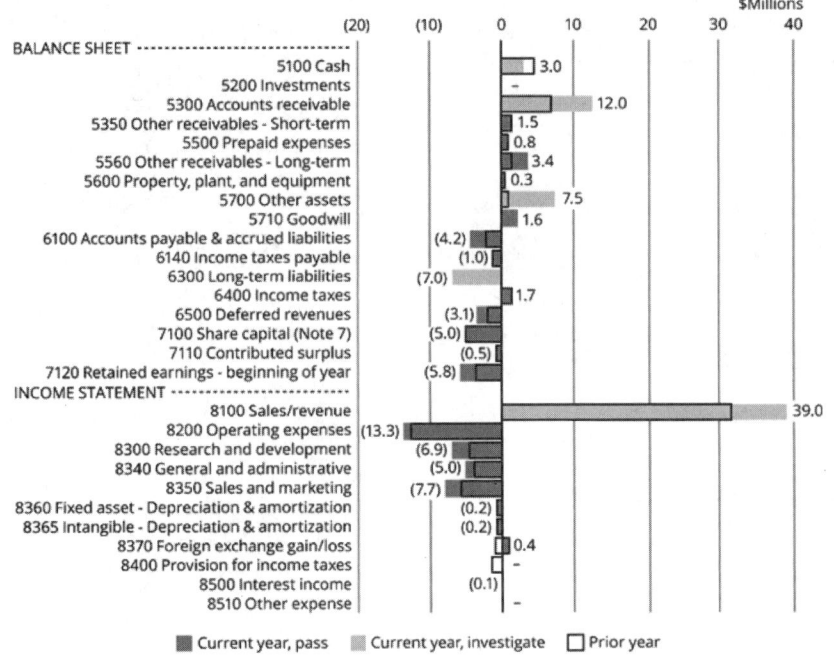

Comparative Analysis

Divergent bar charts are good for showing data that have both positive and negative values.

Graphic Source: AICPA ADA Guide, Exhibit A-4

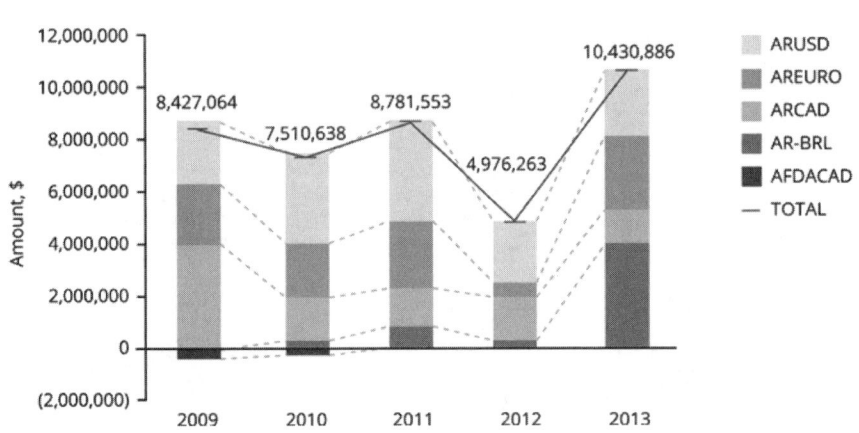

Trend Analysis

Stacked column charts show how the parts make up the whole, and the *trend lines* show how they have changed over time.

Graphic Source: AICPA ADA Guide, Exhibit A-5

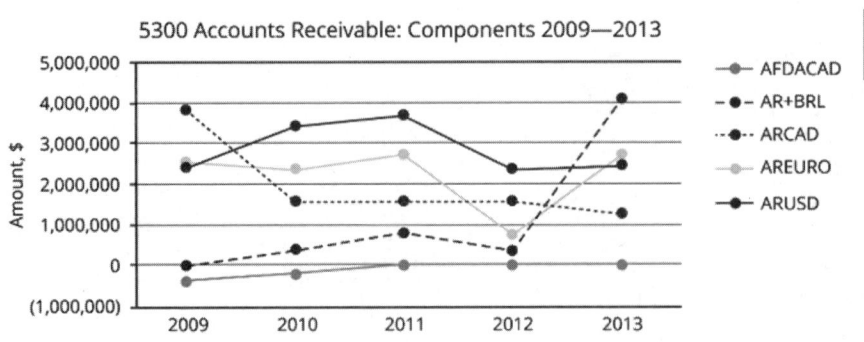

Trend Analysis

Multiple-line charts can be used to show and compare the trends in data over time.

Graphic Source: AICPA ADA Guide, Exhibit A-5

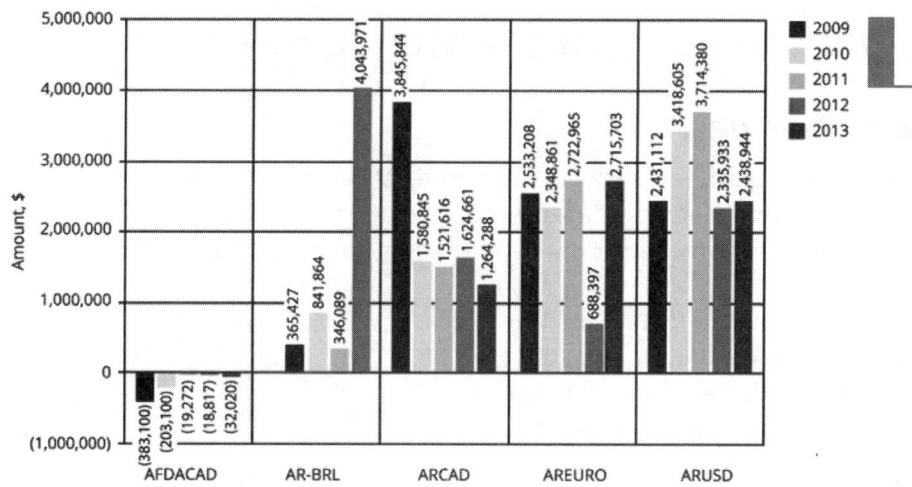

Trend Analysis

Grouped column charts are used to compare different categories of different groups of data.

Graphic Source: AICPA ADA Guide, Exhibit A-5

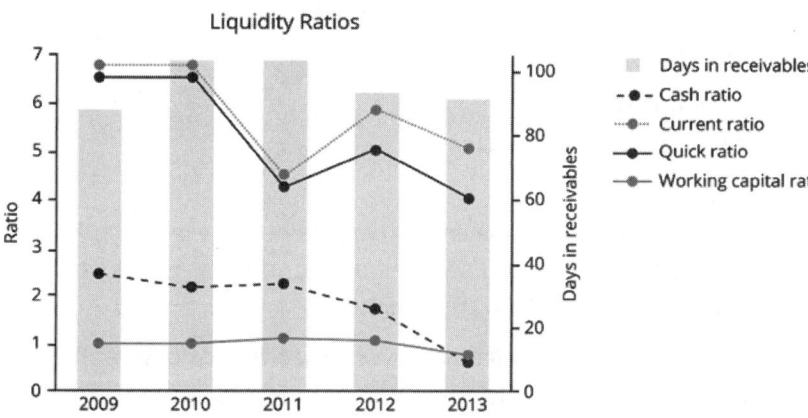

Ratio Analysis

Column & line charts (aka, dual-axis chart) can be combined to show the correlation over time between variables with different scales of measurement.

Graphic Source: AICPA ADA Guide, Exhibit A-6

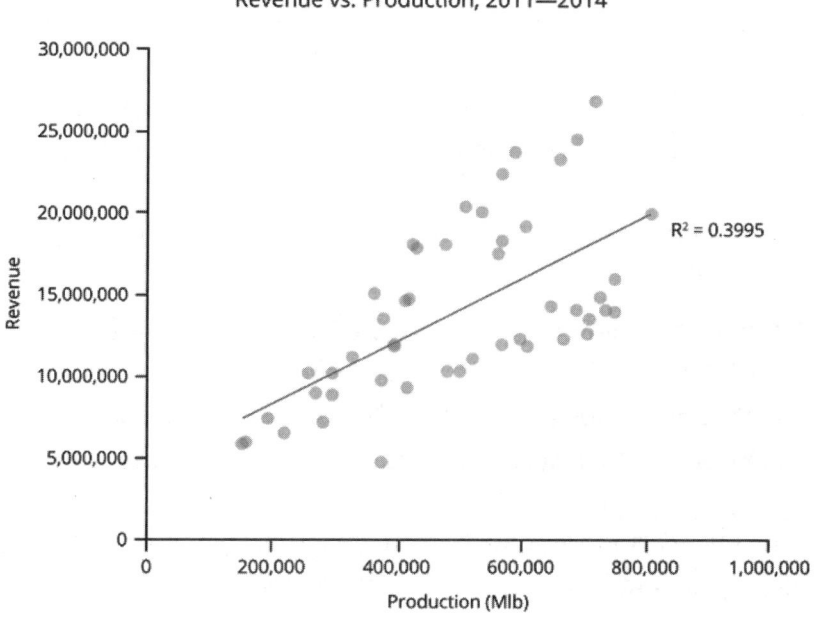

Regression Analysis

Scatterplots and *regression lines* show the correlation (R^2) between two variables. The closer R^2 is to 1, the stronger the correlation and the more precise a prediction of the dependent variable (Y) based on the independent variable (X) will be. Here, R^2 means that only 39.95% of the variance in Revenue can be explained by the regression model in relation to Production (ie, a weak correlation).

Graphic Source: AICPA ADA Guide, Exhibit B-4

Lecture 4.03 – Data Governance & Management

Data Governance: Overview

Data is an asset that must be managed, secured, and assessed. **Data governance** helps maximize the return on data and data-related assets (eg, databases, computers, and other data-related hardware) by coordinating and communicating data-related roles, responsibilities, and obligations.

You might recall from our IT governance discussion that governance is the process of **EDM**: **E**valuating the strategic options based on stakeholder needs, **D**irecting management on the chosen strategies, and **M**onitoring management's implementation of those strategies. Data governance is similar except that the process starts with the evaluation of business needs in terms of data.

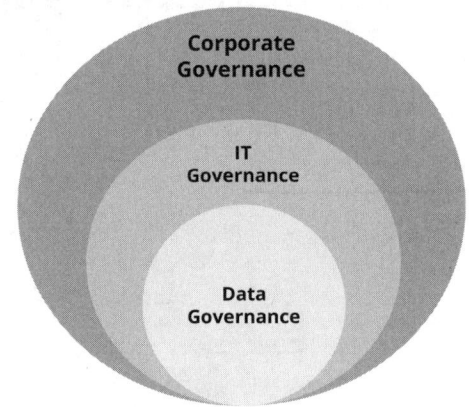

Data Governance: Evaluation

The evaluation process (ie, planning) establishes the foundation for data governance and management activities. Such foundation should define the following:

- The **strategic goals** for data governance – *What is the entity trying to accomplish with the data it collects?* How an organization classifies, handles, and secures data and data assets has a meaningful financial, and potentially legal, impact on the business.
    - The broad business objectives of data governance are to **standardize and streamline data operations** (eg, through reduced data redundancy and more efficient use of servers and other data-related hardware). This objective is primarily focused on creating and maintaining practices that ensure the availability of **timely, high-quality data**.
    - High-quality data can benefit the organization in many ways. For example, it allows management to:
        - Use **data analytics** to make more informed decisions, which may result in increased competitive advantage, reduced costs through more efficient usage of resources, and better-managed risk
        - Provide **data assurance** with respect to the reliability and accuracy of data to auditors and other users of data
        - Comply with **contractual, legal, and regulatory requirements**, such as those that involve data privacy and retention
- The **data needed** by the organization – *What data will be collected?* For example:
    - The marketing department needs certain customer data to enhance customer service and maximize sales.
    - The purchasing department needs supplier data to manage the supply chain effectively.
    - The human resources department needs employee retention data.
    - The accounting department needs financial data for reporting purposes.
    - Management needs various business data that enables better predictions, budgets, allocation of resources, etc.
    - Certain data may be needed for internal control and compliance purposes.

- A **plan for implementing** and incorporating data governance into existing strategic plans, workflows, technology, and business operations
    - *What technology is required?* Data governance evaluation should ensure that the data needs of the business are met and can provide for growth outlined by strategic goals. Good data governance also recognizes that resources are finite and should be used in the most efficient manner.
    - *What data management framework will be used?* Data governance should have a robust framework (eg, COBIT 2019) to ensure that data needs are met while minimizing risks.
    - *Who will be responsible for data governance and data management activities?* Roles must be established at the strategic, tactical, and operational levels to achieve data governance strategic goals through proper oversight and controls.
- Data **policies** and **standards** – These policies determine how data will be collected, stored, and used. There are several *ethical factors* that should be considered regarding the collection and use of data:
    - **Data security and privacy** – Data governance oversees the implementation of public policies (eg, GDPR, HIPAA), as well as company-specific guidelines and rules for handling private and sensitive data. Ethical considerations regarding how private or sensitive data is handled impact risk mitigation, transparency in how sensitive data is used, and how this data is disposed. Data owners are ultimately responsible for establishing operational rules for data privacy and guidelines for data handling and retention.

Examples of Data Privacy Regulations	
Europe	**United States**
Businesses operating in Europe must comply with General Data Protection Regulation (GDPR) laws passed in 2016, which specify that "Controllers and processors of personal data [eg, data owners] must put in place *appropriate technical and organizational measures* to implement the data protection principles."[2]	The Health Insurance Portability and Accountability Act (HIPAA) and the Family Educational Rights and Privacy Act (FERPA) charge businesses and institutions with data protection responsibilities, and specify who, and under what conditions, may access or share private data.

  - **Data retention** – Data should only be retained for as long as it is needed. For example, the validity of transactional data may expire after a few months, while private data, such as Social Security numbers or demographic information on an individual may be valid for years. Some data, however, such as tax information, has legally mandated retention times that a company must adhere to.
  - **Data monitoring and sharing** – Data governance frameworks must consider the ethical factors surrounding the "what, who, and how" of data monitoring. Data monitoring includes activities such as contract compliance and the fair use of data between vendors and business partners.
  - **Data quality** – Data governance creates policies that help ensure consistent data quality. Poor data quality represents an ethical and business risk due to an environment of poor or insufficient data controls, which can lead to faulty or erroneous business decisions by the enterprise or its partners.

---

[2] DIRECTIVE (EU) 2016/680 OF THE EUROPEAN PARLIAMENT AND OF THE COUNCIL of 27 April 2016

- o **Documentation** – Data owners are tasked with creating and maintaining clear documentation and guidelines for data asset handling and protection. The company's privacy practices should be made available to its customers and implicit or explicit consent to collect such data should be obtained.
  - **Measures** and **key performance indicators** that ensure goals are met

Principles

For data governance to be applied successfully, ISACA and Data Management Association (DAMA) International specify eight principles that help all stakeholders resolve data-related conflicts and work cohesively to realize governance goals:

1. **Integrity** – Data owners and stewards are open regarding constraints, options, and potential shortcomings of data-related decisions.
2. **Transparency** – Operations and decisions related to data processes and controls are transparent.
3. **Auditability** – Decisions, processes, and controls are clear and available to internal or external auditors.
4. **Accountability** – Responsibilities for cross-functional data management domains, processes, and controls are defined and maintained.
5. **Stewardship** – The responsibilities and activities of data stewards are transparent to data owners.
6. **Checks-and-Balances** – Accountability and controls are established in a manner that includes checks and balances between the business and IT teams, data creators/collectors and those that use the data, and business standards and compliance requirements.
7. **Standardization** – Data governance supports standardized data throughout the organization.
8. **Change Management** – Data governance supports proactive and reactive changes to activities related to the structure and use of master data and reference data values.

Data Governance: Directing Management

Data governance helps ensure that strategic data goals are achieved by directing management and enforcing accountability for data-related processes throughout the enterprise. This accountability is established through **roles** within the business and IT teams, and is implemented using **oversight** and **control** processes.

Roles

ISACA describes three main **roles** that operate at the strategic, tactical, and operational levels[3]. These categorical roles may be referred to as the strategic, tactical, and operational **data governance committees**. These roles encompass a variety of functional domains and responsibilities and may vary according to the size and needs of the business.

1. At the **strategic level**, **data owners** provide the *overall direction and goals* for the application of data governance within the business. Data owners are senior-level business and IT stakeholders, who are responsible for strategic decisions that determine the resulting value,

---

[3] ISACA, *Rethinking Data Governance and Management: A Practical Approach for Data-Driven Organizations*, USA, 2020

risk, quality, and utility of data. A committee at this level may also be referred to as the **data governance steering committee**.

2. At the **tactical level**, **data stewards** *oversee* the creation, collection, classification, usage, and access to data. Data stewards, who are generally data experts, also monitor and control compliance with data governance policies and procedures.

3. At the **operational level**, **data custodians** *manage* the data. They provide detailed and technical knowledge regarding the composition, use, storage, and protection of data assets, and advise stakeholders of issues or events that affect the data and related processes.

Oversight

The accountability established through the roles above aids in the direction of management by specifying who has authority and control over data assets. The primary goal of data governance oversight activities is to serve as a controller of **data management domains (functions),** which consist of the following processes and workflows*:

- **Data Architecture** – Defines and controls how data and data-related assets are structured
- **Data Modeling & Design** – Used to build, test, and analyze data repositories and assets
- **Data Storage & Operations** – Controls physical data asset storage, backups, maintenance, and recovery
- **Data Security** – Confidentiality, integrity, and accessibility to appropriate parties
- **Data Integration** – Acquisition, extraction, transformation, movement, delivery, replication, federation, virtualization, and operational support
- **Data Quality** – Defining, monitoring, maintaining data integrity, and improving data quality
- **Document & Content Management** – Storing, protecting, indexing, and enabling access to data found in unstructured sources and making this data available for integration and interoperability with structured data
- **Metadata Management** – Collecting, categorizing, maintaining, integrating, controlling, managing, and delivering metadata (ie, data about data)
- **Data Warehousing & Business Intelligence (BI)** – Managing analytical data processing and enabling access to decision support data for reporting and analysis
- **Reference & Master Data Management** – Managing shared data to reduce redundancy and ensure better data quality through standardized definition and use of data values

Note that data governance is also referred to as a data management domain, as it is the foundation of data management; however, we have separated data governance from the other data management activities for simplification purposes.

Control

Control establishes how assets are used within a company. This encompasses everything from **access** to specific data, and who may **add**, **change**, or **remove** data, to how data assets may be used. Control is primarily established through the definition and use of roles (discussed above), responsibilities, and processes for accountability and ownership of data assets.

Data Governance: Monitoring/Measurement

The strategic data governance committee identifies the performance measures that are critical to achieving the defined strategic goals. Data management, discussed in detail below, controls the process of monitoring the implementation of those strategies and reporting to the strategic data governance committee. Metrics may be technical, which refer to items like storage space use, uptime, and network usage; or operational, which focus on process and service measurements.

Data Management

Data management is the implementation of data governance. As previously mentioned, data management encompasses all activities that relate to data, and defines key knowledge areas and processes, called data management domains (functions), that oversee those activities. Data management domains segment the usage and lifecycle of data into processes and workflow components that control data and data-related assets.

Goals of Data Management

The goals of data management align with, and expand upon, data governance goals. While specific data management goals will vary according to the needs of the business, ISACA recommends four broad goals for data-driven enterprises.

- **Establish and evolve the data architecture** – Create data models and structures that incorporate information of strategic and operational importance, and ensure these structures can evolve to meet future business needs.

- **Define, execute, assure data quality and clean polluted data** – Understand the characteristics of the data that the business needs, gather that data from internal and external sources, test and ensure the quality of data in order to support informed business decisions, and clean or replace data (or data sources) that are poor or incomplete.

- **Realize data democratization** – Share the data across the organization to allow for timely analysis and decisions.

- **Focus on data analytics** – Use data to better understand the trends affecting the business and its environment to create effective strategy.

Data Lifecycle

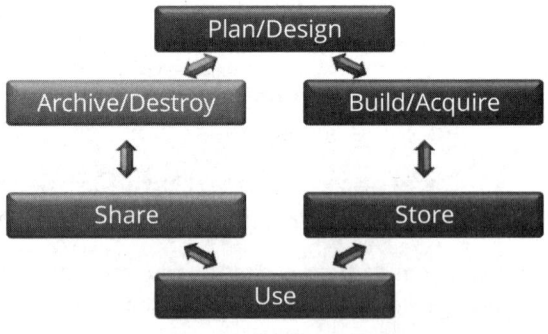

The data lifecycle is made up of several phases, each of which utilizes processes from data management domains. The typical data life cycle phases (as defined by ISACA[4]) are Plan/Design, Build/Acquire, Store, Use, Share, and Archive/Destroy. Many of these phases share knowledge and processes from a single data management domain. For example, elements of data quality and data security are applicable in all data lifecycle stages.

For our discussion, we will focus on the data management domains that have the greatest impact on a specific phase; however, that does not mean that all data management activities associated with a particular domain take place within that data lifecycle phase. The following chart shows how the data management domains correlate with the data lifecycle.

---

[4] ISACA, *Rethinking Data Governance and Management: A Practical Approach for Data-Driven Organizations*, USA, 2020

Data Management in the Data Lifecycle

Phase	Plan/Design	Build/Acquire	Store	Use	Share	Archive/Destroy
Data Management Domains	Data Architecture					
	Data Quality					
	Data Security					
	Data Modeling & Design					
	Reference & Master Data Management					
	Metadata Management					
		Data Integration				
		Data Warehousing & Business Intelligence				
			Data Storage & Operations			
			Document & Content Management			

Data Lifecycle Phase 1: Plan & Design

Data Architecture & Data Security

A business's *data owners* need to plan and design all data-related processes and activities. This phase requires the use of **data architecture**, which defines and controls how data and data-related assets are structured and considers how **data security** processes will be integrated. *Data classification* and *data taxonomy* are central to these domains as they assist in planning *data storage* and *access*, as well as designing appropriate *security* and *privacy* controls.

- Generally the responsibility of a data steward, **data classification** is the process of identifying **sensitive** and **confidential data** categories. This facilitates effective data *protection* and *privacy* requirements, such as those legislated by HIPAA or GDPR.

- The **data taxonomy** provides broad data categories and hierarchies used across the business, such as human resources data, financial data, or operations and product data. This taxonomy lays the foundation for defining the business glossary and the data dictionary. The data taxonomy also is used to design and build master and reference data, which are used in data models (discussed later).

Typical Data Classifications

	Sensitive	Confidential	Internal	Public
Who can access?	Key roles (eg, executive)	Members of a specific group (eg, HR, Legal)	Employees and associates	Anyone
Examples of Data	Strategic plans, intellectual property (IP), trade secrets	Social Security numbers, employee pay stubs	Internal emails, training materials, organization charts, policy guides	Press releases, published annual reports, social media feeds
Data Taxonomy Examples*	Human Resources Data			
	Financial Data			
	Operations and Product Data			

*This is not an all-inclusive list. Some data taxonomy categories may not span all four data classifications.

Reference & Master Data Management

Reference and master data can serve to create a **single source of truth** (SSOT). SSOT means information is structured so that all users access the same data across systems and applications. SSOT models are used to ensure data consistency by limiting data editing to one place and transmitting any data changes to all users. For example, billing data would be hosted in one database and then referenced, or linked, across all data assets that require access to billing data.

- **Reference data** is essential in defining the acceptable values that may occupy certain fields (eg, zip codes, states, countries, codes, etc.). This type of data tends to change slowly over time.

- **Master data** is unique data about customers, employees, suppliers, locations, products, etc. Sometimes collectively referred to as "objects" or "business entities," these people, companies, places, and things provide context to business transactions. This type of data is continually updated.

Metadata Management

Metadata enables data management. A metadata repository is called a **data dictionary**. It describes everything about the data itself, the relationships among the data, who has access, what the data represents (eg, a business process), and the list goes on. While there are several ways to categorize metadata, we'll break it down into two basic types:

- **Business metadata** – Defines business concepts, policies, regulations, data quality standards, etc. for consistency purposes.

- **Technical metadata** – Describes the size, structure of data, relationships between the data, format, origin, data flow, etc.

Data Lifecycle Phase 2: Build & Acquire

Once the planning phase is complete, it is time to implement the plans and collect or acquire data. The acquisition of data is an ongoing process that introduces concerns related to *data modeling* and *data quality*.

Data Modeling

A **data model** helps people visualize the information needed in a dataset, how it will be organized, and what rules, regulations, and conventions are required. These models are commonly created using **Entity-Relationship (ER) diagrams**. ER diagrams are typically used to describe details related to data structures, such as tables in a database, and how those structures relate to each other. As previously discussed, an ER model uses three basic components to diagram data structures: entities, relationships, and attributes.

Data models describe the data according to three levels:

- First, the **conceptual** level defines a very high-level view of what the data contains and which business functions use it. It shows the entities and the relationships between them. A conceptual data model is typically intended for business stakeholders.

- Next, the **logical** level provides more detail. This level adds the attributes and defines the primary and foreign keys. A logical data model is more likely to be used by business analysts or for data architecture purposes.

- Lastly, the **physical** level is developed to describe how the data will be stored within a *specific database system*. Specific naming conventions for tables and columns are applied, and data types (eg, integer, string, etc.) are defined. A physical data model is very technical and typically used by database administrators or developers.

Data Quality

A high degree of data quality provides productivity and financial benefits for an enterprise and is required for public accounting purposes. Data quality maintenance and assurance is the responsibility of the data steward who designs and implements data cleaning and data standardization practices.

Data quality is a key goal of both data governance and IT governance. For example, the COBIT framework (previously discussed) defines the three main **quality criteria categories**:

- **Intrinsic** – Deals with the accuracy, objectivity, reliability, and reputation of the data and data provider
- **Contextual** – Examines the relevance, completeness, currency, consistency, conciseness, ease-of-manipulation, interpretability, and understandability of the data
- **Security/Accessibility** – Examines the availability and access restrictions of data

Specific criteria related to each of the categories and sub-categories are determined based on business context, requirements, levels of risk, etc. For example, financial reports have a heavy emphasis on intrinsic and contextual data quality, and a moderate degree of emphasis on security and accessibility. Weekly performance reports might have more emphasis on contextual data quality and have less stringent requirements related to intrinsic data quality.

Data quality testing relies heavily on standards established by data owners. Such standards determine critical data items, value ranges for good and bad quality data, business thresholds for risk and value tolerances, and how assessment results are reported. Data quality testing also uses metadata from a data dictionary to help ensure that data is free from errors.

Data Lifecycle Phase 3: Store

Data Storage & Operations

The data storage and operations domain is about managing data from the moment it is acquired to the point at which it is destroyed. This is typically the responsibility of a database administrator or network storage administrator and includes controlling the physical data asset storage, maintenance, backups, and recovery, among other things.

Data retention, or how long data is stored, is also an important business consideration, both from legal and resource usage standpoints. Data owners are responsible for creating policies that ensure necessary records and documents are protected, and to indicate how long certain data and records will be maintained once they are no longer needed. For example, the IRS requires payroll data to be retained for a minimum of four years.

Document & Content Management

Document and content management is about managing various forms of data that do not conform to the traditional database, such as documents, video, photos, or other types of unstructured data. Unstructured data presents unique challenges for storing, protecting, indexing, and enabling access to data, primarily due to the quantity and wide variety of data sources and types.

The additional complexity of unstructured data makes standardization and data cleaning processes difficult, which can hinder good data governance and reduce data quality. Making unstructured data available for **integration** with structured data falls under the data management domain of document and content management. This requires extensive **data labeling**, which transforms unstructured data into semi-structured data with informative tags and metadata.

Data that is generated or collected from external sources generally undergoes an **extraction, transformation, and loading** (ETL) process. This process creates data files that can be used in existing systems and applications. Once data has undergone the ETL process and has been placed into a data repository (eg, data warehouse), it must be made visible and accessible for analysis. The ETL process is discussed in more detail in a later section.

Data Integration

To use data most effectively, the data needs to be integrated and standardized in a centralized data repository. This process helps translate and format data into files or datasets that can be used for analysis and decision making. For example, while data stored in individual databases can be used to provide statistics and reports, robust data analytics generally require the combination of data from several sources.

Data Warehousing & Business Intelligence (BI)

The data warehousing and business intelligence (BI) domain oversees the implementation and control of models and structures for data lakes, data marts, and data warehouses. This is also where **data federation** (a type of data integration) occurs. Data federation is the process of creating a common data model, such as a database table or spreadsheet, for heterogeneous data that comes from multiple sources.

For example, a data federation strategy might take customer information from an address book application, product sales information, and business plan data, convert all data fields to a format suitable for loading into database tables (eg, a comma-delimited file), then create the database. To complete this process, the extraction, transformation, and loading (ETL) of data into databases and data warehousing is overseen by the data steward in conjunction with IT roles, such as the database administrator.

Data Lifecycle Phase 4: Use

Data from databases and data warehouses have a wide variety of uses, from providing performance measurements to handling workflows, and providing an overview of day-to-day operations. However, one of the greatest values to an enterprise that is derived from data collection and storage efforts is provided through business intelligence (BI) and data analytics (previously discussed).

Data Lifecycle Phase 5: Share

To realize the goals of making better decisions and reducing costs, data sharing needs to have as few impediments as possible. **Data democratization** facilitates data sharing by publishing what data exists, which datasets are available, where they are located, who owns them, how they are accessed, and who is permitted to use them. This helps identify and reduce the number of data gatekeepers and eliminate sharing bottlenecks so that decision-making processes are expedited and business opportunities are identified.

When using a data democratization system, data owners are responsible for publishing and maintaining the dataset information, while data stewards monitor and control data access according to business rules and processes created by the data owners. Notice this "data democracy" is different from a traditional structure, where the IT department owns and controls data and access.

Data Lifecycle Phase 6: Archive & Destroy

The processes of data archival and destruction of data are used to implement data retention policies and standards.

- When data are no longer *actively* needed for business operations or decisions but still need to be retained, they are **archived**. Archival of data is typically done through physical media, like data tapes and disk drives, although cloud storage is becoming increasingly popular since it offloads the risk of data loss to a third party. Like data retention policies, archival policies are created and maintained by the data owners according to business requirements and regulations.

    Note: Archival of data is not the same as data backups, which are used for data restoration, and separate policies are required for both to be used in tandem (ie, a business still needs a backup of its archive).

- The **destruction of data** is a critical area of data security since destruction translates to permanent data loss, and improper destruction processes create potential security threats. In addition, the portability of data and data access through smartphones and laptops have created a need for an enterprise to be able to implement remote data wiping procedures.

Data wiping is the process of making data unreadable to prevent unauthorized access or use. This is different from **data sanitization**, which includes verification that the data has been removed.

- **Data wiping** makes data unreadable but does not remove it from the device; therefore, it cannot be verified with certainty that all wiped data is fully unrecoverable. This can also apply to the physical destruction of a device, where data storage components may still be recovered.

- A device or file that has been **sanitized** has been proven to render the data **irrecoverable** and is required for data disposal in highly regulated industries. Data that is classified as confidential or sensitive according to the data classification policy and is no longer needed should be sanitized to mitigate unauthorized data access or use.

Summary

The use of data governance to provide a cohesive data strategy and objectives is crucial in an era where the use of data can provide a sustained competitive advantage. Robust data management practices should be used to implement data governance plans, maintain data assets, and ensure optimal performance.

Data Governance (EDM)	Data Management
• *Evaluates* strategic options with respect to data based on stakeholder needs	• *Aligns* data management domains with data governance priorities and strategies
• *Directs* management on strategies chosen	• *Implements* data governance policies, standards, and performance measures
• *Monitors* management's achievement of strategies	• *Monitors and controls* all data-related business and IT processes

Lecture 4.04 – Working with Data (ETL)

Overview

Imagine a retailer wants to analyze sales trends across its entire business. The sales data for its online and brick-and-mortar storefronts are stored in separate systems and in different fields and formats. The retailer also wants to incorporate data from social media and online weather sources to determine if these data affect sales trends. To accomplish this task, a three-step process, called **Extract-Transform-Load (ETL)** is performed.

1. **Extract** – This involves gathering data from various sources. This data could reside in internal or external systems that are developed and supported by different vendors, hosted on different computer hardware, and managed by different employees. In our example, we begin by collecting sales data from the different internal systems, as well as social media and weather data from online sources.

2. **Transform** – This involves converting the raw data gathered from the extract phase into a consistent, useful format for loading the data into the target database.

3. **Load** – This involves inserting the transformed data into the target database for analysis. The target database could be a data mart, data warehouse, data lake, or other form of data repository. The data is now ready to be analyzed.

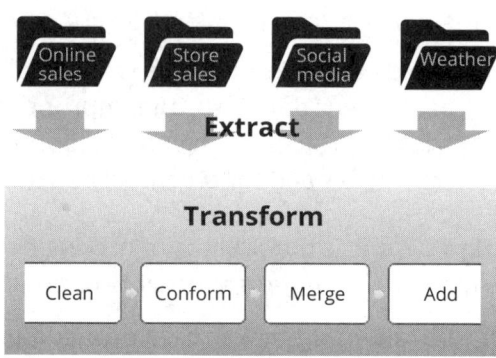

The phases in ETL may be completed *sequentially* or in *parallel*. For example, while the data are extracted, another process that runs in parallel converts the extracted data. Then, a separate data loading process may begin without waiting for the completion of the extract and transformation phases.

Alternatively, the transform and load phases may be reversed, resulting in **ELT**. This sequence is sometimes used to achieve faster loading times with respect to unstructured big data due to its size and variety of formats. ETL, however, is more commonly used than ELT; thus, we will focus our attention on ETL.

Use & Benefits of ETL

ETL initially gained popularity as a technique for migrating data from old legacy systems to new systems. Due to the increase in big data, there is also a need to extract and clean data from a variety of other sources to glean the value of that data in the form of competitive advantage.

Furthermore, many companies store large amounts of information on different platforms, such as Enterprise Resource Planning (ERP) systems, Customer Relationship Management (CRM) systems, and spreadsheets, etc. ETL allows an organization to obtain a unified perspective of the data in these disparate systems.

ETL offers several other benefits:

- It gathers relevant, cleansed data in one place so that it can be mined and analyzed for data analysis purposes. This increases data quality and enables organizations to make better and more informed decisions.
- It allows an organization to combine older data with newer data, which may expose trends that have been occurring over time.
- It creates repeatable processes that can be automated and scaled to perform the ETL process on a regular basis.

Extract

During the extract phase, data from various sources and formats is imported and consolidated in preparation for the transform phase. The objective of this phase is to retrieve all required data for analysis from multiple data sources with as little resources as possible. The extraction phase is important because the transform and load phases depend upon an accurate and complete extraction.

Extracting data from the source system may slow down the source system. To minimize such performance issues, the extraction could be completed during nonbusiness hours.

Examples of Sources and Formats of Data	
▪ SQL (relational) or NOSQL (nonrelational) databases	▪ Data warehouses
▪ Enterprise resource planning (ERP) systems	▪ Spreadsheets and comma separated values (CSV) files
▪ Customer relationship management (CRM) systems	▪ Emails, flat files, text, and portable document format (PDF) files
▪ Supply chain management (SCM) systems	▪ Social media feeds, video and audio files
▪ Internet of Things (IoT) sensors	▪ Extensible markup language (XML) files
▪ Mobile devices and apps	▪ Web pages and services

Extraction Requests

Sometimes end users cannot extract the data they need themselves. In this case, they must request the data from the IT department. A database administrator (DBA) sets up and maintains the database; thus, the DBA is a common point of contact for such requests. Requesting the data may be an interactive process, wherein the end user requests the data and then refines the request over several attempts.

When requesting data, the following should be considered:
- What data is needed (eg, tables, fields, records)?
- What is the business purpose of the data request?
- Why is the data needed?
- How often is the data needed (quarterly, monthly, yearly)?
- What is the desired format of the data (eg, spreadsheet, text file, document)?
- Who is the intended audience for the data?
- Which tool will be used to analyze and process the data?

- What are the risks to data integrity? For example, if the data is incomplete, consider mitigation strategies, such as supplementing your request with additional data.

End User Extraction Methods

Sometimes users can access the data directly without requesting the data from the IT department. A variety of techniques can be used to extract the data. Given the prevalence of relational databases, a common method is to use an SQL (structured query language) query to extract the data. There are two general types of extractions:

1. **Full Extractions** – Full extractions are necessary when the data is *initially* extracted. They may also be necessary for future extractions if the source system cannot identify which data has been changed since the last extraction.

2. **Incremental/Update/Partial Extraction** – Incremental extractions only extract the data that the source system has added or changed since the prior extraction; thus, they are a better option when the source system can identify such changes.

Transform

Data extracted from different sources is often not useable for analysis due to inconsistencies and formatting issues. Thus, a series of transformations are necessary to prepare the data for loading into the target database. At a high-level, the objectives of the transformation phase are to:

- Remove inconsistencies in the extracted data
- Correct mismatches and ensure that columns are in the same order
- Ensure that the data are in the same format
- Enrich datasets by including additional information

Data Transformations

Data cleaning and standardization is an important step in the transform phase. Data cleaning involves removing or correcting extracted data that is incomplete, inaccurate, irrelevant, or duplicated. Data standardization involves merging the formats of data from different systems into one. Examples of these data transformations include the following:

- **Cleaning leading zeroes and removing nonprintable characters** – Leading and trailing zeroes and nonprintable characters should be removed where appropriate as they can cause problems with data analysis. Nonprintable characters include white spaces, page breaks, line breaks, or tabs. This will happen especially when numbers or dates were stored as text in the source files but need to be analyzed as numeric values.

- **Encoding data** – Involves assigning free form values to the data to make them compatible with the target database. Examples include changing NULL values to 0, or changing "M" to "male" and "F" to "female."

- **Decoding data** – Involves standardizing codes for data. One source system may represent customer status as "AC" for active, or "IN" for inactive, whereas another system may represent the same customer status as 1 (active) or 0 (inactive). In the transformation phase, the data would be decoded and then recoded for a consistent format.

- **Integrating data** – Involves assigning each data element one standard name with one standard definition. For example, one data source may assign a customer number with the header CUST_NUM, whereas another system may assign a customer number with the header ACCOUNT_NUM. In the transformation phase, a standard name for customer number would be determined.

- **Splitting data** – Involves dividing data into separate fields or columns. For example, a column with employees' full names can be split into two columns to separate the first and last names.

- **Filtering data** – Involves removing extraneous fields and records. For example, if the source data have three columns (eg, job code, age, salary), then the selection may only take two fields (eg, job code and salary) or the selection could ignore those records where salary is not present (salary is null).

- **Transposing data** – Involves disconnecting rows and columns. For example, columns and rows can be switched or the data can be pivoted by turning multiple columns into multiple rows or vice versa.

- **Joining data** – Involves connecting multiple data points. For example, combining weather data from online sources with internal sales data to forecast sales.

- **Calculate and derive data** – Involves calculating new values from existing data. For example, creating new variables that calculate total cost, profit margin, or total sales.

- **Deduplicating data** – Involves identifying and removing duplicate records or columns.

- **Aggregating data** – Involves summarizing or grouping data (eg, summarizing total sales by store or region).

- **Removing headings or subtotals** – Involves removing unnecessary headers or subtotals.

- **Sorting data** – Involves rearranging the data into a useful order (eg, ascending, descending, or custom).

- **Validating the data** – Involves ensuring that the extracted data are accurate. For example, verify that the postal code from the source exists.

- **Standardizing the data** – Involves formatting the data into tables to match the format of the target database. For example, a field in one source system may be numeric and the same column in the target system may be text. Furthermore, the extracted source data could be in different formats for each data type; hence, all the extracted data should be converted into a standardized format. Specific formatting issues include:

    o **Date/time conversion** – There are many issues surrounding dates because there are many different date and time formats. For example, one source may store dates as Month DD, YYYY while another system uses MM/DD/YYYY.

    o **Numbers** – Numbers can be misinterpreted, particularly if manually entered (eg, 7 or seven). If there are negative numbers in the data, one may need to reformat the numbers to a format required by the data analysis (eg, negative signs vs. parentheses). Also, any data with accounting characters should be reformatted to show the data in raw form (eg, 123.45, not $123.45).

    o **International characters and encoding** – When working with data across countries, it is likely that you will encounter accent marks or special characters or invisible computer characters (eg, line breaks, tabs, returns). These special characters may need to be removed before analysis.

    o **Languages and measures** – Like international characters, data elements may contain a variety of words or measures that have the same meaning. For example, cheese or fromage, ketchup or catsup. To analyze the data, you will need to convert these different words for consistency.

Load

In the loading phase, the data are loaded into the target database (eg, data warehouse, data mart, flat file, or other data repository) after they have been successfully transformed. While loading takes place after transformation, loading for one dataset could take place in parallel with the transform phase of another dataset.

Before loading the data, certain relational database elements, such as referential integrity, triggers, constraints, and indexes, may need to be temporarily disabled.

- Referential integrity is a rule in a relational database management system. It requires that a foreign key value in one table must match an existing value in the corresponding table.

  > For example, consider two tables that are related in a relational database management system: VENDOR table and INVOICE table. The VENDORID field in the VENDOR table is the primary key and the VENDORID is the foreign key in the INVOICE table. Referential integrity would require that all data values for VENDORID foreign keys in the INVOICE table must exist in the VENDORID primary key field in the VENDOR table.

- A database **trigger** is a procedure that is executed when specific actions are made to a table's data. Triggers typically execute after Data Manipulation Language (DML) actions, such as INSERT, UPDATE, and DELETE.

  > For example, suppose that when a salesperson is added to the EMPLOYEE table, a trigger is activated to automatically add this salesperson to the SALESCOMMISSIONS table.

- **Constraints** are rules applied to the data entered into fields in a relational database table. They improve data integrity by limiting what types of data can be entered into a database field.

  > For example, the UNIQUE constraint on a field would require that all data in the field be distinctive.

- A database **index** is a data structure applied to one or more columns in relational database table that improves the speed of data retrieval.

Triggers, constraints, referential integrity, and indexes are valuable in a relational database because they can improve efficiency and data integrity. However, they can slow the load process because they are activated automatically when data are loaded into tables in a relational database. To make the load process more efficient, constraints, triggers, and indexes may need to be disabled during the load and enabled again after the load completes.

Types of Data Loading

- **Initial load** – An initial load is used when loading all the data originally extracted and transformed into the target database.
- **Incremental loading** – After the initial load, updated data can be loaded periodically. This approach compares the newly extracted and transformed data with the data already in the target database and only produces additional or modified records if new and unique records are found. Updating extracted data could be done daily, weekly, or monthly depending on the business need.
- **Full refresh** – If the organization cannot identify which data have been changed, it will need to periodically erase and replace the entire target database.

Data Integrity

After each ETL phase, a series of data validations should be performed to ensure that the data have integrity. Data integrity refers to ensuring data accurately reflect the business events underlying them and that any anomalies are rectified. It is important to ensure that data contain all records needed from the source (ie, completeness), that the transformed data are consistent with the source data, and that the data loaded into the target source properly. Incorrect or invalid data can skew analysis and lead to inaccurate conclusions.

Note that data quality is a subset of data integrity. Quality data is accurate, complete, consistent, valid, and timely. Data integrity includes those characteristics in addition to relevance. That is, data which have integrity are relevant and useful in addition to being complete, accurate, consistent, valid, and timely.

Ways to Assess Data Integrity

- Compare the **record count** of the records extracted to the record count in the source files to see if they are the same.

- If the data were extracted into a tool that limits the number of characters in a string for text fields, **compare the string limits** to be sure that characters were not truncated during the process.

- Compare the average, min, max, median, and sum (ie, **descriptive statistics**) for numeric fields (eg, invoice totals) to ensure that records extracted match those in the source files. This can also be performed for date/time fields (min, max) or numeric values stored as strings (eg, invoice numbers) by converting the data type to numeric.

ETL Tools

Overview

Designing and maintaining the ETL process is time-consuming and resource intensive. Rather than writing custom programming code, many organizations use ETL tools to program reusable scripts that can expedite and **automate** the ETL process. ETL tools can also help with the following tasks:

- In the extract phase, ETL tools can collect, read, and migrate data from multiple sources and across different computing platforms. They include web-scraping capabilities, which allow data to be extracted from websites, as well as the capability to extract data from document files, such as PDFs.
- ETL tools also help with the transform phase by providing data cleaning, joining, filtering, sorting, reformatting, merging and summarizing capabilities through an easy-to-use graphical interface.
- Finally, ETL tools help with the load phase by providing scheduling, version control, and data monitoring capabilities.

Types of ETL Tools

- **Enterprise** – These tools tend to be more expensive and are used by larger companies with more resources.

- **Custom ETL programming** – While time-consuming to develop, writing custom programming code for ETL processes offers more flexibility.

- **Open source** – Free open-source tools for ETL can be modified and shared because their source code is publicly accessible.

- **Cloud** – Various software providers offer cloud-hosted ETL services that are designed to optimize the process of working with cloud-native sources.

- **Batch** – Batch processing ETL tools are designed to move large volumes of data at the same scheduled time, usually when network traffic is low.
- **Real time** – These tools can process data in real time instead of processing data in large batches. They are optimal for data that is streaming or for data that is associated with time-sensitive decision making.

Functionality & Desirable Characteristics of ETL Software

ETL tools should have the following capabilities.

- **Easy to use** – An ETL tool should have a visual drag-and-drop interface, be easy to maintain, and be compatible with components of an organization's existing data solutions.
- **Connectivity/adaptability capabilities** – A good ETL tool allows for data extraction from a variety of files, databases, and cloud sources. It should be able to adapt to the different hardware platforms and existing operating systems, as well as connect to a wide range of data structure types, including relational and nonrelational databases, various file formats, XML, ERP, CRM or SCM applications, standard message formats (EDI), message queues, emails, websites, content repositories, or office automation tools.
- **Data delivery capabilities** – An ETL tool should deliver data to other applications, processes, or databases in various forms, with capabilities for batch, real-time or event-triggered process scheduling.
- **Data transformation capabilities** – An ETL tool needs to be able to join different data sources and perform basic transformations (eg, type conversion, string manipulation, or simple calculations), intermediate transformations (aggregations, summarizations, lookups), and complex transformations such, as free-text analysis.
- **Metadata capabilities & data modeling** – An ETL tool should be able to recover data models from data sources or applications, create and maintain data models, map from a physical model to a logical model, open a metadata repository, synchronize metadata changes in the different components of the tool, documentation, etc.
- **Design capabilities & development environment** – An ETL tool should be able to graphically represent repository objects, data models and data flows, test and debugging support, team capabilities, manage workflow of development processes.
- **Data management capabilities** – An ETL tool should be able to perform data quality checks, data mining, and data profiling (ie, calculating summary statistics based on an examination of the data).
- **Operations & administration capabilities** – An ETL tool should be able to manage, monitor, and control the ETL process. This includes error management, collection of execution statistics, and security controls. It should also be able to automate the ETL process and scale to larger datasets.
- **Security & compliance capabilities** – The best ETL tools encrypt data both in motion and at rest and are compliant with industry or government regulations.

Summary

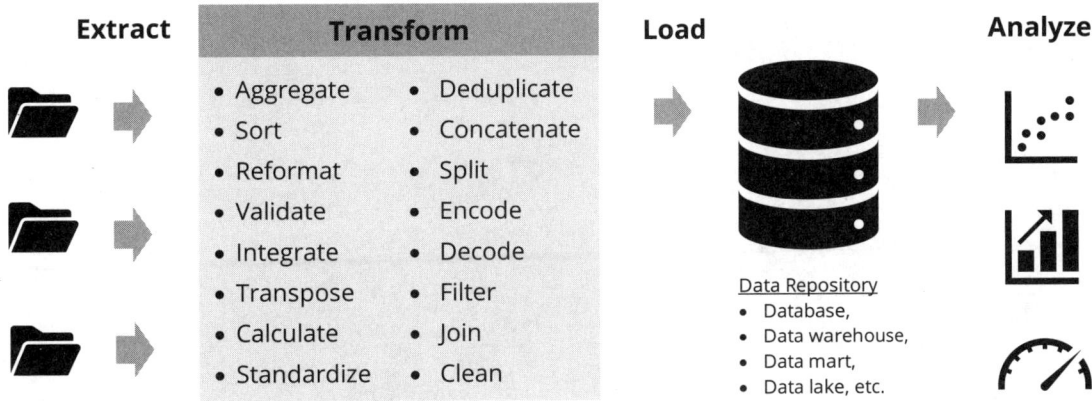

As discussed, ETL is a fairly complicated process of:
- Gathering data from disparate systems,
- Cleaning and converting this data into a useable format, and
- Loading the transformed data into a centralized and unified target database for analysis.

However, ETL could be as simple as saving data downloaded from a database as a CSV file, opening that CSV file in a spreadsheet, changing the names of various columns, and then loading the data into statistical software for further analysis.

As organizations increasingly use big data to make decisions, the importance and complexity of ETL processes will continue to grow.

> 👉 Candidates are **not** required to be able to perform any of these functions in Excel or other software applications on the CPA exam. Rather, candidates are expected to understand:
> - The overall uses and benefits of ETL
> - The tasks involved in each ETL phase
> - Methods for assessing data integrity after each ETL phase
> - The types and characteristics of ETL tools

BEC 5 – Financial Management & Capital Budgeting

Table of Contents

Lecture 5.01 – Managing Working Capital	1
Lecture 5.02 – Managing Cash	3
Lecture 5.03 – Managing Marketable Securities	4
Lecture 5.04 – Managing Receivables	5
Lecture 5.05 – Inventory Management	6
Lecture 5.06 – Present Value: Time Value of Money	8
Lecture 5.07 – Capital Budgeting	11
OVERVIEW	11
CAPITAL BUDGETING TECHNIQUES	11
Lecture 5.08 – Capital Budgeting (Continued)	15
DEPRECIATION TAX SHIELD	15
MUTUALLY EXCLUSIVE, DEPENDENT, OR INDEPENDENT	15
PROJECT NATURE	16
FORECASTING TECHNIQUES	16
RISK ANALYSIS	17
INVESTMENT LIFE CYCLE	18
PRODUCT LIFE CYCLE	18
Lecture 5.09 – Short-Term Debt Management	21
Lecture 5.10 – Long-Term Debt Management	22
DEBT COVENANTS	22
SECURED AND UNSECURED BONDS	22
PROVISIONS AFFECTING THE REPAYMENT OF BONDS	23
BOND INTEREST RATES	23
VARIATIONS ON BOND INTEREST	25
Lecture 5.11 – Advantages & Disadvantages of Debt Financing	26
Lecture 5.12 – Equity	28
COMMON STOCK	28
PREFERRED STOCK	28
LEVERAGE	29
Lecture 5.13 – Cost of Capital	31
WEIGHTED AVERAGE COST OF CAPITAL (WACC)	32
Lecture 5.14 – Asset/Liability Valuation & Ratios	33
APPROACHES TO VALUATION	33
TYPES OF MERGERS	33
KEY RATIOS (PERFORMANCE MEASURES)	33
Lecture 5.15 – Risk Management	37
EXPECTED RETURNS	37
AVERAGE RETURNS	37
STANDARD DEVIATION	38

PORTFOLIO RISK	38
INTEREST RATES & RISKS	41
THE YIELD CURVE	41

Lecture 5.16 – Derivatives   43

RISKS ASSOCIATED WITH DERIVATIVES	43
USING DERIVATIVES TO HEDGE	44
VALUING DERIVATIVES	44

Financial Management & Capital Budgeting

Lecture 5.01 – Managing Working Capital

Financial Management involves five main functions:

- The **financing function** of raising the capital necessary to fund a business.

- The **capital budgeting function** of choosing the best long-term projects to which to dedicate the firm's resources, based on the projects' expected risks and returns.

- The **financial management function** of managing the business's internal cash flows and capital structure (the mix of debt and equity) minimizing financing costs and ensuring obligations can be paid when due.

- The **corporate governance function** of making sure that managerial behavior is ethical (toward all parties) and in the interests of the business's owners.

- The **risk-management function** of identifying and managing the business's various kinds of risk.

Businesses use several financial measures to determine the efficiency with which they use working capital (or liquidity). Managing working capital involves ensuring that the business has the net short-term financial assets necessary to meet the firm's short-term financial obligations. Key elements of managing working capital are managing inventories and receivables.

- **Working Capital =** Current Assets (CA) – Current Liabilities (CL)
- **Current Ratio =** CA/CL
- **Quick (or Acid test) Ratio =** Quick assets / CL
- **Quick assets =** Cash + Marketable securities + Accounts receivable

The **Cash Conversion Cycle (CCC = 2-4)** combines the three calculations below and measures the number of days from when a business pays for its inputs to when the business collects cash from the resulting sales of finished goods. Businesses seek to shorten the CCC to minimize their need for financing. The CCC is also referred to as the "*net operating cycle.*" Shortening the CCC improves profitability because larger CCCs require businesses to use more financing.

- CCC = ICP + RCP – PDP

The **Inventory Conversion Period (ICP = 1-3)** is the average number of days required to convert inventory to sales (assume 365 days in a year unless told otherwise).

- ICP = Average inventory / COGS per day (or sometimes: Sales per day)
- Average inventory = (Beginning inventory + Ending inventory) / 2

The **Accounts Receivable Collection Period (RCP, or average collection period = 3-4)** is the average number of days required to collect accounts receivable.

- RCP = Average accounts receivable / Average credit sales per day
- Also assume 365 days per year unless told otherwise.

The **Accounts Payable Deferral Period (PDP = 1-2)** is the average number of days between buying inventory (including materials and labor for a manufacturing entity) and paying for that inventory.

- PDP = Average payables / Purchases per day (or COGS/365)

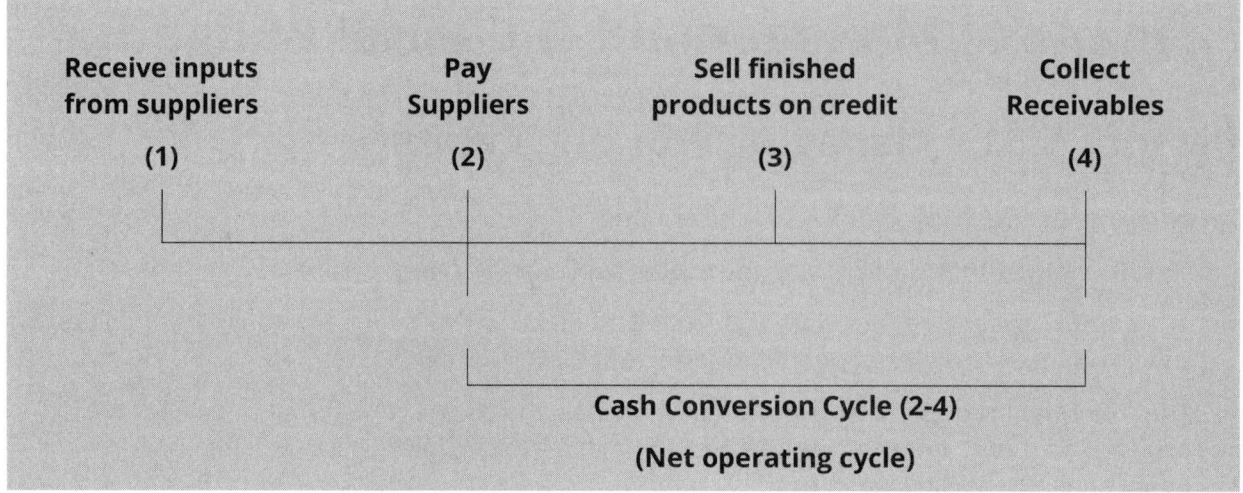

Lecture 5.02 – Managing Cash

Businesses keep cash balances for several purposes:

- **Operations** – Funds to pay for ordinary expenses.
- **Compensating balances** – Banks may require businesses to maintain minimum checking account balances as an alternative (non-cash) form of compensation for bank services and loans.
- **Trade discounts** – Quick payment of bills may result in early payment discounts.
- **Speculative balances** to take advantage of unexpected business opportunities.
- **Precautionary balances** that may be needed in emergencies.

Float refers to the time it takes for checks to be mailed, processed, and cleared. Managing cash involves *maximizing* float on payments to others and *minimizing* float on receipts from others.

- **Pay by Draft (3-party instrument)** – Customers pay by check for slower processing.
- **Zero-balance accounts** – Banks offering these accounts notify their customers each day of checks presented for payment and transfer only the funds needed to cover them.
- **Concentration banking** – Customers pay local branches instead of main offices, so the business gets funds more quickly, reducing float. However, periodic wire transfers from local branches to main offices can be costly.
- **Lock-box system** – Customers send payments directly to the bank to speed up deposits and increase internal control over cash.
- **Electronic funds transfers** – Customers pay electronically for fastest processing. For example, using your debit card at the store. Using electronic funds transfers eliminates float from both payments and receipts.

Lecture 5.03 – Managing Marketable Securities

To maximize their earnings, businesses may choose to use various short-term investments instead of cash (or zero-interest business checking accounts). Choosing among these investments, the most important considerations are *liquidity and risk (safety)*. Some examples include:

- **Treasury bills** (T-bills) are short-term obligations of the U.S. government with original maturities under 1 year. T-bills use a zero-coupon format, under which holders do not receive coupon payments, but instead receive "interest" by buying the securities at a discount from the value that will be paid at maturity. T-bills are one of the largest and most liquid securities markets in the world, so buyers bear virtually no risk of capital losses even if they sell before maturity.

- **Treasury notes** are U.S. government obligations with original maturities between 1 and 10 years. Treasury notes pay coupons (interest payments) semi-annually.

- **Treasury bonds** are the same as notes but with original maturities over 10 years.

- **Treasury Inflation-Indexed Securities (TIPS)** are treasury notes and bonds that pay a fixed real rate of interest by adjusting the principal semi-annually for inflation. These securities retained TIPS as their acronym when the word "protected" was substituted with the word "indexed."

- **Federal agency securities** are offerings that may or may not be backed by the full faith and credit of the U.S. government. They do not trade as actively as Treasury securities but pay slightly higher rates.

- **Certificates of deposit** (CDs) are time deposits at banks with limited government insurance. Interest yields are typically higher on CDs than on U.S. government securities, since, for amounts lower than the FDIC limit, they are not as liquid and, for amounts higher than the FDIC limit, they are not as safe.

- **Commercial paper** is promissory notes issued by corporations with lives up to 9 months.

- **Bankers' acceptances** are drafts drawn on banks that are payable at a specific future due date (not on demand, as checks would be), usually 30-90 days after being drawn. They are usually generated to pay for goods across international borders, and trade in secondary markets at a discount prior to their due dates.

- **Money market mutual funds** invest in instruments with short maturities (ie, under one year), and generally maintain a stable value for investors. During the financial crisis, the Federal Reserve provided temporary insurance for these products.

- **Short-term bond mutual funds** invest in instruments with maturities of under 5 years, generating higher returns than money market mutual funds, but with the potential for fluctuations in value.

- Individual **stocks and bonds** offer substantially higher potential returns, but also greater risk (of losses of up to the whole amount invested).

Financial Management & Capital Budgeting   BEC 5

Lecture 5.04 – Managing Receivables

Managing accounts receivable (receivables or A/R) includes setting up and updating credit approval mechanisms and monitoring the resulting receivables. Businesses' credit policies include four key elements:

- **Credit period** – the time buyers are given to make payments (typically 30 days for business buyers).
    - Seasonal dating is a procedure for inducing customers to buy early by not requiring payment until the selling season begins.
- **Discounts** – Price reductions for paying early (such as a 2% discount for paying within 10 days).
- **Credit criteria** – Financial strength requirements for customers to be granted credit.
- **Collection policies** – Methods employed to collect on receivables that are behind schedule.

To generate immediate cash, a business may do the following with its receivables (A/R financing):

- **Pledging** – The business obtains a loan, offering receivables as collateral.
- **Assignment of A/R** – A lending agreement whereby the borrower assigns an A/R for cash, but must pay interest and usually a service charge on the advance.
- **Factoring w/o recourse** – The business may sell receivables to a financing company, which accepts the risk of non-collection, and charges a percentage fee for accepting that risk (based on an estimate of the uncollectible rate) as well as an interest rate based on the funds advanced prior to the date collection of the receivables is due.

    Factoring receivables generally improves companies' A/R turnover ratio.

    Accounts Receivable (A/R) turnover = $\dfrac{\text{Net credit sales}}{\text{Average A/R}}$

    - **Average accounts receivable** = (Beginning A/R + Ending A/R) / 2
    - Remember to use net credit sales and **not** net sales.

    Number of days of sales in average receivables = $\dfrac{365^*}{\text{A/R turnover}}$

*Use 365 unless a 360-day period is specified.

Lecture 5.05 – Inventory Management

Budgeting for inventory purchase decisions involves determining when to place orders (or start production) to replace inventory, and how much to purchase (or produce). Managing inventories requires weighing many potentially conflicting factors. Higher costs of carrying inventories would push businesses to reduce inventories to the extent possible. Higher costs of placing small orders would likely push businesses to make fewer but larger orders, which would likely increase their inventories. Longer lead times in the delivery of inventories would push businesses to carry larger inventories to avoid running out of products to sell. Higher sales are also typically associated with higher inventory needs.

Materials Requirements Planning (**MRP**) is a computerized system that uses demand forecasts to manage the production of finished goods and the required inventory levels for various raw materials.

Deciding when to order involves calculating the **reorder point**. To do so, the business determines the quantity used per day and the lead time needed for orders to be filled. For example, if the company uses 25 units per day, and an order normally takes 10 days to fill, then an order should be placed, at the latest, when the inventory consists of 25 × 10 = 250 units. Of course, the time it takes to fill an order may vary somewhat, so businesses often use the maximum lead time rather than normal lead time to determine when to place orders. The difference between the two inventory levels is known as the **safety stock**. If, in the above case, the maximum lead time is 15 days, then an order might be placed when there are 25 × 15 = 375 units remaining, and the safety stock is 375 – 250 = 125 units.

Reorder point
Average daily demand
× average lead time
Reorder point without a safety stock
+ safety stock
Reorder point with a safety stock

Businesses may decide the appropriate quantity to order based on a calculation called the **economic order quantity** (EOQ). The formula (which is obtained using calculus) takes into account the Annual Usage of inventory (A), costs involved in Placing orders (P), and Storage costs for carrying inventory (S):

$$EOQ = \sqrt{\frac{2 \times A \times P}{S}}$$

A = Annual Usage of inventory
P = Cost of Placing an order
S = Cost of Storing or carrying an individual unit of inventory for one period, obsolescence cost

If the annual usage of the product is 100 units, it costs $4 to process each order, and $8 to store each unit of inventory for a year, then:

$$EOQ = \sqrt{\frac{2 \times 100 \times 4}{8}} = \sqrt{100} = 10 \; units$$

Some companies follow a **just-in-time (JIT)** philosophy to manage their inventories. To keep their inventories low, these businesses order as little as possible and order as close to the time when inventories are needed as possible. That is, goods are produced on demand rather than based on long-range forecasts of sales. JIT may be used effectively when:

- The costs of storing (non-value-adding operations) inventory are high,
- Lead times are low,
- Needs for safety stock are low because of having good relationships with suppliers who are Very reliable, and
- Costs per purchase order are also low.

In a mature JIT system, units are in process for a relatively short period of time due to the efficiency of the system and the higher speed of manufacturing. As a result, traditional accounting approaches for keeping track of costs in work-in-process are not effective and many companies adopt a *backflush costing* approach.

In a backflush costing approach, costs assigned to jobs will not be tracked in as much detail as in traditional costing systems. Under a **backflush approach** (Delayed or Endpoint costing):

- All manufacturing costs are charged directly to cost of goods sold since little or no inventory is expected to remain at any point in time.
- At the end of an accounting period, the company determines if there are inventories.
- When inventories exist on a reporting date, costs are allocated from cost of goods sold into the appropriate inventory accounts, such as finished goods using standard costs.

Businesses use a wide variety of techniques to manage and assess (audit) their inventories. For instance, traditional "physical inventories" involve counting all actual inventories on a specific date (often requiring production to stop temporarily). In contrast, "cycle counting" focuses on counting small subsets of inventory in specific locations.

Inventory Turnover Ratio = $\dfrac{COGS}{Average \; Inventory}$

o Remember to use cost of goods sold and **not** sales.

Number of days of supply in average inventory = $\dfrac{365*}{Inventory \; Turnover}$

Use 365 unless a 360-day period is specified.

Lecture 5.06 – Present Value: Time Value of Money

Determining the value of a financial instrument that represents a stream of future cash inflows or outflows, such as the exact selling price of a bond, requires using present value concepts. Money that is received at a future date is less valuable than money received immediately, and present value concepts measure future cash flows in terms of the equivalent present dollars. Present value is defined as the current measure of an estimated future cash inflow or outflow, discounted at an interest rate for the number of periods between today and the date of the estimated cash flow. Many decisions require adjustments related to the time value of money:

- The **Present Value of an Amount (lump sum)** is used to examine a single cash flow that will occur at a future date and determine its equivalent value today. Alternatively, it is the amount you need to invest today, for a certain number of years, at a specific interest rate, to get some amount back in the future.

- The **Present Value of an Ordinary Annuity** refers to the value today of repeated cash flows on a systematic basis, with amounts being paid at the *end* of each period (it may also be known as an **annuity in arrears**). Bond interest payments are commonly made at the end of each period and use these factors.

- The **Present Value of an Annuity Due (Now)** refers to the value today of repeated cash flows on a systematic basis, with amounts being paid at the *beginning* of each period (it may also be known as an **annuity in advance** or special annuity). Rent payments are commonly made at the beginning of each period and use these factors.

- **Future Values (compound interest)** look at cash flows and project them to some future date. Future values can be computed using the three variations applicable to present values. The future value factor is the amount that would accumulate at a future point in time if $1 were invested now. As a result, the future value factor is equal to 1 divided by the present value factor.

 For example, an investment of $10,000 in two years at 10% would result in the principal multiplied by the future value factor. In this case the $10,000 × 1/0.8265 = $12,100.

Present and Future Value Tables*

Future Value (Amount) of $1

(n) Periods	6%	8%	10%	12%	15%
1	1.060	1.080	1.100	1.120	1.150
2	1.124	1.166	1.210	1.254	1.323
3	1.191	1.260	1.331	1.405	1.521
4	1.262	1.360	1.464	1.574	1.749
5	1.338	1.469	1.611	1.762	2.011
10	1.791	2.159	2.594	3.106	4.046
15	2.397	3.172	4.177	5.474	8.137
20	3.207	4.661	6.728	9.646	16.367
30	5.743	10.063	17.449	29.960	66.212
40	10.286	21.725	45.259	93.051	267.864

Present Value of $1

(n) Periods	6%	8%	10%	12%	15%
1	0.943	0.926	0.909	0.893	0.870
2	0.890	0.857	0.826	0.797	0.756
3	0.840	0.794	0.751	0.712	0.658
4	0.792	0.735	0.683	0.636	0.572
5	0.747	0.681	0.621	0.567	0.497
10	0.558	0.463	0.386	0.322	0.247
15	0.417	0.315	0.239	0.183	0.123
20	0.312	0.215	0.149	0.104	0.061
30	0.174	0.099	0.057	0.334	0.015
40	0.097	0.046	0.022	0.011	0.004

Future Value (Amount) of an Ordinary Annuity of $1

(n) Periods	6%	8%	10%	12%	15%
1	1.000	1.000	1.000	1.000	1.000
2	2.060	2.080	2.100	2.120	2.150
3	3.184	3.246	3.310	3.374	3.473
4	4.375	4.506	4.641	4.779	4.993
5	5.637	5.867	6.105	6.353	6.742
10	13.180	14.486	15.937	17.549	20.304
15	23.276	27.152	31.772	37.280	47.580
20	36.786	45.762	57.275	72.052	102.444
30	79.058	113.283	164.494	241.333	434.745
40	154.762	259.056	442.592	767.091	1779.090

Present Value of an Ordinary Annuity of $1

(n) Periods	6%	8%	10%	12%	15%
1	0.943	0.926	0.909	0.893	0.870
2	1.833	1.783	1.736	1.690	1.626
3	2.673	2.577	2.487	2.402	2.283
4	3.465	3.312	3.170	3.037	2.855
5	4.212	3.993	3.791	3.605	3.352
10	7.360	6.710	6.144	5.650	5.019
15	9.712	8.559	7.606	6.811	5.847
20	11.470	9.818	8.514	7.469	6.259
30	13.765	11.258	9.427	8.055	6.566
40	15.046	11.924	9.779	8.243	6.642

Present Value of an Annuity Due of $1

(n) Periods	6%	8%	10%	12%	15%
1	1.000	1.000	1.000	1.000	1.000
2	1.943	1.926	1.909	1.893	1.870
3	2.833	2.783	2.736	2.690	2.626
4	3.673	3.577	3.487	3.402	3.855
5	4.465	4.312	4.170	4.037	3.855
10	7.802	7.247	6.759	6.328	5.772
15	10.295	9.244	8.367	7.628	6.724
20	12.158	10.604	9.365	8.366	7.198
30	14.591	12.158	10.370	9.022	7.550
40	15.949	12.879	10.757	9.233	7.638

All values rounded to the nearest thousandth of a percent.

 Actual factors for $1 are typically provided in tables to be multiplied by the cash flows in exam problems.

Converting from an Ordinary Annuity to an Annuity Due - The difference between an ordinary annuity and an annuity due is just the first payment. To convert from an ordinary annuity to an annuity due, you need to add the $1 and 1 year. For example, if you want to figure out the factor for an annuity due for 3 years at 6%, start with an ordinary annuity for 2 years at 6% (1.833) and add the value of $1. So, an annuity due now for 3 years at 6% = 2.833.

Another approach would be to multiply the present value of an ordinary annuity factor by 1 plus the interest rate. For example, the present value of an ordinary annuity at 6% for 2 years = 1.833 × 1.06 = 1.943 (present value of an annuity due for 2 years).

Lecture 5.07 – Capital Budgeting

Overview

Businesses use **capital budgeting** techniques to make long-term investment decisions. For instance, businesses use discounted cash flow techniques to determine the present value (today) of future cash returns from various possible competing investments or projects. While all capital budgeting methods are based on uncertain predictions of future income or cash flows, capital budgeting may be used to help select the most profitable or best investment alternative based on the, unavoidably limited, information available.

The CPA exam likes to test four basic techniques:
- Payback period
- Internal (time adjusted) rate of return (IRR)
- Accounting rate of return
- Net present value (NPV)
    - Profitability index (PI)

Maturity matching (or the self-liquidating approach) to financing assets involves matching asset and liability maturities.

Capital Budgeting Techniques

$$\text{Payback period (\# of years)} = \frac{\text{Initial investment}}{\text{After Tax Annual Net Cash Inflows}}$$

$$\text{IRR: PV Factor} = \frac{\text{Investment}}{\text{Annual Cash Flows}}$$

$$\text{Accounting Rate of Return (or ROI)} = \frac{\text{Accounting Income}}{\text{Average Investment}}$$

$$\text{NPV} = \frac{(\text{PV Cash inflows} - \text{PV Cash outflows})}{\text{Net PV}}$$

$$\text{Profitability Index} = \frac{\text{PV future cash flows}}{\text{Initial investment}}$$

Payback Period

Payback Period is the length of time it takes for an initial cash outlay for the investment to be recovered in cash. Net cash flows are not the same as income, since depreciation is not subtracted in the determination of net cash flows. If the net cash flows are the same each year, then the payback period equals the initial investment divided by the annual net cash inflow. If cash flow is uneven, start with the initial investment, and then subtract each year's cash inflow until the entire investment has been recovered.

Some *disadvantages* of the payback period are that it does not take into account either the project's total profitability or the time value of money. The **discounted payback method** uses the present value of each individual annual net cash flow.

> Payback period = Initial investment / After tax net cash inflows

Internal Rate of Return (IRR)

The Internal Rate of Return (IRR) is the discount rate at which the net present value is zero. Alternatively, the IRR is the rate of interest that equates the present value of cash outflows (commonly referred to, simply, as the project's initial costs) and the present value of cash inflows. It can be used to compare alternative investments. It is also known as the *time-adjusted rate of return* from an investment.

> IRR: PV factor = Investment/annual cash flows

If a business has the funds to launch all the projects that managers were potentially considering, capital budgeting may lead the business to conclude that not all projects should be launched. The business could compare the calculated IRR on each project to pre-specified **hurdle rates** that the business sets as its minimum acceptable rates of return.

Businesses may set several hurdle rates based on market rates of return for projects with similar risk. They would accept projects only if the IRR is greater than the hurdle rate. Businesses commonly use the weighted-average cost of capital (WACC, see below) as the hurdle rate against which they compare projects' IRRs to decide whether to undertake those projects.

Some *advantages* of using IRRs are:
- They take into account the time value of money.
- Hurdle rates may take into account rates of return on investments with similar risk.
- Many practitioners and audiences find IRRs to be more readily understandable than net present values.

Some *disadvantages* of IRRs are:
- Under different assumptions, some cash flow patterns may actually yield multiple IRRs.
- Some cash flow patterns may not have an IRR for which the project's NPV equates to zero.

Accounting Rate of Return (ARR)

The ARR computes an approximate rate of return that does not take into account the time value of money and does not use actual cash flows. ARR is calculated dividing accounting income by the investment. Accounting income is net of all expenses, *including depreciation and income taxes.* The investment usually refers to the initial investment, but occasionally the exam requires the use of the average book value of the investment each year. In the first year, average book value is the initial investment reduced by one-half year of depreciation.

> For example, if an asset costs $1,000, has a 5-year life, no salvage value, and straight-line depreciation is used, depreciation in the first year will be $1,000/5, or $200. The book value at the beginning of the year would be the cost of $1,000. At the end of the year, book value would be $1,000 - $200, or $800. As a result, average book value in the first year is ($1,000 + $800) × ½ = $900.

> ARR = Accounting income / Average (or initial) investment

Since ARRs have the *advantage* of being easy to compute and understand, they are often used to rate managerial performance (simple and intuitive).

Some *disadvantages* of ARRs are:
- ARRs do not take into account the time value of money.
- ARRs do not take into account differences in risk across investments (no project risk).
- Using different depreciation methods yields different ARRs.

Net Present Value (NPV)

Net Present Value (NPV) is the excess of the present value of the cash inflows over the present value of the outflows (typically the investment today). The time value discount rate used is known as the *hurdle rate* of return or cost of capital, and represents the minimum rate of return the company is willing to accept on an investment. A project that earns the hurdle rate of return has an NPV = 0. NPV > 0 means the project earns more than the hurdle rate.

NPV = (Present value of future cash flows − Required investment)

NPVs are the most accepted approach to compare projects financially. Some *advantages* of NPVs are
- NPVs take into account the time value of money.
- NPVs may take into account risk, using higher discount rates for riskier projects.
- NPVs take into account total profitability.
- NPVs yield results in dollars, which may be readily interpreted as the changes in owners' wealth if a project is carried out.

Some *disadvantages* of NPVs are:
- NPVs require more involved computations (not simple and intuitive).
- Some audiences may understand NPVs less readily.
- NPVs do not take into account that managers may not actually follow the originally scheduled investments (or expenses).

Of course, IRRs and NPVs are ultimately different ways to express the same concept. If a project returns more (less) than its discount or hurdle rate, it has a positive (negative) NPV. Summarizing:

NPV	IRR
NPV > 0	IRR > Discount or hurdle rate
NPV = 0	IRR = Discount or hurdle rate
NPV < 0	IRR < Discount or hurdle rate

Profitability Index

The profitability index (or **excess present value index**) is the ratio of the present value of cash inflows to the initial cost of a project. When businesses are faced with several potential projects with positive NPVs, but do not have the funds to carry out all of them, they may use this index to choose which projects to carry out first. If the ratio is > 1.0, then the NPV is positive. To calculate, divide the present value of the annual after-tax cash flows by the original cash invested in the project.

Assume a business is considering buying a machine, and has the following information:

Cost	$900
Useful life	5 years
Salvage value	NONE
Depreciation method	Straight-line
Annual depreciation	$180
Annual net cash flow	$250
Hurdle rate of return	10%

In addition, present value information is available for a 5-year ordinary annuity:

Rate	10%	11%	12%	13%
Factor	3.79	3.70	3.60	3.52

The **accounting rate of return** on the original investment is:

Income / Investment = ($250 - $180) / $900 = $70 / $900 = **7.78%**

The **payback period** is:

Investment / Annual cash flow = $900 / $250 = **3.6 years**

The **net present value** at the 10% hurdle rate of return is:

	Cash	PV Factor	Present Value
Inflows	250	3.79	948
Outflows	900	1.00	900
Net			**48**

The **internal rate of return** is the rate at which the present value of the annual cash inflows of $250 equals the investment of $900, and this occurs when the present value factor for the annuity is $900 / $250 = 3.6, at **12%**. Notice that the net present value at 12% is zero:

	Cash	PV Factor	Present Value
Inflows	250	3.60	900
Outflows	900	1.00	900
Net			-0-

Lecture 5.08 – Capital Budgeting (Continued)

Depreciation Tax Shield

When determining cash outflows and inflows for payback, NPV, and IRR analysis, the effect of depreciation expense on cash flows must be considered if the given information starts with net income, rather than cash inflows and outflows. (Presumably, income from all projects will be taxed at the same marginal rates.) While depreciation is not a cash expense, it affects the cash paid for taxes (ie, it produces tax savings).

In other words, the noncash expense shields what would otherwise be taxable income, resulting in a reduced cash outflow for taxes. The depreciation tax shield can be simply calculated as the tax rate × depreciation.

> Assume estimated annual net income before taxes from a project is $100,000; the estimated annual depreciation expense is $30,000; and the estimated marginal tax rate is 40%. The estimated annual taxes are 0.40 × $100,000 NI = $40,000. Thus, the estimated annual cash inflow is equal to net income before taxes with the noncash expense of depreciation added back, less taxes: $100,000 NI + $30,000 dep. – $40,000 taxes = $90,000 inflow.
>
> Without the depreciation deduction, annual taxes would be 0.40 × ($100,000 + $30,000) = $52,000 taxes; thus, the cash inflow would be $100,000 NI + $30,000 dep. – $52,000 taxes = $78,000 inflow.
>
> The depreciation tax shield is the $12,000 difference ($52,000 – $40,000) between the tax amounts with and without the depreciation deduction. It can also be calculated as 40% × $30,000 dep. = $12,000.

We meet this tax shield concept again when considering the debt/equity mix for a business. Interest expense is tax deductible, but dividends are not.

Mutually Exclusive, Dependent, or Independent

Projects may be classified by whether they are mutually exclusive, dependent, or independent.

- **Mutually exclusive** – The entity can implement only one of two or more projects. For instance, a company owns a restaurant with a kitchen not in compliance with the health code and an outdated, but operable, dining area. The entity can either sell the property or upgrade the kitchen and open the restaurant for business, but not both.

- **Dependent** – A dependent project's cash flows are influenced by another project. For instance, a company owns a restaurant with a kitchen not in compliance with the health code and an outdated, but operable, dining area. Redecorating the dining area of the restaurant is dependent on upgrading the kitchen since without an operable kitchen, the dining area will not have cash flows.

- **Independent** – The entity can implement an independent project regardless of the status of the other projects. For instance, assuming sufficient resources, opening restaurants in two different cities are independent projects.

In a sense, all projects are mutually exclusive as capital to be invested is limited. The NPV, IRR, and profitability index (a refinement of the NPV method) readily accommodate ranking mutually exclusive projects. When conflicts between NPV and IRR exist, the NPV ranking generally is more reliable as it does not assume that project earnings are reinvested at the same rate that the project earns.

Project Nature

Projects also may be classified by the nature of the projects. Entities may require less analysis for projects of some natures than for others. Low-analysis projects typically include mandated projects. High-analysis projects typically include development of a new product with unknown market demand.

Categories include:

- Maintenance-of-business replacements
- Cost reduction replacements
- Expansion of existing projects or markets
- Development of new projects or markets
- Mandated projects (due to license, safety, or environment regulations)
- Strategic (providing differentiation from competitors, etc.)
- Other (mixed-purpose projects for which deciding on a category exceeds any benefit)

Forecasting Techniques

Businesses use forecasting techniques to develop projections of the environment in which they will operate in the future, including:

- Economy-wide conditions such as interest rates, inflation, unemployment, economic growth, retail sales etc.,
- Conditions in their sector of the economy such as sector-specific sales and prices, and
- Cash flows specific to the business, to specific subsidiaries, and to existing and proposed projects, etc.

Interpolation & Extrapolation

Interpolation involves using available data to "fill in gaps" in data relevant to a business. For instance, if a business has reliable data that customers with credit scores in the 500-520 range have loan delinquency rates of 10% and customers with credit scores in the 540-560 range have loan delinquency rates of 8%, then interpolation might lead a business to forecast, project, assume, and/or conclude that customers with credit scores in the 520-540 range would have loan delinquency rates of about 9%.

Extrapolation involves using available data to make projections outside the range for which there is available data. Continuing with the earlier example, using the relationship between credit scores and loan delinquencies, a simple extrapolation would conclude that customers with credit scores in the 480-500 range would have delinquency rates of 11% and customers with credit scores in the 460-480 range would have delinquency rates of 12%.

In general, the results from interpolation are far more reliable than those for extrapolation. In addition, extrapolation becomes less reliable the further one moves from the range of actual data. However, the precise boundary between interpolation and extrapolation is often quite blurred.

For instance, a company with retail outlets in many cities and data about both sales in each outlet and city characteristics might use forecasting techniques to project what sales might be in a retail outlet in a new city. This projection could be considered interpolation if the new city falls within the range of the characteristics of many cities where the business already operates. The projection could be considered extrapolation if the city is in a region, or country, where the business has little experience.

Univariate & Multivariate Forecasting

Univariate forecasting uses the past relationship between only one variable to be projected (the dependent variable) and actual or projected values for only one other variable (the independent variable). An example would be using credit scores to project expected delinquency rates.

Multivariate forecasting uses past relationships between the variable to be projected (dependent variable) and multiple independent variables. An example would be using credit scores, income, change in income, wealth, etc.) to predict delinquency rates.

These forecasting techniques typically employ variations of regression analysis (discussed later).

Trends, Momentum & Mean Reversion

While forecasting techniques may be more or less computationally sophisticated, ultimately, they involve determining past relationships among various variables and making projections based on:

- The assumption that past relationships (ie, **trends**) will continue and/or
- Specific judgments about how some particular variables might behave in the future.

Consequently, forecasts tend to be most accurate when economic conditions are most stable, and routinely miss turning points in business cycles. That is, they commonly fail to predict recessions and often underpredict the strength of recoveries.

Some forecasting techniques seek to combine both the principles of **momentum** (ie, that short-term trends will continue) and **mean reversion** (ie, that deviations from long-term patterns will eventually be corrected).

For example, over short periods, if home prices are climbing (or falling) quickly, one may readily expect that trend to continue (ie, momentum). Eventually, however, if prices become too high, younger families may find prices too high for their income, and/or lenders may find it too risky to engage in further lending, leading to a period of falling prices (a reversion of prices from high levels closer to their long-term means).

Despite this understanding of momentum and mean reversion, existing forecasting techniques are far from being able to determine when mean reversions will take place.

To address the common shortcomings in forecasts, some forecasters provide not only a "central" forecast (eg, inflation will most likely be 2%), but also a range of possible values and probabilities for the various values. For example, there might be a 10% probability of inflation below 0%, a 20% probability of inflation between 0% and 1%, a 40% probability of inflation between 1% and 3%, a 20% probability of inflation between 3% and 10%, and a 10% probability of inflation higher than 10%.

Risk Analysis

When applying capital budgeting techniques to evaluate whether to accept a project, one factor to consider is the risk associated with that project. Risk analysis involves identifying risks that might impair the ability of the entity to achieve the expected results from a particular project and estimating the probability that the risk will actually have an adverse effect and measuring the expected amount of the increase in cost, or reduction in return that will be experienced.

> For example, an entity is considering a project involving the acquisition of a piece of equipment that has a reputation for failing periodically. The entity will:
>
> | | |
> |---|---|
> | ▪ Estimate the probability that the equipment will fail | 25% probability |
> | ▪ Estimate the additional cost that will be incurred because of the failure | An overhaul is expected to cost $10,000. |
> | ▪ Multiply the probability by the amount to estimate the expected cost of the risk event | $10,000 × 25% = $2,500 |

Investment Life Cycle

When evaluating an investment's rate of return, all phases of the investment life cycle will be considered as will such factors as acquisition cost, the cost of managing the investment, cash flows, appreciation, deprecation, and costs of disposal.

When an entity makes an investment, the actions it takes over the period during which it is involved with the investment is considered the investment life cycle.

- **Pre-commitment Evaluation** – An entity plans for the acquisition of an investment, including the evaluation as to whether the investment is likely to meet the entity's investing criteria. This includes the investment's cost, volatility, expected return, and whatever other factors the entity considers when comparing investments.
- **Acquisition of Investment**
- **Management** – Manage the investment with an emphasis on growth, earnings, tax benefits, cash flows, or some other factor relevant to the entity. Some investments (eg, ownership of a business, product line, or division) require ongoing decisions; others (eg, a U.S. Treasury bond) are more passive.
- **Monitoring** – Re-evaluate the investment to determine if there are diminishing returns, suggesting the investment either no longer meets the criteria or may no longer be the best alternative.
- **Disposal of Investment**

Product Life Cycle

A product's life cycle is from the time it is introduced to the time when it is withdrawn. Not all products make it to all phases. For instance, some go from introduction to decline.

Introduction

- Few and intermittent sales
    o Limited production capacity

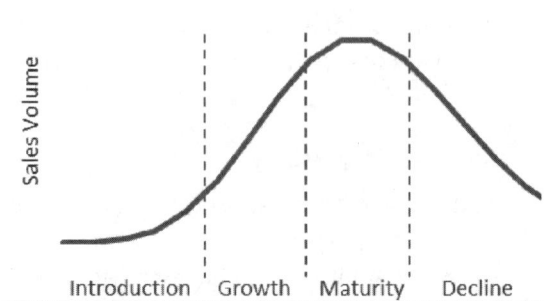

- Lack of appropriate retail outlets
- Consumer resistance to change to the established consumption patterns
- Highest proportional promotional expenses (ie, small volume of sales to offset high promotion efforts to create demand)
  - Informing potential and present consumers of the new and unknown product
  - Inducing a trial of the product
  - Screening distribution network
- Highest product prices possible
  - Low volume to absorb fixed costs
  - Technological problems not fully resolved
  - Few or no competitors
  - Sales to higher income groups/first adopters

Growth

- Rising sales as consumers accept the product
  - Prices may remain high to recover some of the development costs.
  - High profits encourage competitors to enter the market.
  - Consumer resistance fades.
  - Distribution network solidifies.
  - Production is optimized.
- High promotional expenses
  - Expenses shift from informing consumers to brand identification.
  - Special offers/allowances are made to consumers/dealers.
- Product improvements
  - Competitors do not incur the same extent of research and development or promotional costs as the originator.
  - Competitors or originator gain advantage by modifying products.
  - Competitors or originator gain advantage by reducing prices.

Maturity

- Sales accelerate at a declining rate.
  - Market reaches saturation.
  - Prices soften and become more uniform.
  - Competition intensifies as each manufacturer tries to maintain production at a viable level.
    - The more capital-intensive the product is to produce, the more important it is to maintain high output to cover fixed costs at lower prices.
    - The Internet has lengthened the life cycle for many products.
- Normal promotional expenses as competition squeezes margins. Manufacturers try to "milk the cash cow" for all it is worth.
- Extension strategies: Substantial product modification can have the revised product re-enter the introduction phase to re-start the cycle.
  - Development of new markets for existing product

- o Development of new uses for existing product
- o Development of more frequent use for existing product
- o Development of wider range of products (more flavors, colors, etc.)
- o Development of style change (slightly different product)

Decline
- Sales decline rapidly.
  - o Prices fall.
  - o Over capacity pushes manufacturers to cease production.
  - o Conceivably, this could be a very profitable period for a producer with low fixed costs.
- Little or no promotional expenses.

Financial Management & Capital Budgeting — BEC 5

Lecture 5.09 – Short-Term Debt Management

Businesses may obtain short-term financing by purchasing goods on **Trade Credit.** For instance, *3/15, net 45* would mean a 3% discount if the balance due is paid within 15 days, otherwise the entire balance would be due within 45 days. If the business does not delay paying, the business does not pay the higher price; ie, it does not pay the equivalent of interest. To calculate the *cost of NOT taking the discount*:

Annual Financing Costs (AFC) = $\dfrac{\text{Discount \%}}{(100\% - \text{Discount \%})} \times \dfrac{365 \text{ (or 360)}}{(\text{total pay period} - \text{discount period})}$

Compensating Balances are demand deposit balances (set as a percentage of loans) that lenders may require as a condition for receiving loans. Having to maintain compensating balances in practice increases the effective interest rate paid on the net part of the loan that borrowers get to use. To calculate the effective cost of the loan:

Cost of the loan = $\dfrac{\text{Interest paid}}{\text{Net funds available (or Principal} - \text{Compensating Balance)}}$

Lecture 5.10 – Long-Term Debt Management

Private Debt (variable interest) includes business obligations that may not be readily resold to (ie, traded with) the general public. Private debt largely includes loans from banks, other financial institutions, or from syndicates of lenders. Most business loans have variable interest rates that are set at a premium over some base rate or *index*. Some businesses may also sell bonds to qualified (ie, large or sophisticated) investors in "private placements" that may not be readily traded to other parties.

- The **Prime Rate** is the rate that each lender charges its most creditworthy customers. Since the mid-1990's, most banks have set their prime rates 3% above the federal funds rate. Other business customers may obtain loans at some premium above the prime rate (eg, Prime plus 2%).

- The **London Interbank Offered Rate (LIBOR)** is also a common base rate for many business (and consumer) loans both abroad and in the U.S. LIBOR computes rates for many (short) maturities and currencies, including the U.S. dollar.

Public Debt (fixed interest) includes business obligations that may be readily resold (ie, traded with) the general public in markets (eg, exchanges) that the **Securities and Exchange Commission (SEC)** regulates. Public debt largely includes bonds that, typically large, corporations may issue directly to retail and institutional investors. Issuing bonds permits corporations to borrow from sources other than banks, paying interest rates that may be fixed and, depending on their credit history, may actually be lower than those that banks would charge.

- **Eurobonds** are bonds denominated in U.S. dollars that are sold abroad (ie, despite their name, not only in Europe). Some countries have less stringent registration and disclosure requirements than those of the SEC.

Debt Covenants

To convince lenders, or investors, to lend, borrowers often agree to restrictions on their financial behavior or debt covenants.

Positive covenants stipulate what the *borrower must do* and might involve:
- Providing annual audited financial statements to the lender.
- Maintaining various financial ratios within preset parameters (eg, a minimum ratio of current assets to current liabilities).
- Maintaining life insurance policies for officers or key employees of the company.

Negative covenants stipulate what the *borrower may not do* and might involve:
- Not borrowing additional sums during the time period from other lenders.
- Not selling various listed assets of the business.
- Not exceeding certain levels of dividend payments to shareholders.
- Not exceeding certain compensation limits for executives.

Secured and Unsecured Bonds

Debt obligations may be secured by certain collateral or may specifically be placed behind other forms of debt in the priority of repayment. For instance, larger firms sometimes float public debt offerings collateralized by the firms' accounts receivable. The creation of such asset-backed securities is sometimes called **securitization of assets**. In roughly declining order of safety (and increasing order of interest rate), there are:

- **Mortgage bonds** are secured by real estate owned by the borrower.
- **Collateral trust bonds** are secured by financial assets owned by the borrower.
- **Debentures** are unsecured bonds.
- **Subordinated Debentures** are unsecured bonds that, in a liquidation of the business, receive any repayments only after all other more senior creditors have been paid in full.
- **Income bonds** make interest payments only if the business has earnings in excess of some preset level.

Provisions Affecting the Repayment of Bonds

- **Term bonds:** the face value is repaid on a single maturity date.
- **Serial bonds:** a fraction of the face value is repaid on several dates (installments) throughout the life of the bond (eg, every year for a 10-year bond).
- **Sinking funds:** Throughout the life of the bond, the borrower sets funds aside to cover the repayment of the face value of the bond.
- **Convertible bonds:** The bondholder may convert the bonds to the common stock of the company as repayment instead of holding them to maturity.
- **Redeemable bonds:** The bondholder may demand repayment in advance of the normal maturity date should certain events occur (such as the buyout of the company by another firm).
- **Callable bonds** – The borrower may repay the bondholders before the normal maturity date (force to redeem). As compensation for early redemptions, call provisions require borrowers to repay bondholders some premium over the face value of the bond.

Bond Interest Rates

- **Stated rate** – The fixed interest payment calculated from the face value of the bond. It is also known as the **coupon rate, face rate,** or **nominal rate.**
- **Current yield** – The fixed interest payment divided by the current selling price of the bond. When the bond is trading at a discount, the current yield will be higher than the stated rate, and when the bond is trading at a premium, the current yield will be lower than the stated rate. The current yield should be interpreted with some caution, since it reports the interest payment as a percentage of the current price, not taking into account the fact that the principal repayment of the bond will not be the current selling price, but the face value.

$$\frac{\text{Annual interest paid}}{\text{Bond market price}} = \text{Current Yield}$$

- **Yield to maturity** – The interest rate at which the present value of the cash flows of interest and principal will equal the current selling price of a bond. For a bond selling at a discount, yield to maturity will be higher than the current yield, since it accounts for the "bonus" interest payments reflected in the discount. For a bond selling at a premium, yield to maturity will be lower than the current yield, since it reflects the loss of the premium when the face value is repaid. Yield to maturity is also known as the **effective rate** or **market rate**. The formula for calculating the **Effective Annual Interest** rate (**EAR**) is:

$$EAR = (1+r/m)^m - 1$$

r = Stated interest rate

m = compounding frequency

- The **yield curve** illustrates the relationship between short- and long-term interest rates. These relationships are important in determining whether to use long-term fixed or variable rate financing.

- The price of a bond depends on the economy-wide, risk-free interest rate and the credit risk involved in that bond. Bond rating agencies analyze bonds to assess their credit risk. *Some of the credit risk categories, as rated by Moody's investor service,* include:

Aaa	Aa	A	Baa	Ba	B	Caa	Ca	C
Lowest Risk								*Highest Risk*
(Investment grade)								*(Speculative grade, junk, or high yield)*

To calculate the **Present Value (PV) of the proceeds** for a bond, two amounts need to be PV'd.

- **PV of the Face Value** of the bonds (Face value × PV of a lump sum using the Effective interest rate)

- **PV of the interest payments** as an annuity (Face value × stated rate × time = interest × PV of an ordinary annuity at the effective interest rate)
  - The sum of these two amounts represents the PV of the bond.
  - If semi-annual interest is being paid, take the years × 2 and the interest rate/2
    - Ex. 5 yr bonds at 10% semi-annual. Use the PV table for 10 periods @ 5%.

Let's assume a Bond with a stated rate of interest of 8% and a market rate of 10% was issued. Because the stated rate of 8% is lower than the market rate (Yield/Effective rate) of 10%, the only reason someone would purchase this bond is if the bond effectively yields 10%. In order to do so, the issuer must sell the bond at a **DISCOUNT** (the actual cash proceeds must be precisely computed using present value factors and are only estimated in this journal entry).

Cash	900,000	
Discount	100,000	
Bonds Payable		1,000,000

The **discount must be amortized** over the life of the bond. Let's assume we are using straight-line amortization of $20,000 year (100/5yrs=20).

Interest expense	100,000 (10%)	
Discount		20,000
Cash		80,000 (8%)

Variations on Bond Interest

Zero-coupon bonds do not make coupon payments but only pay the face value on the date of maturity. A common example of zero-coupon bonds are short-term U.S. *Treasury Bills*. Zero-coupon bonds *sell at a discount*, with the return to be bondholders arising from the difference between the price at which the bond is bought and the face value paid at maturity.

Floating rate bonds do not have fixed coupon payments. Payments instead fluctuate with some general index of interest rates. In **reverse floaters,** payments actually increase when the general interested rate index goes down and payments decrease when the index goes up. These unusual bonds are one more tool through which businesses may hedge their interest-rate risks.

Registered bonds use a register in which the borrower has the names and addresses of bondholders, such that the borrower may send payments directly to the bondholders (ie, not through a broker). In such cases, an actual bond certificate will usually not be issued.

Junk (high yield, or speculative grade) bonds are those issued by companies that credit rating agencies assess as more likely to default, and thus pay much higher interest rates. In the ratings of Moody's Investors Service, bonds with ratings lower than Baa are considered junk bonds. Some bonds are initially issued as investment-grade bonds but are subsequently downgraded to junk bonds.

Foreign bonds have interest and face value payments in another currency.

Lecture 5.11 – Advantages & Disadvantages of Debt Financing

Some of the *Advantages* of using debt to finance a business are:

- Interest is tax-deductible.

- With certain caveats, the obligation (ie, interest and principal payments) is generally fixed (eg, assuming that the debt was fixed-rate, that we are considering only nominal interest rates, and considering only the period until the maturity date of the debt).

- If current owners issue debt instead of new shares of stock, the current owners avoid giving up control to the new shareholders.

- If the business has excess earnings, those earnings will accrue to owners, not to debt holders.

- Debt is less costly than equity; so, the cost of capital will be lower.

- During inflationary periods, the debt is paid back with less valuable dollars.

Some of the *Disadvantages* of using debt to finance a business are:

- The business must make pre-determined interest and principal payments independently of its performance.

- While debt holders do not gain any formal control of the business (like new shareholders), by agreeing to the terms of loan and bond covenants, businesses effectively forgo some control (ie, flexibility).

- High debt levels increase the risk that the business may fail, wipe out owners' claims, and, thus (despite their sometimes positive effects on returns on equity), high debt levels may reduce stock prices.

Leasing vs. Buying

Businesses may also finance their operations through leases rather than buying or borrowing to buy assets. From the lessee's point of view, there are generally two types of leases: Operating leases and Finance leases. With the issuance of ASC 842, the accounting for operating and finance leases have become more similar; that is, they are both recognized on the balance sheet now, but most of the benefits of leasing versus buying remain unchanged:

- Capital that could be used to acquire an asset could be put to another use.

- Businesses unable to obtain credit to purchase an asset may be able to lease it instead.

- A loan may violate a debt covenant while an operating lease should not.

- Leases often do not involve down payments.

- A lease provides an additional source of capital with level payments, sometimes over a longer term.

- Leases are generally less expensive in that the lessee is not paying the entire amount of the asset's cost; thus, payments are generally lower than a loan, meaning lease payments may fit the cash flow budget better than loan payments to purchase the same asset.

- Terms in lease agreements are often less strict than in bond indentures.

- In bankruptcy, creditors have weaker rights over some assets financed by leases (eg, real estate).

- Leases may transfer the tax benefits of debt financing to lessors, prompting lessors to reduce the cost of leases to lessees.
- Some leases provide maintenance services, making management of the asset easier and possibly less expensive.
- Leasing an asset vs. buying it provides a hedge against obsolescence; that is, a lease provides more flexibility, thus, reducing risk to the lessee.
- Disposal of the asset at the end of its useful life remains with the lessor.

Lecture 5.12 – Equity

Common Stock

Businesses are ultimately owned by their common shareholders (or stockholders). They control the business (ie, they may appoint and remove management through elections to a board of directors) and have a claim to the residual (or leftover) assets and income after the claims by all creditors and preferred shareholders are satisfied. While most companies have only one class of common stock (class A), companies may have a second class of common stock (class B) with different rights to vote or to receive dividends. Common stock is generally issued at Par value, unless there is no par value, then Stated value is used.

Some **advantages** of common stock to the business are:

- Businesses have the flexibility that dividend payments to common shareholders are not fixed; ie, they may be increased or decreased depending on performance.
- Businesses with more equity pose less risk to lenders, thus reducing businesses' borrowing costs.
- Many investors find common stock to be very attractive since it entitles them to businesses' future profit growth.

Some **disadvantages** of common stock to the business are:

- The costs of issuing common stock are larger than those for debt.
- Current owners dilute their ownership and control with each new issuance of stock.
- While tax law considers interest a tax-deductible cost, common dividends are not tax-deductible (out of retained earnings).
- Shareholders ultimately receive a much higher return than lenders if the business is successful, so relying more on common stock results in a higher cost of capital for the business.

Common stock trades in different markets:

- **Primary market** – new issues market (initial price offerings, IPOs)
- **Secondary market** – where already outstanding shares are resold
- **Over-the-counter** – market for unlisted securities

Preferred Stock

Preferred shareholders (or stockholders) must be paid a preset dividend before any dividends may be paid to common stockholders. In a liquidation, preferred stockholders must be paid in full before any payments are made to common stockholders; that is, preferred have priority (or are "preferred") over common stockholders. Some possible features of *preferred stock* are:

- **Cumulative dividends** – Under this feature, if the business "skips" preferred dividends (**arrears**) for any period, the business must pay all previously skipped dividends before it may pay any dividends to common shareholders.
- **Redeemability** – Under this feature, stockholders may demand repayment of the face value at a specific date. In some cases, redemption is automatic. Such shares more closely resemble debt and are often presented before equity in the balance sheet.

- **Callability** – Under this feature, the business may force to repay the stockholders the face value of the stock and extinguish any future obligations (call features can typically be exercised only after a minimum number of years).
- **Convertibility** – Under this feature, preferred stockholders may convert their shares into common stock.
- **Participation** – Under this rare feature, preferred stockholders receive higher dividends when common dividends are increased.
- **Floating rate** – Under this feature, preferred dividends may vary, for instance, based on an interest or inflation index.

Some **advantages** of preferred stock are:

- The business has the flexibility of being able to skip preferred dividends (even if those dividends may have to be paid later when the business wants to pay common dividends).
- Businesses with more equity pose less risk to lenders, thus reducing businesses' borrowing costs.
- Issuing more preferred stock does not entail common stockholders giving up control over the business's decision making.
- If the business has more earnings, preferred stockholders rarely receive any of them.

Some **disadvantages** of preferred stock are:

- The costs of issuing preferred stock are larger than those for debt and the dividend rates paid on preferred stock are higher than the interest rates paid on debt.
- While tax law considers interest a tax-deductible cost, preferred dividends are not tax-deductible.
- A business that has accumulated skipped dividends (arrears) over extended periods of time may encounter difficulties reducing that backlog and/or finding new sources of funding.

To make appropriate financing decisions, businesses take into account leverage and the cost of capital.

Leverage

The degree of **Operating leverage (DOL)** measures how the size of a business's *fixed costs* affects its performance when revenues change.

- Higher fixed costs (relative to total costs) mean there is greater risk of low (or negative) earnings should revenues (sales volumes) fall below expectations. The risk that profits may be lower than anticipated is commonly known as **Business Risk** and is measured by the degree of operating leverage (DOL).

$$\text{DOL} = \frac{\text{\% change in EBIT (Earnings before Interest and Taxes)}}{\text{\% change in Sales volume}}$$

- Increases in revenues for businesses with high fixed costs (ie, a high DOL) result in proportionately larger increases in return on equity. Having lower variable costs, increases in revenues result in proportionately larger increases in profits.

The degree of **financial leverage (DFL)** measures how much a business relies on *debt financing*. Using more debt can increase returns on equity, but also increases risks for stockholders. Because debt is generally cheaper than equity, businesses have an incentive to increase their reliance on debt. However, ever larger increases in debt increase leverage, risk, and ultimately the interest rate demanded by subsequent lenders. Of course, financial leverage is an extension of operating leverage that purely focuses on one type of fixed cost, the interest costs resulting from debt financing.

- Higher debt means higher interest and principal obligations for repayment, increasing risk if performance is not up to expectations.
- Debt financing costs less than equity financing and doesn't increase with greater performance, so overall profit potential and asset growth potential are greater.

$$DFL = \frac{\% \text{ change in Earnings per Share}}{\% \text{ change in EBIT}}$$

A leveraged buyout (**LBO**) is a method of financing the acquisition of all or a voting majority of the outstanding shares of a company. LBOs are financed primarily with debt secured by the assets of the target company.

Lecture 5.13 – Cost of Capital

A business's cost of capital is the average of the costs of its debt and equity (including preferred stock, common stock, and retained earnings), each weighted by its market value. These costs are expressed as percentages per annum.

The word *capital* can have different meanings in different contexts. In some contexts (eg, bank regulation), capital is roughly equivalent to equity and excludes most liabilities (eg, deposits and senior bonds). In the context of calculations of the cost of capital, project selection, etc., capital means all sources of funds, including both debt and equity.

Cost of Debt Financing

The Cost of Debt financing is the after-tax cost of interest payments as measured by yields to maturity. It can be calculated in *two ways*:

- Yield to maturity × (1 – effective tax rate)
- (Interest expense – Tax deduction for interest) / Carrying value of debt

Cost of Preferred Stock Financing

The Cost of Preferred stock financing is the stipulated dividend divided by the net issue price of the stock.

- Cost of Preferred stock = *Dividend/Net issue price*

Cost of Existing Common Stock (Equity) Financing

The Cost of *Existing* Common stock (equity) financing represents the expected returns of common shareholders, and is difficult to estimate. Some techniques:

- The **Capital Asset Pricing Model (CAPM) (Security Market Line),** assumes that the expected return of a particular stock depends on its *volatility* relative to the overall stock market *(beta)* (describes relationship between risk and expected return).
  CAPM = *(Beta × Excess of Normal Market Return over Risk Free Investments) + Return on Risk Free Investments.*
    - The **Beta coefficient** of an individual stock is the correlation between changes in the stock's price and changes in the price of the overall market. If, for example, the market goes up 5% and the individual stock's price goes up 10%, the stock's beta coefficient is 2.0.
    - **CAPM** = Risk free rate + [(expected market rate – risk free rate) × Beta]
- The **Arbitrage Pricing Model** is a more detailed version of CAPM that uses separate excess returns and betas for various factors contributing to a stock performance.
- The **Bond Yield Plus** method is based on the historical relationship between equities and debt and, thus, simply adds 3% to 5% to the interest rate on the business's long-term debt.
- The **Dividend Yield plus Growth Rate** method adds the current dividend (as a percentage of the stock price) and the expected growth rate in earnings.

$$\frac{\text{Next expected dividend}}{\text{Current stock price}} + \text{expected growth in earnings} = \textbf{Dividend Yield Plus Growth Rate}$$

Cost of New Common Stock

The Cost of New Common stock is a little higher than that of existing stock, since the business must recover the cost of issuing the new shares (selling or flotation costs).

$$\frac{\text{Next expected dividend}}{\text{(Current stock price − flotation costs)}} + \text{expected growth in earnings} = \textbf{Cost of new Common stock}$$

Weighted Average Cost of Capital (WACC)

The Weighted average cost of capital (WACC) is a calculation of a firm's effective cost of capital taking into account the portion of its capital that was obtained as debt, preferred stock, and common stock. Businesses with capital structures that result in low WACCs have lower required rates of return, or hurdle rates, and are more likely to find projects that add to shareholder wealth. Therefore, businesses seek capital structures that minimize their WACC.

The optimal capital structure for a business involves a tradeoff between the fact that equity is typically higher cost than debt, and the fact that higher debt-to-asset ratios result in higher interest rates for an individual business. Thus, at very low debt-to-asset ratios, businesses may make their capital structure more optimal (reduce their WACC) by relying more on debt. However, at very high debt-to-asset ratios, businesses may make their capital structure more optimal (reduce their WACC) by relying less on debt. While conditions change, in general, determining the optimal capital structure for a business involves finding the debt-to-assets ratio that minimizes WACC.

> For example, if 40% of capital was obtained through long-term debt at an effective cost of 6%, 10% of capital was obtained by issuing preferred stock with an effective cost of 8%, and 50% of capital was obtained by issuing common stock expected to return 11% to shareholders, the weighted average cost of capital is:
>
> 40% × 6% + 10% × 8% + 50% × 11%
>
> = 2.4% + 0.8% + 5.5%
>
> = 8.7%

Financial Management & Capital Budgeting — BEC 5

Lecture 5.14 – Asset/Liability Valuation & Ratios

Approaches to Valuation

Businesses use valuations for evaluating investments, capital budgeting, financial reporting, tax reporting, mergers and acquisitions, and litigation. The three major approaches to valuation are:

1. **Using Actual Prices for Identical Assets Traded in Liquid Markets** – If an asset is actively traded in a liquid market, the most commonly recognized value for the asset is simply its market price.

2. **Using Prices of Similar Assets Traded in Liquid Markets** – To use this approach, one must carefully adjust for differences between the item being valued and the one that traded in a liquid market. These adjustments often require using financial models.

3. **Using Valuation Models** – If neither the asset nor similar ones trade in liquid markets, businesses use valuation models to develop estimates of fair values for the asset. These models generally use assumptions about future conditions to estimate future cash flows and incomes. Since using different assumptions may yield widely different estimates, businesses must consider these assumptions carefully to ensure that they are broadly reasonable and in line with current and/or past market and economic conditions and experience.

Types of Mergers

- **Horizontal mergers** involve businesses that are in the same market (ie, competitors).
- **Vertical mergers** involve businesses acquiring others in the same supply chain (ie, a supplier or customer).
- **Conglomerate mergers** involve businesses acquiring others in unrelated markets (ie, not direct competitors, *suppliers, or customers*).

Valuing potential merger targets, businesses may use:

- **Discounted cash flow analysis** to determine the present value of the cash flows expected from the acquisition of the company, discounted at the cost of equity capital.
- The **market multiple method** multiplies the current earnings of the company times a price-earnings ratio that is appropriate to that company (based on factors such as the typical ratio in that industry).

Key Ratios (Performance Measures)

Profitability Ratios

Gross Margin = Gross profit / Net sales

Operating Profit Margin = Operating profit / Net sales

Free Cash Flow = Net operating profit after taxes (NOPAT) + Depreciation + Amortization
– Capital expenditures – Net increase in working capital

Residual income = Operating profit – Interest on investment

- **Interest on investment** = Invested capital × required rate of return

Economic Value Added (EVA) = NOPAT − Cost of financing
- **Cost of financing** = (Total assets − Current Liabilities) × WACC

Economic Rate of return on Common stock (Total Return)
- (Dividends + change in price) / beginning price

Return on Investment (based on assets) = Net income / Average assets or Average invested capital

DuPont ROI analysis: ROI = Return on sales × Asset turnover
- **Return on sales** = Net income / Sales
- **Asset turnover** = Sales / Total assets

Return on Assets = Net income / Average total assets
- **Average total assets** = (Beginning total assets + Ending total assets) / 2

Return on Equity = Net income / Average common stockholders' equity
- **Common stockholders' equity** = Stockholders' equity − Preferred stock liquidation value

Used in isolation, different financial ratios have various advantages and disadvantages. For instance, businesses that set managerial and employee compensation based on ROIs focused on the short term may obtain results that maximize short-term ROIs by ignoring, and forgoing, projects that have short-term costs (and therefore less attractive short-term ROIs), but that overall, or long-term, would have positive net present values and, thus, add to shareholder wealth.

Asset Utilization Ratios

Receivable Turnover = Net credit sales / Average accounts receivable
- **Average accounts receivable** = (Beginning A/R + Ending A/R) / 2
- Remember to use net *credit* sales and **not** net sales.

Receivables Collection Period = Average accounts receivable / Average credit sales per day
- Use 365-day year unless told otherwise.

Inventory Turnover = Cost of goods sold / Average inventory
- Remember to use cost of goods sold and **not** sales.

Inventory Conversion Period = Average inventory / Average cost of goods sold per day

Total Asset Turnover = Sales / Average total assets

Fixed Asset Turnover = Sales / Average net fixed assets
- Remember that net fixed assets is after subtraction of accumulated depreciation.

Debt Utilization Ratios

Debt to Total Assets = Total liabilities / Total assets

Debt to Equity Ratio = Total debt / Total equity

Times Interest Earned Ratio = Earnings before interest and taxes (EBIT) / Interest expense

Financial Management & Capital Budgeting

Liquidity Ratios

Current Ratio = Current assets / Current liabilities

Quick (or Acid Test) Ratio = Quick assets / Current liabilities
- **Quick assets =** Cash + Marketable securities + Accounts receivable

Market Ratios

Market Capitalization = Common stock price per share × Common stock shares outstanding

Market/Book Ratio can be calculated in two ways:
- Common stock price per share / Book value per share
- Market capitalization / Common stockholders' equity

Book Value per Share = Common stockholders' equity / Common stock shares outstanding

Price/Earnings (PE) Ratio = Common stock price per share / Earnings per share (EPS)

Many other ratios may be computed. Some ratios are, of course, more widely used than others. Other examples of less commonly used ratios include:
- The **Sales to Cash Flow Ratio**, which is generally interpreted to be a measure of financial strength.
- The **Investment Turnover Ratio** = sales / book value (or net worth)

It is important to understand the ratios and their *Purpose or Use*.

Ratio	Formula	Purpose or Use
Liquidity – Measures of the company's short-term ability to pay its maturing obligations.			
1. Working Capital	Current assets - Current liabilities	Measures ability to meet current expenses
2. Current ratio	Current assets / Current liabilities	Measures short-term debt-paying ability
3. Quick or acid-test ratio	Cash, marketable securities, and receivables (net) / Current liabilities	Measures immediate short-term liquidity
4. Current cash debt coverage ratio	Net cash provided by operating activities / Average current liabilities	Measures a company's ability to pay off its current liabilities in a given year from its operations
Activity – Measures how effectively the company uses its assets.			
5. Receivables turnover	Net credit sales / Average trade receivables (net)	Measures liquidity of receivables
6. Inventory turnover	Cost of goods sold / Average inventory	Measures liquidity of inventory

Ratio	Formula	Purpose or Use
7. Asset turnover	$\dfrac{\text{Net sales}}{\text{Average total assets}}$	Measures how efficiently assets are used to generate sales
8. Number of days' supply in average inventory	= 365 / Inventory Turnover **or** = Average (ending) inventory / Average daily cost of goods sold	Measures number of days required to sell inventory
9. Number of days' sales in average receivables	= 365 / Receivables Turnover	Measures number of days required to collect receivables

Profitability – Measures of the degree of success or failure of a given company or division for a given period of time.

Ratio	Formula	Purpose or Use
10. Profit margin on sales (Gross margin)	$\dfrac{\text{Net income}}{\text{Net sales}}$	Measures net income generated by each dollar of sales
11. Rate of return on assets	$\dfrac{\text{Net income}}{\text{Average total assets}}$	Measures overall profitability of assets
12. Rate of return on common stock equity (Return on equity)	$\dfrac{\text{Net income minus preferred dividends}}{\text{Average common stockholders' equity}}$	Measures profitability of owners' investment
13. Earnings per share	$\dfrac{\text{Net income minus preferred dividends}}{\text{Weighted shares outstanding}}$	Measures net income earned on each share of common stock
14. Price-earnings ratio	$\dfrac{\text{Market price of stock}}{\text{Earnings per share}}$	Measures the ratio of the market price per share to earnings per share
15. Payout ratio	$\dfrac{\text{Cash dividends}}{\text{Net income}}$	Measures percentage of earnings distributed in the form of cash dividends

Coverage – Measures of the degree of protection for long-term creditors and investors.

Ratio	Formula	Purpose or Use
16. Debt to equity	$\dfrac{\text{Total debt}}{\text{Stockholders' equity}}$	Shows creditors the corporation's ability to sustain losses
17. Debt to total assets	$\dfrac{\text{Total debt}}{\text{Total assets}}$	Measures the percentage of total assets provided by creditors
18. Times interest earned	$\dfrac{\text{Income before interest expense and taxes}}{\text{Interest expense}}$	Measures ability to meet interest payments as they come due
19. Cash debt coverage ratio	$\dfrac{\text{Net cash provided by operating activities}}{\text{Average total liabilities}}$	Measures a company's ability to repay its total liabilities in a given year from its operations
20. Book value per share	$\dfrac{\text{Common stockholders' equity}}{\text{Outstanding shares}}$	Measures the amount each share would receive if the company were liquidated at the amounts reported on the balance sheet

Lecture 5.15 – Risk Management

Expected Returns

The total return of an investment includes cash distributions (interest, dividends, rents) and the change (growth) in the value of the asset (Total Return = Distribution Rate + Growth Rate). This model, known as the **Gordon Growth Model**, assumes that the reinvested assets will increase distributions by the amount of reinvestment, so that the growth in the assets will be the growth rate of future dividends. Eventually, all earnings are going to be distributed over the life of the company.

For example, an investment of $100 that pays a dividend of $3 and grows in value to $107 at the end of the year has a total return of 10% (3% distribution + 7% growth). With $107 in assets, the company should be able to pay out a dividend of $107 × 3% = $3.21 next year, and add $107 × 7% = $7.49 to the value of the asset, increasing it to $114.49, on which an even higher 3% dividend can then be paid in the third year, and so on.

A group of investments (whether in similar types of assets or not) is known as a **portfolio**. The expected return on a portfolio is a weighted average of the expected return of the individual investments.

For example, if a portfolio is invested 60% in Asset A, which is expected to return 10%, and 40% in Asset B, which is expected to return 5%, the expected return (ER) of the portfolio is:
(60% × 10%) + (40% × 5%)
= 6% + 2%
= 8%

Average Returns

Since investors cannot know the future, estimates of investments' expected returns (ER) are commonly simply the averages of historical (or past) rates of return. Average historical rates of return can be computed arithmetically (simple average) or geometrically (taking into account the effects of compounding):

- The **arithmetic (simple) average return rate** simply adds the returns for several periods and divides by the number of periods.

- The **geometric average return rate** is the single annual compound rate of return required to turn the initial value of an investor's investment into its final value over the number of periods intervening. Geometric averages are lower than arithmetic averages, except for the case when all single-period rates are identical.

For example, if an investment grew by 44% in one year and 0% in the next, then $100 would have grown to $144 in the first year and remained there in the second.
- Arithmetic average return = 22% (the average of 44% and 0%)
- Geometric average return = 20% (an investment of $100 earning a consistent 20% each year would grow to $120 after one year and $144 after two years).

Standard Deviation

A very common measure of investment risk is the **standard** deviation (SD, or the lower case Greek letter sigma, σ), which is a measure of the volatility of an investment. (The variance, σ², is simply the standard deviation squared, or multiplied times itself). To calculate SD, take the following steps:

1. Determine the arithmetic average return.
2. Calculate the difference from the average for each individual period.
3. Square those differences.
4. Determine the average of the squared values.
5. Calculate the square root of this average.

Since most investors are **risk averse**, investors demand higher expected returns from investments with a higher standard deviation (eg, common stocks) and demand lower expected returns from investments with a lower standard deviation (eg, bonds).

> Assume an investment has returned 7%, 15%, and 8% in 3 different periods.
>
> 1. (7% + 15% + 8%) / 3 = 10% arithmetic average return.
> 2. –3%, +5%, –2% are the differences from the average in the 3 periods.
> 3. 9%, 25%, 4% are the squares of the differences.
> 4. (9% + 25% + 4%) / 3 = 12.67% average of the squared values.
> 5. Square root of 12.67% = 3.56% = the standard deviation (SD)
>
> Notice that the SD of 3.56% is slightly higher than the average of the absolute values of the differences: (3% + 5% + 2%) / 3 = 3.33%. This result follows because the calculation of the SD gives disproportionate weight to bigger differences.

The **Coefficient of Variation** (CV) is another common measure of risk. Standard deviations (SDs) are somewhat related to the averages from which they are computed (eg, SDs computed among values in the billions are typically going to be much larger than SDs computed among values in the thousands). The CV seeks to address this shortcoming in SDs and provide a measure of Relative Risk that is readily comparable across investments of different sizes (ie, whether in the billions or thousands).

To compute the CV (or relative risk) for an investment, one would divide the standard deviation (SD) of the investment's returns by the investment's average (or expected) return (ER). Depending on their degree of risk averseness, investors will weigh the expected returns (ER) and relative risks (CV) of their investment options, generally preferring some combination of higher ERs and lower CVs.

Portfolio Risk

Investors once largely assumed that portfolios consisting of individually riskier investments would be riskier, and that to reduce risk portfolios had to include safer investments. In 1951, Harry Markowitz revolutionized the investment field launching **Modern Portfolio Theory (MPT)** pointing out that the standard deviation of a portfolio of investments will generally be much smaller than the standard deviation of the individual investments, since the prices of various individual investments do not each move up and down at exactly the same time.

The measure of the degree to which various (ie, typically more than two) investments move together may be captured by a **covariance matrix.** Since interpreting a covariance matrix is not straightforward, investors often focus on the **correlation coefficients** between pairs of investments (ie, between only one investment and only one other investment at a time). We addressed correlation coefficients above, but repeat the key points here adapted for the case of portfolio theory.

- *Correlation coefficient = 1.00* When one investment goes up, the other always goes up. When one goes down, the other always goes down.
- *Correlation coefficient = 0* There is no identifiable relationship between the two investments, whether one goes up or down does not reliably predict whether the other goes up or down.
- *Correlation coefficient = -1.00* When one investment goes up, the other always goes down. When one goes down, the other always goes up.

Whenever the correlation coefficient between two investments is less than 1.00, the standard deviation of the portfolio will be lower than the average of the standard deviations of the individual investments. This result follows because the differences in the investments' price fluctuations somewhat offset each other.

By combining investments that have low covariances with each other, an investor can largely eliminate **unsystematic (unique) risk**, or the risk that pertains to one investment (eg, a single company) or even to a group of similar investments (eg, mining stocks). What remains is the unavoidable or **systematic risk** that cannot be diversified away and that results from market-wide factors and economy-wide fluctuations in GDP, inflation, interest rates, etc.

According to MPT, investors may expect some reward from bearing systematic risk in the form of the market's average (or expected) returns. In contrast, investors bearing unsystematic risks (ie, portfolios that are not properly diversified) may expect only lower average (or expected) returns since they are bearing risks that may be avoided.

Investors may use the **mean-variance optimization** technique, combining the expected returns of various investments and their covariances with each other, to identify the portfolio that will:

- For any level of desired volatility, have the highest possible expected return; or,
- For a particular expected return, have the lowest level of volatility.

The portfolio with the highest average (or expected) return for a particular level of volatility is known as the most **efficient portfolio** for that level of variance. An **efficient frontier** plots the combinations of assets that yield the most efficient portfolios for various levels of risk (technically efficient frontiers exist in multi-dimensional space for multi-investment portfolios, but efficient frontiers are commonly shown for simplified two-asset portfolios (eg, stocks vs. bonds) in graphs with "only" the standard two vertical and horizontal axes).

Beta is a standardized measure of investments' systematic risk. **Beta risk** measures how changes in the value of an individual investment compares with changes in the value of an overall or market-wide portfolio (commonly the S&P 500 stock index). Thus, Beta measures (or compares) the volatility of an individual investment relative to that of the portfolio (or the market) as a whole.

- A beta of 1 indicates that the investment moves up and down at approximately the overall rate for the portfolio (or market).
- A beta of 0.5 indicates that it moves up and down only half as much.
- A beta of 2 indicates that it goes up and down twice as much as the overall portfolio.

> For instance, when the overall stock market goes up by 10%, a stock with a beta of 0.5 would be expected to go up only by 5%, and a stock with a beta of 2 would be expected to go up 20%. Similarly, a 10% market drop will result in drops of 5% and 20%, respectively.

The **Capital Asset Pricing Model** (CAPM) suggests that investments with higher betas have higher expected returns to compensate for the extra volatility. The degree to which a portfolio does better or worse than the return predicted by its beta is known as **alpha**. Alpha is considered to be a measure of the degree of success or failure of the individual portfolio manager.

One implication of the CAPM is that the **asset allocation** of a portfolio (eg, the percentage of a person's investments devoted to stocks vs. bonds) is overwhelmingly the most important factor in determining the returns an investor can expect.

Many academics conclude that markets generally reflect the combined knowledge of their participants, and that individual variations from an alpha of zero are largely a matter of luck. The conclusion that individuals cannot outperform market averages over long periods of time except by luck is known as the **Efficient Market Hypothesis** (EMH).

This hypothesis led to the development of **index funds**, which buy all available investments in a category instead of trying to determine which ones will appreciate the most. For example, an S&P 500 stock index fund buys all 500 stocks in the Standard & Poor's market average. If unsystematic risk isn't rewarded reliably—and there are no particularly large costs for buying the smallest, least liquid stocks—buying less than all 500 would theoretically result in extra risk for no extra return.

Also, since the strongest form of the EMH assumes that prices reflect the best judgment of the participants, the index fund should not invest equal amounts in each of the index components, but hold stocks in proportion to the total market values of the different companies—eg, more in Apple (large total valuation) than in Disney (smaller total valuation).

In practice, most analyses find that increasing the number of stocks in one's portfolio to 30 or 40 yields almost all the gains from reducing unsystematic risk. Of course, the 30-40 stocks would need to be chosen to be somewhat representative of the overall selection of 500 stocks. Buying 30-40 technology stocks would expose one to the unsystematic risks of the technology sector, and not to the systematic risk of the market as a whole.

More recently, there have been several challenges to both the CAPM and EMH. Beta has not proven to be a very good predictor of returns, and there is even some evidence that higher betas often result in lower expected returns. For example, initial public offerings (IPOs) generally represent relatively new and untested companies that are much more volatile than average, but they have consistently had worse-than-average subsequent performance in the market, combining high volatility and low returns.

There is also some evidence that stocks with low prices in relation to earnings and assets (**value stocks**) do better than stocks with high relative prices (**growth stocks**)—even though the latter are more volatile, and stocks with a smaller total market capitalization do better than those with larger total market values, regardless of volatility.

The EMH counterargument is that value stocks generally represent companies and industries that aren't growing quickly, and face more **business risk** (risk of bankruptcy or other failure), and that small companies are similarly far more likely to fail than large ones. Others believe these differences represent evidence of consistent bias by the participants in the market that may occasionally be exploited to gain higher-than-average returns by those who resist these biases (this view is studied by **Behavioral Finance Theory**).

Investors often use the term *market trend* to refer to the direction in which financial markets are moving. The terms **bull market** and **bear market** describe upward and downward movements in the market, respectively, and can be used to describe either the market as a whole or specific sectors and securities.

- A bear market normally refers to a period during which prices have fallen by more than 20% from their previous peak.

- A bull market normally refers to a period during which prices have risen by more than 20% from their previous trough (during the previous bear market).

Multi-year periods of sustained price growth (even if they contain some bear markets) are commonly referred to as "secular bull markets" (eg, the early 1980s to the late 1990s). Multi-year periods without sustained price growth (even if they contain some bull markets) are commonly referred to as "secular bear markets" (eg, the mid-1960s to the early 1980s, and the late 1990s to the later 2000s).

Interest Rates & Risks

Through loans (and bonds) borrowers may use funds that they would otherwise not have and lenders forgo the use of those funds. In compensation, borrowers pay lenders interest. To provide funds to riskier projects (or borrowers), lenders (and investors) demand higher rates of return. Common risks that lenders (and investors) may consider include:

- **Credit (or default) risk** – The risk that borrowers will not abide by the terms of their contracts (eg, fail to make some payments of interest or principal).
  - **Sector risk** – The fraction of a borrower's credit risk associated with being in its industry.
- **Concentration of credit risk** – The credit risk resulting from lending to only a few borrowers or only to borrowers (even if a large number of them) in related industries. Lenders (and investors) may reduce this risk by diversifying their portfolios of loans (and bonds).
- **Market risk** – The risk that worsening economy-wide conditions will depress the value of all pre-existing assets (independently of whether credit risk worsens).
- **Interest rate risk** – The risk that rising interest rates will depress the resale value of pre-existing bonds (or loans).

The Yield Curve

The **yield curve** presents U.S. Treasury interest rates (yields) in the y-axis (vertical) and terms (or maturities, usually 3 months to 30 years) in the x-axis (horizontal). Most non-government bonds and loans are more or less loosely priced in reference to the yield curve, such that changes in the yield curve affect interest rates in almost all markets throughout the U.S. economy.

- **Normal yield curve** – Interest rates are higher for longer terms.
  According to the **liquidity preference theory**, interest rates would normally be higher for longer terms than for shorter terms since investors demand more compensation for long-term investments that are more subject to various risks (such as inflation or interest rate risk).

- **Inverted yield curve** – Interest rates are lower for longer terms.

According to the **expectations theory**, long-term interest rates reflect future expected short-term interest rates. An inverted yield curve usually reflects investors' expectations of upcoming declines in economy-wide interest rates, usually because investors expect falling inflation rates and/or worsening economy-wide conditions (eg, a recession).

- **Flat yield curve** – Interest rates are similar across terms. Of course, normal yield curves typically flatten before becoming inverted, and inverted yield curves typically flatten before returning to normal.

Moreover, according to the **market segmentation theory**, some participants in bond (and loan) markets may focus on lending at different terms. Thus, different changes in conditions for each set of participants (eg, different levels of credit losses, capital, or regulatory differences) may result in interest rates, at least temporarily, changing in different directions for different terms. For instance, depository institutions focus more on short-term bonds and loans, while some institutional investors (eg, life insurance companies and pension funds) focus more on longer-term bonds and loans.

In practice, yield curves may not always be "straight lines." **Changing expectations** about the future and the **relative liquidity** of bond (and loan) markets at various terms may even cause the yield curve to become temporarily "**humped**," with higher rates for intermediate terms than for short or long terms.

Note that the term "normal" does not mean to imply either "common" or "preferable." Normal simply means that shorter terms have lower rates. During periods of expansionary monetary policy, shorter terms are typically pushed lower, making the yield curve look "normal." In contrast, during periods when monetary policy is neutral, yield curves often look rather flat.

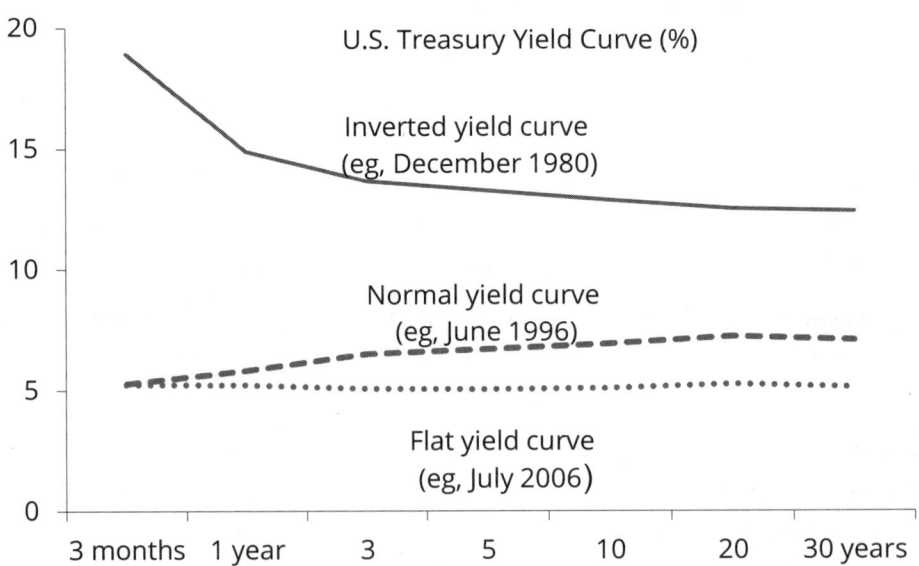

Predicting macroeconomic conditions and interest rates is inherently difficult. Thus, determining the ideal set of maturities and loan types (eg, fixed vs. variable rates) for a firm to use is also difficult. For instance, a borrower using mostly long-term, fixed-rate debt would forgo the benefits of falling interest rates, should interest rates fall. A borrower using mostly short-term (and thus effectively variable rate) debt will experience more liquidity risk, may suffer more earnings volatility, and may, thus, be charged higher rates by lenders. Prudent financial policy would, thus, likely call for diversifying a firm's debt maturities and types.

Financial Management & Capital Budgeting   BEC 5

Lecture 5.16 – Derivatives

Derivatives are financial instruments that derive their value from other underlying assets or prices (commodities, indices, stocks, exchange rates, interest rates, etc.).

- Derivatives are commonly settled through transfers of cash or other liquid assets, taking into account how the prices of the underlying asset evolved relative to the terms set in the original derivative contract.

- Derivatives are financial instruments that have the following **three** characteristics: (**NUNS**)
  o <u>N</u>o net investment
  o An <u>U</u>nderlying and a <u>N</u>otional amount
  o Net <u>S</u>ettlement
    - There is an Underlying price to be used to settle the contract and a Notional amount to calculate the settlement. Little or no payment takes place at origination and the derivative can be settled in a net amount.

Common types of derivatives include:

- **Options** allow (but do not require) holders to *buy (call)* or *sell (put)* an underlying asset at a pre-specified price during a pre-specified period of time (American options) or at a specified date (European options).

- **Forwards** are negotiated contracts in which two parties agree to purchase and sell an underlying asset at a pre-specified price at a future date. The parties may tailor the contract for any amount or date.

- **Futures** are standardized versions of forwards for standardized amounts (eg, X tons of grade Y steel) and dates (eg, the last day of the quarter).

- **Swaps** are agreements by which two parties agree to swap certain streams of payments. In a **currency swap**, the parties may swap flows in two currencies, potentially removing exchange rate risk for both parties. In **interest rate swaps**, the parties may swap a fixed rate flow of payments and a variable rate flow of payments. **Swaptions** are contracts that give holders the option to enter into new swaps, or extend or terminate existing swaps.

Risks Associated with Derivatives

Derivatives may be used for two different purposes:

- **Speculation** – Businesses may use derivatives to raise revenues by shouldering other parties' risks, hoping that the losses feared by the counterparty do not materialize; eg, issuer of credit default swaps (CDS) for subprime mortgages charge a premium to protect others against defaults. The issuer will make profits if the defaults do not take place.

- **Hedging** – Businesses may use derivatives to reduce their risks; eg, an American company with costs in the U.S. but an expected future stream of revenues in Japanese Yen may use currency derivatives to lock in those future revenues as dollars using current exchange rates, thus eliminating its exchange rate risk.

Various business risks are associated with the use of derivatives.

- **Credit (or counterparty) risk** – the counterparty in a contract not honoring its obligations.
- **Market risk** – Adverse changes in economy-wide conditions will affect the fair value of the derivative. This risk is only applicable to derivatives used for speculation.
- **Legal risk** – Legislative or regulatory changes may alter or void the derivative's contracts.
- **Basis risk** – Changes in the value of the derivative may not match exactly changes in the value of the asset (or flows) that is being hedged. In this case, the derivative will fail to hedge risks completely.

Using Derivatives to Hedge

Three common uses of derivatives to hedge are:

- **Fair value hedges** against changes in the value of an asset or liability that the firm has or expects to have.
- **Cash flow hedges** against fluctuations in future cash flows.
- **Foreign currency hedges** against the effects of fluctuations in the value of a foreign currency on the value of assets, liabilities, or cash flows.

According to the Accounting Standard Codification, derivatives must be reported at **fair value**. However, changes in the value of derivatives that qualify as hedges may be used to offset changes in the value of the hedged items. Unrealized gains and losses are reported as follows:

- **Fair value hedges** – If a fair value hedge is completely effective, changes in the value of the derivative and in the value of the item being hedged will offset one another perfectly, and neither change needs to be reported in earnings (the income statement). If the hedge is not completely effective, only the net effect of the changes in the value of the derivative and in the value of the item being hedged will be reported in earnings.
- **Cash flow hedges** – In contrast, for cash flow hedges, both the effective and ineffective portions of the hedge are reported as other comprehensive income to be accumulated on the balance sheet in stockholders' equity until the expected event occurs. Once the event being hedged occurs, the offsetting amounts are reported in net income.

Valuing Derivatives

Derivatives that trade on public markets are reported at their quoted prices. For derivatives that do not trade on public markets, fair values are commonly estimated using various valuation models such as:

- **Black-Scholes** – used to estimate the value of stock options.
- **Monte Carlo simulations**
- **Binomial trees**
- **Zero-coupon method** – used to estimate the value of interest rate swaps.

The calculations used in these models are generally complex and require specialized knowledge or computer programs.

Next, we work through an example of using derivatives.

Financial Management & Capital Budgeting

Assume your client is an oil distributor. On October 1, it purchased 1 million gallons of gasoline from its supplier (a refinery) paying $3.30 per gallon (a wholesale price). The client plans to sell oil to various airlines in early January, but is concerned that, in the meantime, the price of oil might drop considerably from the current selling price of $3.50 (a retail price). To protect from losses in the value of its inventory, the client sells a gasoline futures contract based on a wholesale gasoline price index per gallon (the underlying) times 1 million gallons (the notional amount), with a settlement date of January 2. Assume the price of the index drops $0.20 (or 20 cents) per gallon by the end of the year.

The purchase of the inventory by the distributor from the refinery is recorded as follows (assume immediate payment and entries in millions of dollars):

10/1	Inventory	3.30	
	Cash		3.30

When the futures contract is established, there is no entry, since no cash is involved. This is a **fair value hedge**, since the distributor is hedging against an existing asset.

As of the end of the year, the decline of $0.20 per gallon in the price of oil results in a loss on the inventory of $200,000. The futures contract, however, is now expected to result in a collection of $200,000 upon settlement. The entries are:

12/31	Loss on market decline in inventory	0.2	
	Inventory		0.2
	Receivable on derivative	0.2	
	Gain on fair value hedge		0.2

Both the loss on inventory and gain on the fair value hedge are included in the computation of net income, so there is no net income effect. This, of course, was the goal of the hedge.

Let's now go back to October 1 and consider the issues from the point of view of the airline that is planning on purchasing the gasoline in early January. The airline might enter into a mirror image of the very same contract to hedge against a price increase. However, for the airline, it would be a **cash flow hedge**, since, as yet, there is no asset (like the inventory), liability, or fixed commitment for the purchase.

On October 1, the airline enters into a derivative based on the gasoline index with the same notional amount of $1 million gallons. There is **no entry** on that date.

On December 31, the price decline of $0.20 per gallon in the index means that the airline expects to have to pay $200,000 on the settlement date. The entry is:

12/31	Other comprehensive income – loss on cash flow hedge	0.2	
	Payable on derivative		0.2

Note that the loss is **not** included in the calculation of net income. The reason why, is that the decline in gasoline is expected to reduce the cost of inventory in the next period; so, this loss will be offset by a reduction in the cost of sales in the next period. Since the offsetting event is not yet reflected in net income, neither can the hedge.

To summarize, when derivatives are used as speculation or fair value hedges, gains and losses are reported in net income (in the case of a fair value hedge, there will be offsetting amounts on the asset or commitment being hedged). When derivatives are used as cash flow hedges, gains and losses are reported in other comprehensive income (they are transferred to net income when the expected events occur, and offsetting amounts are reported in net income).

Derivatives Summary

Speculation (nonhedge)
- Acquired to take on risk, hoping for profit.
- Gain or loss in income from continuing operations **(I/S)**.

Fair value hedge
- Acquired to hedge against a recognized asset or liability or a firm purchase commitment.
- Gain or loss in income from continuing operations **(I/S)**.
- Should be offset by loss or gain on hedged item.

Cash flow hedge
- Acquired to hedge against a forecasted future transaction.
- Gain or loss in other comprehensive income (OCI) **(B/S)**.
- Nothing included in net income until forecasted activity occurs.

Foreign currency hedge against an investment in foreign operations
- Acquired to hedge against currency risk from a major investment in a company with a local currency (currency in which books are maintained) other than the U.S. dollar.
- Gain or loss in other comprehensive income (OCI) **(B/S)**.
- Offsets translation losses or gains from investment in foreign operations.

BEC 6 - Decision Making

Table of Contents

Lecture 6.01 – Cost Accounting: Cost Definitions	1
Lecture 6.02 – Cost Classifications	2
Cost Systems	3
Lecture 6.03 – Predetermined Overhead Rate	4
Lecture 6.04 – Flow of a Cost System	5
Lecture 6.05 – Variable & Absorption Costing	8
Lecture 6.06 – Cost Volume Profit	10
Lecture 6.07 – Special Decisions	13
Overview	13
Special Orders	13
Make or Buy	15
Sell or Process Further	16
Scrap or Rework	16
Retain or Eliminate	17

Decision Making

Lecture 6.01 – Cost Accounting: Cost Definitions

A primary purpose of cost measurement is to allocate the costs of production (direct materials, direct manufacturing labor, and manufacturing overhead) to the units produced. It also provides important information for management decisions, such as product pricing decisions.

Cost Definitions

y = A + Bx   [TC = Fixed + Var (X)]

In this formula:

- The **y** is equal to **total cost** and is referred to as the *dependent variable* since its amount is dependent on the other factors.

- The **x** is equal to **volume** and is referred to as the *independent variable* since it can be increased or decreased at the company's discretion. This is also often referred to as the **cost driver** as the amount of costs incurred will be largely dependent on the volume of this variable.

- The **A** is equal to **fixed costs** and remains constant at any volume as long as the company is operating within a given range of volume.

- The **B** is equal to the **variable cost** per unit.

Note: These cost assumptions only remain valid within the **Relevant Range**.

- **Mixed cost** (Semi-Variable – Fixed and Variable Component).

- **High-Low Method** – This method computes the slope for the variable rate based on the highest and lowest observations. The difference in cost is divided by the difference in activity to obtain the variable cost.

Hi-Low Method	
Total Cost	**Hours**
$ 110,000	30,000
$ 80,000	20,000
$ 30,000	**/10,000 = $3hr**

Total Cost/Hours = $3 per hour
TC = F + V(X)

110 = F + 3(30,000)
 F = 20

TC = 20 + 3(X)

Fixed   Variable   Total Costs

Lecture 6.02 – Cost Classifications

Cost accounting refers to the calculation of the cost of manufactured inventory. There are three types of *Product costs* included:

- **Direct materials** – These are the materials that are physically included in the final manufactured product. For example, if a company is manufacturing metal paper clips, the only direct material is the metal. Some costs might include freight in, insurance in transit, storage, import duties and purchasing and receiving dept costs.

- **Direct labor** – These are the wages paid to those employees working with the direct materials to change them from their raw state to finished goods.

- **Overhead** – All other costs related to manufacturing are reported here. These include *indirect materials* (for example, sandpaper used to smooth edges of the paper clips and cleaning supplies to keep the assembly line in good condition) and *indirect labor* (eg, supervisors and maintenance workers in the factory building). Other examples of overhead include payroll taxes and fringe benefits for manufacturing employees, rent and depreciation on factory assets, lubricants, shop supplies and utilities to keep the factory in operation.

Direct materials and direct labor are known as the **prime costs** of manufacturing. Direct labor and overhead are known as the **conversion costs** of production.

Manufacturing costs are often called **product costs** since they are matched to the product and not expensed until the product is sold. Costs that are not associated with manufacturing, such as selling, general, and administrative expenses, are often described as **period costs**, as they are *expensed* in the period incurred. *Normal spoilage* in a manufacturing process is treated as a product cost, while *abnormal spoilage* is expensed as a period cost.

- **Manufacturing costs** – Product costs (added to the cost of the finished product)
    - DM (Direct materials – an integral part of the product)
    - DL (Direct Labor – The labor to convert a raw material to a finished good)
    - **Manufacturing Overhead** (Mfg O/h) (all factory costs except DM & DL)
        - Indirect materials
        - Indirect labor
    - Prime costs = DM + DL
    - Conversion costs = DL + MFG O/h

- **Non-MFG** costs – Period costs
    - Selling, General and Administrative costs (SG&A)
    - Marketing costs, freight out, re-handling costs
    - Abnormal spoilage
    - An expense in the period

- **Other Cost Classifications**
    - Relevant Costs - An anticipated future cost that differs among alternative plans.
    - Avoidable Costs – Costs that will not be incurred if a planned activity is changed or discontinued.
    - Marginal Costs – Additional costs incurred owing to one more output unit.

Cost Systems

- **Actual cost system** (DM, DL & Mfg O/h are all actual)
- **Standard cost system** (All costs based on standards)
- **Normal cost system** (DM & DL based on actual, Mfg O/h based on standards)

Lecture 6.03 – Predetermined Overhead Rate

Accounting for manufacturing overhead is an important part of a costing system. The distinguishing feature of manufacturing overhead is that while it must be incurred in order to produce goods, it cannot be directly traced to the final product as can direct material and direct manufacturing labor. Therefore, overhead must be applied, rather than directly charged, to goods produced.

$$\frac{\underline{\text{Estimated}} \text{ O/h costs}}{\underline{\text{Estimated}} \text{ DL \$/Hrs}} = \text{Predetermined O/h rate} \times \text{actual production} = \textbf{applied O/h}$$

Applied O/h

WIP Control	300	
Factory O/h Applied		300

Actual O/h

Factory O/h Control	500	
Cash		500

Underapplied

Factory O/h Applied (a temporary account)	300	
Expense – *COGS* (Underapplied)	200	
Factory O/h Control		500

Lecture 6.04 – Flow of a Cost System

The **calculation of cost of sales** in a manufacturing company (one that manufactures the products that it sells) is more complicated than the equivalent computation for a merchandising company (one that purchases from outsiders the products that it sells).

- For a **merchandising** company, the calculation is:

    Beginning inventory
    + Purchases
    = Cost of goods available for sale
    - Ending inventory
    = **Cost of goods sold**

- For a **manufacturing** company the **flow of a cost system** looks as follows:

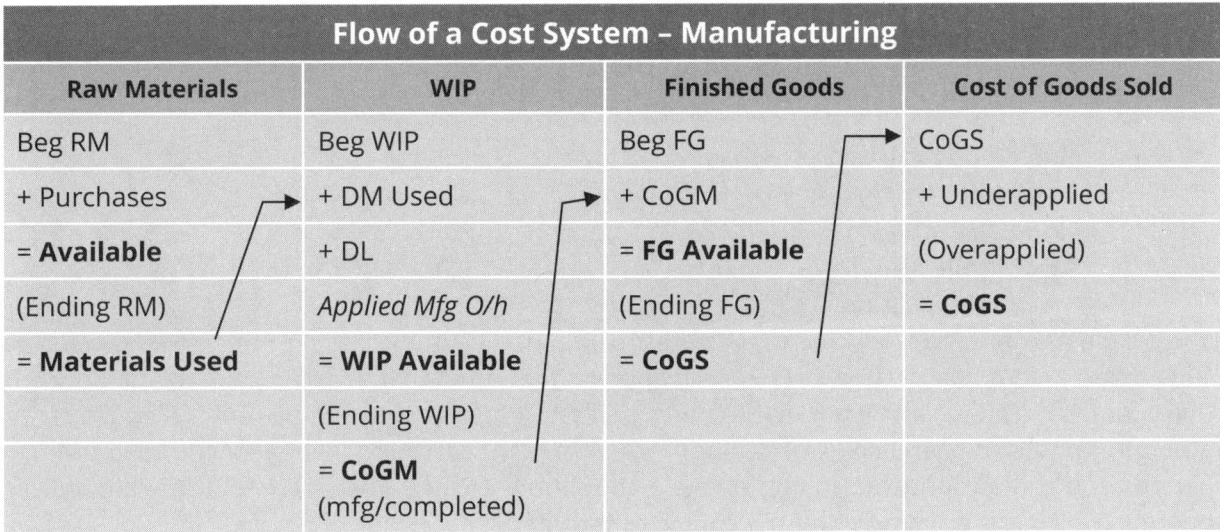

Flow of a Cost System – Manufacturing			
Raw Materials	**WIP**	**Finished Goods**	**Cost of Goods Sold**
Beg RM	Beg WIP	Beg FG	CoGS
+ Purchases	+ DM Used	+ CoGM	+ Underapplied
= **Available**	+ DL	= **FG Available**	(Overapplied)
(Ending RM)	Applied Mfg O/h	(Ending FG)	= **CoGS**
= **Materials Used**	= **WIP Available**	= CoGS	
	(Ending WIP)		
	= **CoGM** (mfg/completed)		

To determine **Direct Materials used**, the calculation is:

Beginning direct materials inventory
+ Direct materials purchased
– Ending direct materials inventory
= Direct materials used

To determine **Cost of Goods Manufactured**, the calculation is:

Direct materials used
+ Direct labor incurred
+ Overhead applied
= Costs added to production
+ Beginning work-in-process inventory
– Ending work-in-process inventory
= Cost of goods manufactured

To determine **Cost of Goods Sold:**

Beginning finished goods inventory
+ Cost of goods manufactured
= Cost of goods available for sale
− Ending finished goods inventory
= **Cost of Sales**

In the computation of cost of goods manufactured, **overhead is applied** to production. This is not the same as the actual overhead costs incurred during the period. The reason is that the matching principle requires an approach to overhead that systematically and rationally allocates it to the benefits, and companies normally do not have the same amount of production in every period.

For example, assume a company is leasing factory equipment with rental payments of $500 per quarter ($2,000 per year) paid to the lessor. Over the course of the year, the company manufactures 1,000 units, so rental costs are $2,000 / 1,000 units = $2 per unit that year. Production is not paced evenly, however, since demand for the product varies through the year. Unit production and actual rent per unit each quarter are:

Quarter	1st	2nd	3rd	4th	Total
Actual Rent	500	500	500	500	2,000
Units	125	250	125	500	1,000
Rent / Unit	$4	$2	$4	$1	$2

The problem with this approach is that the calculation of inventory cost per unit varies considerably from quarter to quarter, and it appears that rent is extremely high in the first and third quarters and extremely low in the fourth quarter. In fact, however, the rent is a stable amount. To follow the matching principle, more of the rent costs should be recognized in the periods of higher production. In this example, the simplest way is to apply rent at the rate of $2 per unit, which is the average over the course of the year:

Quarter	1st	2nd	3rd	4th	Total
Units	125	250	125	500	1,000
Rent / Unit	$2	$2	$2	$2	$2
Applied Rent	250	500	250	1,000	2,000

In the first and third quarters, only $250 of rent is applied, even though $500 is paid, so the rent is underapplied by $250 in both of those quarters. In the fourth quarter, $1,000 is applied, even though $500 is paid, so the rent is overapplied by $500. By the end of the year, however, total applied and actual rent are the same, as long as actual production equals the number of units estimated at the beginning of the year, when the application rate of $2 was determined.

Overhead costs are not usually applied based on *units of production*, the method used in the example. One reason is that it can be difficult to determine the number of units that have been produced, especially with three different types of inventory: raw materials, work-in-process, and finished goods. Another is that most overhead costs are closely related to direct labor, so this might be a more accurate way to match costs. For example, payroll taxes and fringe benefit costs are overhead costs clearly associated with the amount of labor and not necessarily the productivity of those laborers. By applying overhead based on direct labor, it is more likely that applied overhead will be close to actual overhead.

The most common base selected is **direct labor hours**, which is usually easy for the company to determine, since these hours are necessary for wage computations. A company may also use **direct labor dollars**, though this requires the added step of applying wage rates to hours, and is not as popular as a method of allocating overhead as a result. For a company that is highly automated, overhead is occasionally computed based on **machine hours**, but this is quite rare on the CPA exam.

> For example, assume the company paying $2,000 of rent on factory equipment and expecting to produce 1,000 units during the year also estimates that it requires approximately 2 hours for each unit to be produced, and expected wage rates to average $10 per hour. If the company chooses to apply overhead based on *direct labor hours*, then it will use:
>
> $2,000 / 2,000 hours = $1 per direct labor hour
>
> If the company chooses *direct labor dollars*, the result is:
>
> $2,000 / $20,000 = 10% of direct labor cost

Lecture 6.05 – Variable & Absorption Costing

Two Income Statements for a Manufacturing Co.	
Absorption/Full costing/ GAAP	**Direct/ Variable/Prime/CM/Internal**
Sales	Sales
(Var COGS)	(Var COGS)
(Fix COGS)	(Var SGA)
Gross margin	CM (contribution margin)
(Var SGA)	(Fix Mfg. Costs)
(Fix SGA)	(Fix SGA)
Operating Income	Operating Income

Variable and absorption costing methods of accounting for fixed manufacturing overhead differ: under variable costing, fixed manufacturing overhead is expensed whereas under absorption costing, such amounts are treated as a product cost and inventoried. The treatment of fixed manufacturing overhead often results in different levels of net income between the absorption and variable costing methods. The differences are timing differences, which result from recognizing the fixed manufacturing overhead as an expense.

- **Variable costing** - *In the period incurred*
- **Absorption costing**- In the period in which the units to which fixed overhead has been applied are *sold*

Inventoriable Costs	Absorption Costing	Variable Costing
DM	Y	Y
DL	Y	Y
V O/h	Y	Y
F O/h	Y	**N**
V SGA	N	**N**
F SGA	N	**N**

Under direct (Variable) costing, whether a cost is included in inventory has nothing to do with whether it is expensed as a variable or fixed cost. Variable selling expenses are not included in inventory, but are included in the computation of contribution margin. Variable manufacturing costs are included in inventory and are included in the computation of contribution margin. Neither fixed manufacturing costs nor fixed selling expenses are included in inventory nor in the computation of contribution margin.

The calculation of operating income on a manufacturing company's income statement normally looks as follows, using what is commonly called **absorption costing:**

> Sales
> − Cost of sales
> **Gross profit**
> − Selling and administrative expenses
> Operating income

For internal purposes, a company may also prepare an income statement using the **direct costing** approach:

> Sales
> − Variable costs
> **Contribution margin**
> − Fixed costs
> Operating income

The direct costing statement differs in two ways: (1) variable selling expenses are matched to sales along with the variable manufacturing costs and (2) fixed overhead costs are expensed as incurred along with the fixed selling and administrative expenses. The first difference doesn't affect total operating income, since selling expenses are the result of sales, and will be the same amount in either statement. The second difference does affect total operating income, however, and is the reason direct costing statements *violate GAAP* and may only be used internally.

> Assume a company incurred $100 of fixed overhead during the year and produced 100 units, applying fixed overhead at the rate of $1 per unit produced*. If the company sells only 90 of the 100 units produced, then only $90 of the fixed overhead will be in cost of sales that year, and the remaining $10 will be absorbed into ending inventory on the balance sheet when using absorption costing.
>
> Under direct costing, however, the entire $100 is expensed as a fixed cost, causing operating income to be understated by $10. Direct costing normally understates income as inventory levels rise and overstates income as inventory levels fall, due to the different treatment of fixed overhead costs.
>
> *For simplicity, we're assuming overhead is applied based on units and not direct labor, but the results are effectively the same either way.*

The difference in operating income will be equal to the fixed manufacturing overhead per unit multiplied by the increase/decrease in units in inventory.
- When ending inventory *equals* beginning inventory, both methods will result in the same operating income.
- When ending inventory is *greater than* beginning inventory, absorption costing will result in higher operating income.
- When ending inventory is *lower than* beginning inventory, variable costing will result in higher operating income.

Lecture 6.06 – Cost Volume Profit

Cost-volume-profit (CVP) analysis provides management with profitability estimates at all levels of production in the relevant range (the normal operating range).

In making decisions about offering new products or services, companies often rely on cost-volume-profit analysis. The exam tests *three common applications* of this technique:

- Determining sales needed to break even
- Determining sales needed to achieve a particular dollar profit
- Determining sales needed to achieve a particular return on sales

$$\text{Break Even in Units} = \frac{\text{Fixed costs + Profit (Loss)}}{\text{SP - VC(CM)}}$$

$$\text{Break Even in Sales dollars} = \frac{\text{Fixed costs + Profit (Loss)}}{\text{CM Ratio (cm/sales price)}}$$

The information needed to apply this form of analysis is typically obtained from an income statement prepared using the direct costing approach.

> Assume a budget has been prepared for a product based on estimated sales of 100 units per period, selling price of $10 per unit, variable costs of $6 per unit, and fixed costs of $300 per period. A direct costing statement based on this information follows:
>
> | | |
> |---|---:|
> | Units | 100 |
> | Sales (10) | 1,000 |
> | – Variable costs (6) | 600 |
> | Contribution margin (4) | 400 |
> | – Fixed costs | 300 |
> | Operating profit | 100 |
>
> The **breakeven point** occurs when the operating profit is $0. Since fixed costs are always $300, contribution margin must also be $300 in order to achieve breakeven. To figure out the number of units that must be sold for contribution margin to equal fixed costs, the following formula is used:
>
> Fixed costs / Contribution margin per unit = $300 / $4 = 75 units.
>
> To figure out the number of dollars of sales needed, contribution margin can be expressed as a percentage of sales (or contribution margin per dollar of sales). In this information, that is 40% (either $4 / $10 or $400 / $1,000), so the formula is:
>
> Fixed costs / Contribution margin percentage = $300 / 40% = $750.

Of course, these are related, since 75 units at a $10 selling price equals $750 in sales. Let's look at the breakeven statement next to the original budget:

Units	<u>100</u>	<u>75</u>
Sales (10)	1,000	750
-Variable costs (6)	<u>600</u>	<u>450</u>
Contribution margin (4)	400	300
-Fixed costs	<u>300</u>	<u>300</u>
Operating profit	100	-0-

Determining the level at which a **desired profit** is achieved is actually not much more complicated than determining the breakeven point. All that is needed is to increase contribution margin so that it exceeds the fixed costs by the desired profit. The formula for the sales in units is:

(Fixed costs + Desired profit) / Contribution margin per unit

The formula for the sales in dollars is:

(Fixed costs + Desired profit) / Contribution margin percentage

In the example, the sales in units needed for a $20 profit are:
($300 + $20) / $4 = $320 / $4 = 80 units.

Again, let's list the income statement next to the previous ones for budget and breakeven point.

Units	100	75	80
Sales (10)	1,000	750	800
- Variable costs (6)	<u>600</u>	<u>450</u>	<u>480</u>
Contribution margin (4)	400	300	320
- Fixed costs	<u>300</u>	<u>300</u>	<u>300</u>
Operating profit	100	-0-	20

Finally, to determine the point at which a **desired return on sales** is achieved, use an algebraic approach to desired profit:

(Fixed costs + Desired profit) / Contribution margin % = Sales

With a desired return on sales of 10%, the equation is expressed as:
    (300 + 10% of sales) / 40% = Sales or
    (300 + .1x) / .4 = x or
    300 + .1x = .4x or
    300 = .3x or
    1,000 = x

This is the sales level of the original budget above, with a $100 profit that is 10% of sales.

The **Margin of Safety** is the excess of budgeted (or Actual) sales over the break-even volume of sales. It states the amount by which sales can drop before losses begin to be incurred in an organization. If, for example, a company had sales of $3,500,000 and a breakeven volume of $3,200,000, the margin of safety would be $300,000.

When a company that is operating at a profit experiences an increase in costs, whether variable or fixed, the breakeven point is increased and the margin of safety is decreased.

The Margin of Safety can also be expressed in percentage form. This percentage is obtained by dividing the Margin of Safety in dollar terms by total sales.

Total sales – Break even sales = *Margin of Safety*

Lecture 6.07 – Special Decisions

Overview

Less common applications involve mere variations of the cost-volume-profit techniques:

- Determining whether a special order should be accepted.
- Determining whether to make or buy a product.
- Determining whether to sell a product or process it further.
- Determining whether to scrap or rework defective products.
- Determining whether to retain or eliminate a product line or division.

The general rule for these situations is to consider only the *relevant* revenues and costs (ie, the revenues and costs that change between the alternatives). If the facility is at full capacity, an opportunity cost—the benefit (ie, revenues – costs) forgone for an alternative not chosen—is involved.

Special Orders

The special order type of question typically involves an order at a lower than usual price, sometimes reducing regular sales. If the facility is not at full capacity, accepting a special order at a price lower than the absorption unit cost (including fixed costs) may make sense, as long as the variable costs are covered, because the total fixed costs already are borne by the regular units. When regular sales are impacted, this will not necessarily be the case.

> For example, Flexco originally prepared an annual budget for a product based on estimated sales of 100,000 units with a per unit sales price of $100, variable manufacturing costs of $35, fixed manufacturing costs of $15, variable selling and administrative (S&A) costs of $20, and fixed S&A costs of $10, resulting in per unit operating income of $20. This budget does not use Flexco's full annual capacity of 105,000 units and neither increases nor decreases year-end inventory counts.
>
> Big Mart offers to buy 10,000 units at $80 per unit; filling this order will not affect regular sale prices nor change fixed manufacturing costs and fixed and variable selling and administrative expenses; however, it will eliminate 5,000 units of regular sales, since Flexo has insufficient capacity for them. An analysis of revenues and costs that change shows that Flexo will increase its operating income by accepting the order:
>
> | | |
> |---|---:|
> | Revenues due to special order ($80/unit x 10,000 units) | $800,000 |
> | Less: special order manufacturing costs ($35/unit x 10,000 units) | (350,000) |
> | Less: reduction in revenues from regular sales ($100/unit x 5,000 units) | (500,000) |
> | Plus: reduction in variable manufacturing costs ($35/unit x 5,000 units) | 175,000 |
> | Plus: reduction in variable S&A costs ($20/unit x 5,000 units) | 100,000 |
> | **Increase in operating income** | **$225,000** |

A comparison of financial statements (*$ in 1,000s) for the two options will confirm this:

	Regular sales only			Total	=	Regular sales w/ order			+	Special order		
	#	$/#	$*	$*		#	$/#	$*		#	$/#	$*
Sales	100,000	100	10,000	10,300		95,000	100	9,500		10,000	80	800
Var. mfg.	100,000	35	3,500	3,675		95,000	35	3,325		10,000	35	350
Var. S&A	100,000	20	2,000	1,900		95,000	20	1,900				
Cont. margin			4,500	4,725				4,275				450
Fixed mfg.	100,000	15	1,500	1,500				1,500				
Fixed S&A	100,000	10	1,000	1,000				1,000				
Oper. Inc.			2,000	2,225				1,775				450

The fact that fixed manufacturing costs amount to $15 per unit and fixed S&A expenses amount to $10 per unit at a volume of 100,000 units indicates that fixed manufacturing costs are $1,500,000 per period, and fixed S&A expenses are $1,000,000 per period, regardless of the number of units produced and sold and regardless of whether or not a special order is accepted.

If Flexo does not accept the order and continues at a volume of 100,000 units at regular prices, revenues, costs and expenses will be as follows:

Revenue (100,000 units x $100/unit)	$10,000,000
Variable manufacturing costs (100,000 units × $35/unit)	3,500,000
Variable S&A expenses (100,000 units × $20/unit)	2,000,000
*Contribution margin	4,500,000
Fixed manufacturing costs ($1,500,000)	1,500,000
Fixed S&A expenses ($1,000,000)	1,000,000
Operating Income	$ 2,000,000

If Flexo does accept the order, the volume will consist of 10,000 units included in the special order and 95,000 units to be sold through normal channels, for a total of 105,000 units. Revenues, costs and expenses will be as follows:

Revenue regular (95,000 units × $100/unit)	$9,500,000
Revenue special (10,000 units × $80/unit)	800,000
Variable manufacturing costs (105,000 units × $35/unit)	3,675,000
Variable S&A expenses (95,000 units × $20 /unit)	1,900,000
*Contribution margin	4,725,000
Fixed manufacturing costs ($1,500,000)	1,500,000
Fixed S&A expenses ($1,000,000)	1,000,000
Operating Income	$2,225,000

*This calculation can be further simplified. The contribution margin represents the amount that the sale of a unit contributes to covering fixed costs or, once covered, to profit. It is measured as the difference between the revenue that will be generated by the sale of a unit and the variable costs that will be incurred in relation to it.

Flexo's units sold at the normal sales price of $100 have a contribution margin of $45 per unit, taking into account variable manufacturing costs of $35 per unit and variable S&A expense of $20, for a total of $55. The units sold under the special order will have a sales price of $80 per unit and variable manufacturing costs of $35, resulting in a contribution margin that is also $45 per unit. There will be no variable S&A costs since the customer initiated the transaction and incremental selling and administrative expenses were not necessary.

As a result, if Flexo does not accept the special order, the contribution margin will be 100,000 units at $45, for a total of $4,500,000. If the special order is accepted, the contribution margin will consist of 95,000 units at $45 per unit, and 10,000 units at a contribution margin of $45 per unit, for a total of 105,000 units at $45 per unit, which is $4,725,000, an increase of $225,000.

Fixed costs, including both fixed manufacturing costs and fixed S&A expense, remain the same regardless of the number of units produced or sold as long as the volume falls within the entity's normal range of operations, referred to as the relevant range.

Make or Buy

The Make or Buy type of question typically involves a component that can be produced in-house or by a subcontractor. The Sell or Process Further type of question typically involves a component that can be sold in an early stage or processed further before being sold. The Scrap or Rework type of question typically involves defective parts that could be either reworked and sold or merely sold for scrap. In analyzing these situations, add the opportunity cost of using the facilities for another purpose (if any) to the in-house costs.

For example, Miller & Baker Company (MBC) uses 13,000 units of Part 1322 monthly. The per unit costs are $4 for direct material, $2 for direct labor, $2 for variable overhead, and $4 for fixed overhead (FOH). If MBC buys the parts, they will cost $13 apiece, but the company will eliminate $3 of FOH costs per unit.

The remaining FOH remains regardless of whether MBC purchases or makes the part. The facilities used to manufacture Part 1322 alternatively could be used to manufacture Part 668 at a monthly profit of $50,000. An analysis of revenues and costs that differ between the two options indicates that it is more profitable to buy the part and use the facilities to manufacture Part 668:

	Make	**Buy**
Direct material	$4	
Direct labor	2	
Variable overhead	2	
Fixed overhead subject to elimination*	3	
Relevant unit costs	$11	$13
Units	13,000	13,000
Relevant costs for 13,000 units	$143,000	$169,000
Opportunity cost of making Part 1322	50,000	-0-
Total relevant costs	$193,000	$169,000

*Note: The remaining $1 of FOH that cannot be eliminated is irrelevant to this decision.

If the alternative equipment use for Part 668 were not an option ($50,000 opportunity cost), it would be $26,000 ($169,000 − $143,000) more profitable to make the part in-house; however, because of the $50,000 opportunity cost, it is $24,000 ($193,000 − $169,000) more profitable to buy the part and use the equipment to make Part 668.

Sell or Process Further

Again, the sell or process further type of question typically involves a component that can be sold in an early stage or processed further before being sold.

> For example, Sailor & Pirate Company (SPC) makes products X, Y, and Z jointly. Each product may be processed further or sold at the split-off point. Joint production costs of $100,000 are allocated using the relative-sales-value at split-off method. Additional per-unit information is as follows.
>
> | | X | Y | Z |
> |---|---|---|---|
> | Sales value at spilt-off | $25 | $50 | $10 |
> | Additional processing cost | 20 | 10 | 15 |
> | Final sales value | $100 | $60 | $20 |
>
> An analysis of revenues and costs that change for the two alternatives for each product indicates that it is most profitable to process product X further and sell product Z. For product Y, there is no difference.
>
> | | X | Y | Z |
> |---|---|---|---|
> | Final sales value | $100 | $60 | $20 |
> | Less: Sales value at spilt-off | 25 | 50 | 10 |
> | Incremental revenue | 75 | 10 | 10 |
> | Less: Incremental costs | 20 | 10 | 15 |
> | Additional profit (loss) | $55 | $0 | $(5) |
>
> By processing product X further at a cost of $20, revenue will increase by $75 ($100 – $25), resulting in a net benefit of $55 ($75 revenue increase – $20 cost increase), making it more profitable to process product X further before sale.
>
> By processing product Y further at a price of $10, revenue will increase by $10 per unit ($60 – $50), resulting in no net difference between processing product Y further and selling it at the split-off point ($10 revenue increase – $10 cost increase).
>
> By processing product Z further at a cost of $15, revenue will increase by $10 per unit ($20 – $10), resulting in a net reduction in income of $5 per unit ($10 revenue increase – $15 cost increase). Product Z will not be processed further.
>
> The joint production costs are irrelevant to this decision, as they will remain the same regardless of whether any of the products are processed further or not.

Scrap or Rework

The Scrap or Rework type of question is another instance of sell or process further.

> For example, Sneak & Rogue Company (SRC) has 20,000 defective units of product Loot with a total cost of $18,000. As scrap, they can be sold for $1,500. If they are reworked for $10,000, they may be sold for $12,000. The rework option is the more profitable alternative, contributing more to net income than the scrap option.
>
> | | Scrap | Rework |
> |---|---|---|
> | Incremental revenue | $1,500 | $12,000 |
> | Less: Incremental costs | 0 | 10,000 |
> | Additional profit (loss) | $1,500 | $ 2,000 |
>
> The total cost of the defective units before rework is irrelevant; this sunk cost is the same between the two alternatives.

Retain or Eliminate

The retain or eliminate type of question typically involves an unprofitable product line or division. One must consider whether the at-risk line or division helps the other more profitable divisions cover the fixed costs—generally allocated from corporate or administrative sources—that do not cease with the product line or division elimination. In other words, in some cases, the reason the product line or division is not profitable is due to costs allocated to that product line or division that will continue to be incurred after the product line is discontinued or the division is closed.

If, for example, the CEO's salary is allocated among all four products that an entity manufactures, and one of the four products is discontinued, the CEO's salary will not be reduced proportionately; it will be allocated among the remaining products. As a result, when performing such an analysis, only those revenues and costs that will change should be considered.

> For example, Roving Epicure Company (REC) has four product lines: quality fruits, game meats, fine wines, and fine cheeses. For the past three years, the fruit line has seen dwindling profits; this trend seems unlikely to reverse. Additional information (in 1,000s) is as follows:
>
> | Product line | Fruit | Meat | Wine | Cheese |
> |---|---|---|---|---|
> | Revenue | $4,000 | $2,000 | $6,000 | $2,000 |
> | Variable costs | 3,000 | 1,000 | 2,000 | 1,000 |
> | Contribution margin | 1,000 | 1,000 | 4,000 | 1,000 |
> | Avoidable fixed costs | 200 | 400 | 2,000 | 300 |
> | Unavoidable fixed costs | 1,000 | 200 | 400 | 100 |
> | Net income | $(200) | $400 | $1,600 | $600 |

While the $200,000 of net loss from the fruit line can be eliminated, the $1,000,000 unavoidable fixed costs borne by the fruit line cannot be eliminated. These fixed costs remain to be allocated to the remaining product lines. In other words, even though the fruit product line appears to be unprofitable, it should be retained.

If the fruit line is eliminated, revenues will be reduced by $4,000,000. Variable costs will be reduced by $3,000,000, and avoidable fixed costs of $200,000 will no longer be incurred. The unavoidable fixed costs will continue to be incurred and will be allocated to the other product lines. As a result, the reduction in revenues ($4,000,000) exceeds the reduction in costs ($3,200,000) by $800,000, thus reducing company profitability if the fruit product line is eliminated.

The following chart is expressed in 1,000s:

Product line	With	Without	Reduction
Revenue	$14,000	$10,000	$4,000
Variable costs	7,000	4,000	3,000
Contribution margin	7,000	6,000	1,000
Avoidable fixed costs	2,900	2,700	200
Unavoidable fixed costs	1,700	1,700	0
Net income	$2,400	$1,600	$800

BEC 7 – Cost Accounting

BEC 7 – Cost Accounting

Table of Contents

Lecture 7.01 – Cost Accounting 1
   Standard Costing 1
   Variance Analysis 2

Lecture 7.02 – Overhead Variances 4
   Overhead Applied 4
   Overhead Spending Variance 4
   Overhead Efficiency Variance 5
   Overhead Production Volume Variance 5

Lecture 7.03 – Two Costing Systems: Job Order vs. Process Costing 7
   Job Order Costing 7
   Process Costing 7

Lecture 7.04 – Joint Product Costing 12
   Relative Sales Value Method 12
   By-products 14

Cost Accounting

Lecture 7.01 – Cost Accounting

Standard Costing

Standard costs are predetermined target costs which should be attainable under efficient conditions. Standard costs are used to aid in the budget process, pinpoint trouble areas, and evaluate performance. Cost accounting developed in response to internal concerns, rather than as a standardized tax or financial reporting framework with uniform terms. The industry (and hence, the CPA exam) commonly uses more than one name for some variances.

In setting internal goals for the efficient production of inventory, companies establish standards for the components that determine direct materials, direct labor, and overhead. At the end of the period, these standards are compared with actual results in order to determine **variances**. The standards include:

- **Standard cost** – The unit purchase price of direct materials. Differences between standard cost and actual cost produce **direct materials price variances**.

- **Standard quantity** – The number of units of direct materials used to produce each unit of inventory. Differences between standard quantity allowed and actual quantity used produce **direct materials usage variances**.

- **Standard rate** – The hourly rate of pay for direct labor. Differences between standard rate of pay and actual rate of pay produce **direct labor rate variances**.

- **Standard hours** – The number of hours of direct labor used to produce each unit of inventory. Differences between standard hours allowed and actual hours used produce **direct labor efficiency variances**.

- **Predetermined overhead rate** (also called the standard fixed application rate, or **SFR**). The amount of overhead to apply (usually based on direct labor hours). Differences between applied overhead and actual overhead produce overhead variances. There are several different ways to compute overhead variances.

> Assume a company manufactures collectible life-size figurines, which are sold for $1,000 each. Typically, a single figurine is completed in a day, and the **standard** costs involved in the manufacture of each figurine are:
>
> Direct materials – 20 pounds of clay at $5 per pound
> Direct labor – 5 hours of labor at $10 per hour
> Overhead – Applied at $19 per direct labor hour
>
> The estimated cost of manufacturing on a normal day (one figurine) is:

	Normal
Direct materials	$100
Direct labor	$50
Overhead	$95
Total cost	$245

Assume that, on a particular day, the company manufactures **two** figurines, and incurs the following **actual** costs:

>   Direct materials – 36 pounds of clay at $4 per pound
>   Direct labor – 12 hours of labor at $11 per hour
>   Overhead - $255

It is not appropriate to compare the normal costs with the actual costs, since the **normal costs are based on expected production** (one figurine). Instead, the actual costs are compared with **standard costs allowed based on actual production** (two figurines), as follows:

	Normal	Standard	Actual	Variance
Direct materials	100	200	144	56 F
Direct labor	50	100	132	32 U
Overhead	95	190	255	65 U
Total cost	245	490	531	41 U

The variances that result from actual costs being lower than standard costs are identified as *favorable* and those resulting from actual costs being higher are *unfavorable.*

The variances identified in the right column are not the ones usually requested on the exam. Instead, the 4 standards related to the direct costs each result in a variance:

Variance Analysis

(SAD → Standard – Actual = Difference)

DM	DM **Price** Variance = (purchasing)	AQ (SP – AP)	While in the factory, can I control the quantity used? YES (use Actual quantity)
	DM **Usage** Variance = (production)	SP (SQ – AQ)	While in the factory, can I control the price? NO (use Standard price)
DL	DL **Rate** Variance = (personnel)	AH (SR – AR)	While in the factory, can I control the hours worked? YES (use Actual quantity)
	DL **Efficiency** Var = (production)	SR (SH – AH)	While in the factory, can I control the pay rate? NO (use Standard price)

SQ × SH = Standard allowed for actual production

The **direct materials price variance (DMPV)** is the difference resulting from the actual cost per unit (AC) of the direct materials ($4 per pound) being different from the standard cost (SC) per unit

Cost Accounting

($5 per pound). It is based on the total quantity actually purchased (AQP). Assuming that the company maintains no inventories, it needs to purchase 36 pounds (if purchases are different from usage, the exam question will indicate that the calculation should be based on purchases). The variance is:

$$\text{DMPV} = \text{AQP} \times (\text{SC} - \text{AC}) = 36 \times (5 - 4) = 36 \times 1 = 36 \text{ F}$$

The **direct materials usage variance (DMUV)** is the difference resulting from the actual quantity used (AQU) of direct materials (36 pounds) being different from the standard quantity allowed (SQA) based on production (40 pounds for 2 figurines). It is based on the standard cost per unit, since there is already a separate price variance to take into account the effect of the actual cost per unit being different. (This also may be called the direct materials efficiency variance.) The variance is:

$$\text{DMUV} = \text{SC} \times (\text{SQA} - \text{AQU}) = 5 \times (40 - 36) = 5 \times 4 = 20 \text{ F}$$

The **direct labor rate variance (DLRV)** is the difference resulting from the actual rate of pay (AR) for the direct laborers ($11 per hour) being different from the standard rate of pay (SR) for those laborers ($10 per hour). The total difference is multiplied by the actual number of hours (AH) that the laborers worked (12 hours). The variance is:

$$\text{DLRV} = \text{AH} \times (\text{SR} - \text{AR}) = 12 \times (10 - 11) = 12 \times -1 = 12 \text{ U}$$

The **direct labor efficiency variance (DLEV)** is the difference resulting from the actual hours worked (12 hours) being different from the standard hours allowed (SH) based on actual production (10 hours for two figurines). The total difference is multiplied by the standard rate of pay, since there is already a separate variance that takes into account the effect of the actual rate of pay being different. (This also may be called the direct labor usage variance.) The variance is:

$$\text{DLEV} = \text{SR} \times (\text{SH} - \text{AH}) = 10 \times (10 - 12) = 10 \times -2 = 20 \text{ U}$$

Notice that the sum of the two unfavorable direct labor variances is $32 (DLRV $12 + DLEV $20), equal to the total direct labor variance.

Lecture 7.02 – Overhead Variances

Overhead Applied

When companies apply a standard cost system to overhead, the amount of overhead applied will be determined on the basis of the standard amount of the allocation base that should have been used in the production process based on the number of units produced. If overhead is allocated, for example, on the basis of direct labor hours, **overhead applied** (OA) can be calculated as follows:

$$\text{OA} = \text{SDLH} \times \text{POHR}$$

In the formula above, POHR is the **predetermined overhead rate** including both the variable and fixed components. It is calculated in a three-step process:

1. The total of the base is estimated. For example, if the company expects to produce 50,000 units at 2 standard direct labor hours per unit, the estimate for the base is 100,000 hours.
2. Second, total overhead is estimated on the basis of expected fixed overhead for the period and variable overhead per unit of the base. If, for example, the entity paid rent of $400,000 per year and utilities of $1 per hour, at 100,000 hours, total overhead would be $400,000 (rent) + $100,000 (utilities calculated as 100,000 hours at $1 per hour), for a total of $500,000.
3. Finally, total estimated overhead is divided by the number of units in the base to establish a rate. At $500,000 for 100,000 hours, the POHR would be $5 per hour ($500,000/100,000 DLH), which includes $4 per hour fixed and $1 per hour variable costs.

Many companies will further analyze overhead using a 2-variance, 3-variance, or 4-variance approach. The most common is the 3-variance approach, dividing the total variance into a Spending variance, an Efficiency variance, and a Volume variance.

Overhead Spending Variance

The overhead Spending variance (OSV) measures whether the amount of variable overhead being spent per hour is more or less than the amount expected and whether the amount of fixed overhead incurred is more or less than the budgeted amount. The overhead spending variance (aka, flexible budget variance) is the difference between the amount of overhead that would be budgeted based on actual hours worked and the amount actually spent on overhead. It is calculated as follows:

$$\text{OSV} = (\text{ADLH} \times \text{PVOHR} + \text{Budgeted fixed overhead}) - \text{Actual overhead}$$

In the above formula, if OSV is a positive number, the variance is favorable. The overhead spending variance can also be segregated into a fixed and a variable component.

In addition to spending, the total overhead variance includes a portion related to usage. The variable component is referred to as the **overhead efficiency variance**, which measures the extra variable overhead spent if the entity worked more hours than expected or the variable overhead saved if the entity worked fewer. The fixed component is referred to as the **volume variance** since it is better to spread fixed overhead over a greater number of units, resulting in a lower cost per unit, than a smaller number.

Overhead Efficiency Variance

The overhead Efficiency variance (OEV) is similar to the labor efficiency variance. It measures whether the units manufactured required more or less than the number of hours expected. Since variable overhead is incurred with each direct labor hour spent, the amount can be calculated as follows:

$$OEV = PVOHR \times (SDLH - ADLH)$$

In the formula above, PVOHR is the predetermined variable overhead rate. If OEV is a positive number, the variance is favorable.

Overhead Production Volume Variance

The overhead Production Volume variance (OVV) is the one over which the manufacturing department has the least control. This is due to the fact that the variance measures whether the company produced as many units as expected. The amount can be calculated as follows:

$$OVV = (SDLH \times PFOHR) - \text{Budgeted fixed overhead}$$

In the formula above, PFOHR is the predetermined fixed overhead rate which is calculated by dividing the budgeted fixed overhead by the standard direct labor hours based on expected production. When more units were produced than were anticipated, the amount of overhead applied will exceed the budgeted amount, resulting in a favorable volume variance.

Total Overhead Variance

The total of the Spending variance, the Efficiency variance, and the Volume variance is the total overhead variance.

Budget to Actual Comparison
Flexible Budget Equation (FBE) = TC = F + v (X)
TC = total costs, F = fixed cost, v = variable cost

Budgeted overhead costs:
- Fixed Rent = $400,000 (ie, $4 × 100,000 hrs budgeted)
- Variable Electricity = $1 × 100,000 hrs budgeted
- **FBE = $400,000 + $1 (X)**
- X = Actual production × Actual Hrs, or Actual production × Std hrs allowed for actual production.

Actual costs:
- Fixed Rent = $390,000
- Variable Electricity = $1.01 (97,000 hrs)

Actual at Budget			
	50,000 units (2 hrs) =	100,000 hrs	Budget
	48,000 (2.02) =	97,000 hrs	Actual
	48,000 (2) =	96,000 hrs	Standard allowed for Actual production

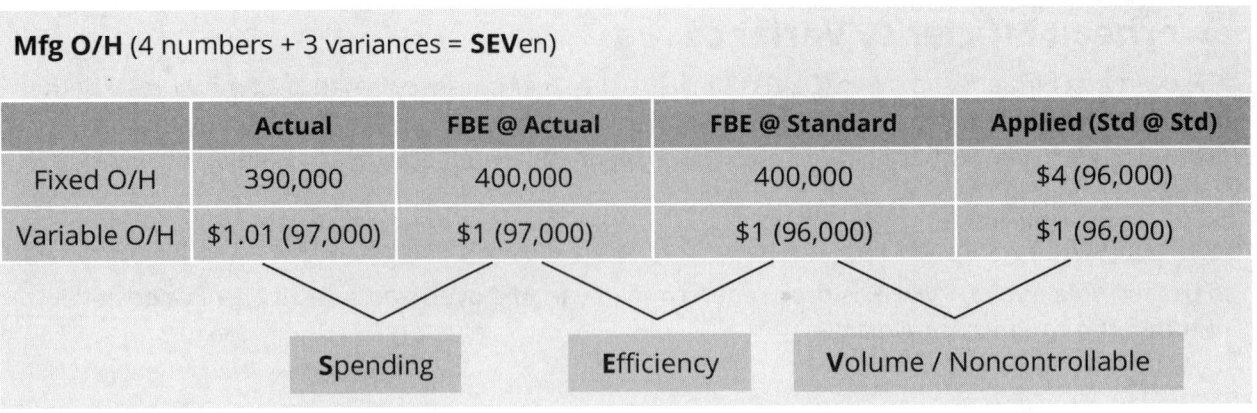

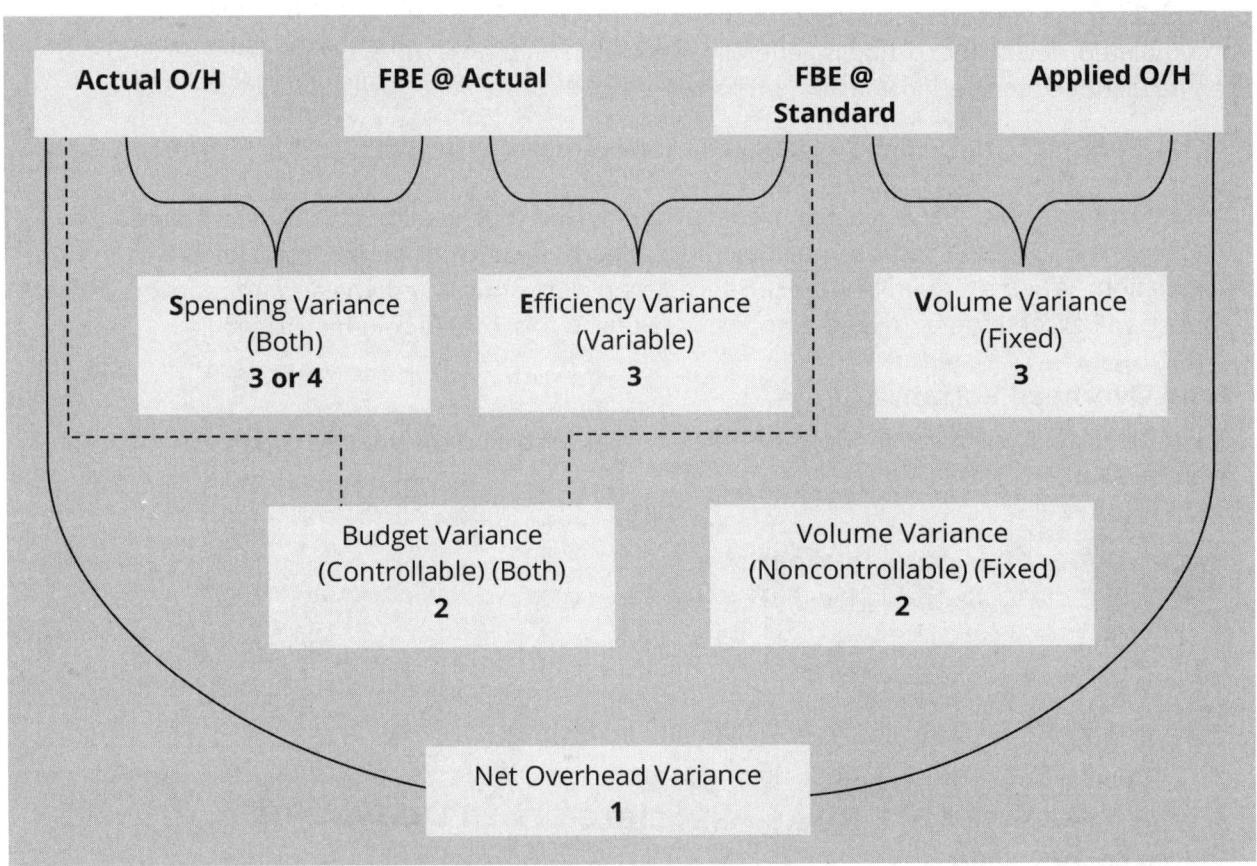

1 – One-variance method	Net O/H variance
2 – Two-variance method	Flexible Budget (Controllable) / Volume (Noncontrollable)
3 – Three-variance method	Spending / Efficiency / Volume
4 – Four-variance method	Fixed Spending / Variable Spending / Efficiency / Volume

Lecture 7.03 – Two Costing Systems: Job Order vs. Process Costing

There are two methods of accumulating production costs in a manufacturing company and for allocating the costs to work in process, finished goods and cost of goods sold:

- Job order costing
- Process costing

Job Order Costing

Job order costing is a system for allocating costs to groups of unique products. It is applicable to the production of customer-specified products. Each job becomes a cost center for which costs are accumulated. Job order costing is generally used when units are relatively expensive and when costs can be identified to specific units or batches of units. Because costs are traced to specific jobs, certain items that might otherwise be classified as manufacturing overhead (overtime premiums paid to accommodate a customer change order, for instance) are classified as direct costs.

- **Job order costing** – expensive, heterogeneous – cost based per **Job.**

Process Costing

Process costing, in contrast to job order costing, is applicable to a continuous process of production of the same or similar goods. Since the product is uniform, there is no need to determine the costs of different groups of products and each processing department becomes a cost center. Process costing is generally used when units are relatively inexpensive and when it is difficult to trace costs to specific units being produced, such as when units are mass-produced in large quantities.

- **Process costing** – inexpensive, homogeneous - costs per **Period.**
    - Equivalent "whole" units (80 × ¾ cc = 60 whole units) (cc = Conversion Cost)
        - Weighted average method (beginning + started)
        - **FIFO** (beginning first/ then started)

There are two methods of applying process costing to production. These are the weighted average method and FIFO.

Weighted Average

Under the weighted average approach, equivalent production for a period will include units that are **completed** during the period, considered whole units as to all costs, and units in process at the end of the period. The ending work-in-process (WIP) will be converted into equivalent units based on the level of completion.

Total equivalent production will be divided into costs for the period to determine an average cost per equivalent unit. The costs included will be the costs associated with beginning inventory and the costs incurred during the period.

FIFO

Under the FIFO approach, equivalent production for a period will include the units that are **started and completed** during the period, considered whole units as to all costs. Both beginning and ending WIP inventory will be converted into equivalent whole units.

- For beginning inventory, the portion of the work that needed to be completed during the period will be multiplied by the number of units to determine equivalent production.
- For ending inventory, the percentage of completion will be multiplied by the number of units to determine equivalent production.

Total equivalent production will be divided into costs for the period to determine an average cost per equivalent unit. The costs included, however, will only be those costs that were incurred during the period.

Comparing Weighted Average to FIFO

The difference between weighted average and FIFO is the handling of beginning WIP inventory. When there is no beginning inventory, both will have the same result. When there is a beginning WIP inventory, the weighted average approach will yield a number of equivalent units that will be equal to or greater than equivalent production under FIFO.

- When costs are incurred at the end of the process, or at some point in the process that the beginning inventory had not yet reached, equivalent production will be the same under both approaches.
- When costs are incurred uniformly during the process, at the beginning of the process, or at some point in the process that the beginning inventory had already reached, equivalent production under weighted average would be greater than FIFO.

Weighted Average
TC/Total Equivalent Units = Cost per Unit

FIFO
Costs **this Period**/Units Worked on **this period** = Cost per Unit

Equivalent Production

One significant aspect of process costing is the computation of equivalent units. The objective is to analyze the period's production, including units completed and units partially completed, and determine the number of whole units the production is equivalent to.

The calculation of equivalent production will depend on the point in time at which costs are incurred.

- When costs are incurred at the beginning of the process, partially completed units will be considered equivalent to whole units as soon as they are started.
- When costs are incurred at a specific time during the process, such as when units are 40% complete, partially completed units will be considered equivalent to nothing until they reach that point and equivalent to whole units when that point is reached.
- When costs are incurred at the end of the process, partially completed units will be considered equivalent to nothing until completed, at which time they will be equivalent to whole units.
- When costs are incurred evenly throughout the process, the percentage of completion will be multiplied by the number of units in process to determine the number of equivalent whole units.

When a company has more than one manufacturing department, the costs are assigned to WIP and to goods transferred to the next department. In the subsequent department, the units transferred from a previous department are considered similar to a raw material that is added to the production cycle at the beginning of the process.

Cost Accounting

 The Alexes Co. is the first of a two-stage production process. The following information concerns the conversion costs in May 20X3:

	Units	Conversion costs
Beginning work in process (60% complete)	30	$68
Units started	60	96
Spoilage — normal	0	$164
Units completed and transferred	50	
Ending work in process (80% complete)	40	

Using the Weighted-average and the FIFO methods, calculate equivalent whole units, the cost of goods completed and transferred, and ending inventory.

Weighted Average (Total Costs/Total Equivalent Whole Units)

	units	% complete CC	Equivalent whole units	Costs
Beg. Units	30	60%		$ 68
Started	60			$ 96
Units to acct for	90			$ 164
Completed	50	100% =	50 × $2 = $100	
Spoilage	0			
End	40	80% Complete =	32 × $2 = $64	
			$164	
Units to acct for	90		82 equiv. units	$164

Same under Both → (applies to End row)

W/A → What did you finish? Do not care where it came from.
TC/EU → EU = 50 completed + 40 (0.8) = 82 equiv. Whole units
= $164/82 = $ 2 per unit
50 × $2 = $100 (COG completed)
32 × $2 = 64 (Ending Inventory)
$164

FIFO (Costs incurred this period/Units actually worked on this period)

	units	% completed CC	Equivalent whole units	Costs
Beg. Units	30	60%		$ 68
Started	60			$ 96
Units to acct for	90			$ 164
Completed	50	30 × 40% = 12	12 × $1.5 = 18	
		20 × 100% = 20	20 × $1.5 = 30	
			$48	
			+ started 68	
			Cogc $116	
Spoilage	0			
End	40	80% Complete =	32 × $1.5 = $48	
			$164	
Units to acct for	90		64 equiv. units	$164

Same under Both → (applies to End row)

©UWorld, LLC

FIFO → What work did you perform *this period*?
  Costs this period/Units Worked on this period
  Units Worked on this period =

What did it take to make it 100% complete? Came in with 60%, so 40%.

The 30 units in beginning inventory were already 60% complete and the remaining 40% was required to complete them.

If 50 units were completed, 30 of which were from beginning inventory, there were 20 units that were started and completed in their entirety during the period.

Ending inventory is treated the same under FIFO as under weighted average. There are 40 units that are 80% complete.

Cost of goods completed will consist of:
- The costs in beginning inventory
- The cost to complete the units in beginning inventory (EU × cost per EU)
- The cost of units started and completed during the period (EU × cost per EU)

30 (from beginning) (.40) = 12 + 20 (100%) = 32 + ending 40 (.80) = 64 equiv. whole units
  = $96/64 = $1.5 × 32 = $48+ 68 = 116 (COG completed)
       $1.5 × 32 = 48 (Ending Inventory)
            $164

When a company produces large quantities of identical goods, it will often use **process costing** to determine the average cost per unit of products. When using this approach, costs are accumulated in WIP until the end of the period, and then a calculation is made of the cost per equivalent unit of products completed and incomplete at the end of the period.

Assume that a company had work-in-process (WIP) at the beginning of the month of $30, associated with 2 units that were 50% complete at the time. During the month, it spent $150 and started an additional 8 units. At the end of the month, WIP consisted of 4 units that were 75% complete. Assume there was no spoilage in the production process.

The total cost in WIP before allocating is $30 + $150 = $180. With 2 units at the start and 8 more begun during the month, there were 10 units to account for at the end of the month. Since 4 were in process, 6 must have been completed.

The **equivalent units** include the 6 that were completed and 4 × 75% = 3 equivalent units for the ending WIP, for a total of 9 equivalent units. The costs of $180 are allocated over 9 equivalent units at $20 per equivalent unit. Ending WIP is $20 × 3 equivalent units, or $60, and the remaining $120 must represent the costs associated with the 6 units completed and transferred to finished goods.

Cost Accounting

	Units	Costs	Cost / EU	
Beg WIP (50%)	2	30		
Added	8	150		
To account for	10	180	180	
		EU		

	Units	Costs	Cost / EU	Allocation @ $20
End WIP (75%)	4	3		60
Completed	6	6		120
Accounted for	10	9	9	180
Cost / EU			20	

For costs added at the beginning of a process, the equivalent units are the same for WIP as they are for completed units. For example, if raw materials are added at the beginning of the process, the 4 units in process at the end of the month already have all the raw materials, and are assigned 4 equivalent units instead of 3.

Lecture 7.04 – Joint Product Costing

Joint products are two or more products produced together up to a split-off point where they become separately identifiable. They cannot be produced by themselves. When more than one product is being produced, certain costs are associated with the production of more than one product, and are known as **joint product costs**. These costs are allocated to the different products using an appropriate method. One method is called **units of volume of output**, but this method is not as frequently tested.

Relative Sales Value Method

The most popular is the **relative sales value at split-off** approach. The total sales value of the products involved is determined, and is reduced by separate costs incurred in the manufacture of each product after the split from the joint process. The result is the approximate sales value of each product at the point the joint process ended. This is referred to as the sales value at split-off or the synthetic sales value and is used to allocate the joint costs.

Under the Relative Sales Value Method:

- The **sales value** of each joint product is determined by multiplying the amount produced by the sales price per unit.

- The sales value is reduced by **separable costs**. Separable costs are the costs incurred after the mutual manufacturing process is complete. They are the costs necessary to prepare a joint product to be sold. Not all joint products will have separable costs.

- The resulting reduced amount is considered the **relative sales value** of the joint product **at split-off point**. The split-off point is that point, at the conclusion of the joint manufacturing process, when individual joint products can be identified.

- The relative sales values for each of the joint products are combined to obtain a total amount.

The joint product costs to be allocated to a specific joint product will be determined by the relative sales value method using the following formula:

$$\frac{\text{Sales value of product at split-off}}{\text{Total of sales values of all products at split-off}} \times \text{Joint product costs}$$

Sometimes, in addition to joint products, companies may have by-products that result from a process. By-products are output from the joint process that do not contribute significantly to the firm's revenue and are not products that the company is manufacturing by intent. Joint costs may be allocated to **by-products** in a variety of ways:

- An amount equal to the net proceeds from the disposal of by-products may be allocated such that the by-products are sold at breakeven.

- Joint costs may be allocated to by-products in the same manner as to joint products using the relative sales value method, as if it were an additional joint product.

- No costs may be allocated to the by-product.

Cost Accounting

A company has joint product costs of $54,000 at split-off. There are 2 main products, A and B, and one by-product, Z. Division A has $30,000 of additional costs after split-off in order to sell all output for $80,000. Division B has $30,000 of additional costs after split-off in order to sell all output for $60,000. By-product Z has $1,000 of additional costs in order to sell for $5,000. How much of the joint product costs should be allocated to products A, B and by-product Z?

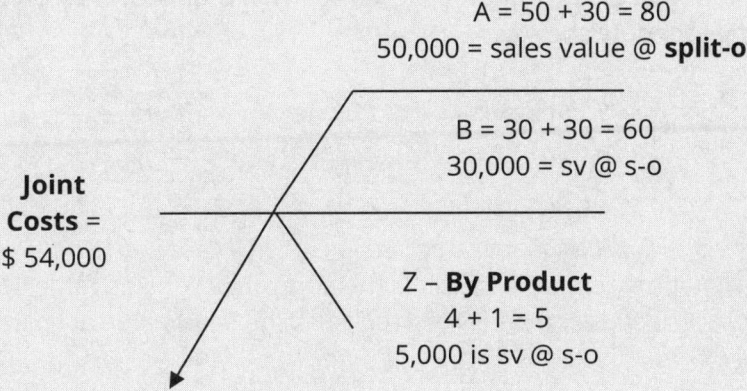

Sales-Value at Split-Off

Separable Costs (Work Backwards)
A → **$50,000** + $30,000 = $80,000
    If work on it more (put in an extra cost of $30,000), it could be worth $80,000.
    The $50,000 represents the synthetic sales value at split off.

B → **$30,000** + $30,000 = $60,000
    If work on it more (put in an extra cost of $30,000), it could be worth $60,000.
    The $30,000 represents the synthetic sales value at split off.

If we add those two synthetic values up, we get $50,000 + $30,000, or $80,000. We would then allocate the joint costs as follows:

A → 50,000/80,000 × (54,000)
B → 30,000/80,000 × (54,000)

Z → **$4,000** + $1,000 = $5,000
    Can use to offset cost or add to revenue.
    $54,000 − $4,000 = $50,000 Joint Costs to be allocated

- Product A would be allocated 50/80 × $50,000 = $31,250
- Product B would be allocated 30/80 × $50,000 = $18,750
                                                 $50,000
- Product Z would show zero revenue as the $4,000 was reduced from the $54,000 of joint product costs that needed to be allocated between products A and B.

Assume a company produces a standard and deluxe version of a product. The standard version is produced starting in department A and finishing in department B. The deluxe version is produced starting in department A and finishing in department C. The total sales are $30 of the standard version and $50 of the deluxe. The costs incurred are $10 in department A, $6 in department B, and $34 in department C.

While it is not a problem to determine total gross profit for the company, a breakdown by product line is more difficult, as the following schedule shows:

	Standard	Deluxe	Total
Sales	30	50	80
Separate costs	6	34	40
Sales value at split-off	24	16	40
Joint costs	?	?	10
Gross profit	?	?	30

Using the sales value at split-off approach, the standard version is allocated $24 / $40 = 60% of the joint costs of $10, or $6, and the deluxe version is allocated $16 / $40 = 40% of $10, or $4.

By-products

If one of the products resulting from production is considered a by-product, and is only being produced as an incidental result of production of the main product or products, then the net realizable value of the by-product is simply subtracted from the cost of production of the main.

For example, oil refining involves the removal of impurities from crude oil. The impurities are actually useful in the manufacture of glue, so oil companies sell them and subtract the net proceeds (sales price less costs of disposal) from the cost of refining oil.

If there are two or more main products in addition to a by-product, the net realizable value of the by-product is subtracted from the joint product costs, which are then allocated to the main products based on relative sales value at split-off approach or a comparable method. Sometimes, rather than recognizing by-product market value as a reduction of production costs, it is recognized when sold and disclosed as ordinary income, other income, or as a contra to cost of sales.

BEC 8 – Planning, Control & Analysis

Table of Contents

Lecture 8.01 – Master & Static Budgets	**1**
FLEXIBLE BUDGETING	2
Lecture 8.02 – Correlation & Regression Analysis	**4**
RESPONSIBILITY ACCOUNTING	5
Lecture 8.03 – Performance Measures	**9**
BALANCED SCORECARDS	9
PROFITABILITY RATIOS	10
BENCHMARKING	11
QUALITY CONTROL	11
Lecture 8.04 – Business Process Management (BPM)	**14**

Planning, Control & Analysis

Lecture 8.01 – Master & Static Budgets

Managers use a variety of tools for their organization's internal financial planning, control, and analysis.

- **Strategic planning** refers to setting long-term overall goals and policies, which help guide the organization's long-run operations.
- **Tactical planning** focuses on short-term objectives and temporary techniques.

Strategic planning often begins with preparing a **mission statement** identifying the organization's purpose and highest values. The next step in strategic planning is to identify goals and objectives that flesh out more fully the organization's mission. In the next step, specific **performance measures** are associated with each of the goals and objectives, so that the organization may measure its performance (ie, whether it is achieving its goals and objectives). Finally, the organization will design **tactics**, that is, the specific actions to be used to meet these goals.

To assist in their management, companies often use several specialized budgets. Companies use a **master budget** (a static budget for the company as a whole) to summarize various individual budgets. The two major budgets that the master budget summarizes are:

- **An operating budget**, or a projected (or budgeted or future) income statement with its various supporting schedules.
- **A financial budget**, comprising projected (or budgeted or future) capital budget, cash budget, balance sheet, and statement of cash flows. This budget is usually for 1 year, but could be a rolling budget as well.

Static budgets serve to analyze conditions for a specific level of activity (eg, what would our labor costs be if our level of sales were X?). Thus, static budgets do not change (or are recalculated) each time some volume (eg, of sales) changes. Static budgets are normally set up for extended periods of time (eg, before each year begins). Large companies may set up static budgets for:

- A division within the company
- The company as a whole

Under **Kaizen budgeting**, managers make cost projections that incorporate their expectations for future improvements. Of course, if those improvements do not take place, the budget (goals) cannot be met. The term "Kaizen" generally refers to an originally Japanese management approach that focuses on continually identifying and implementing small improvements (instead of focusing on major breakthroughs or large structural changes).

Preparing a Master Budget

1. Estimate (future) sales volumes (this is the *First* step in budgeting).
2. Use sales volumes to estimate (future) revenues.
3. Use collection histories to estimate (future) collections.
4. Estimate the cost of sales based on the number of units sold.
5. Use current finished goods inventory, budgeted ending inventory, & cost of sales to estimate the number of units to be manufactured.

6. Use units manufactured to estimate the organization's (future) material needs, labor costs, & overhead costs.
7. Use material needs, current raw materials inventory, & budgeted ending inventory to budget (future) purchases.
8. Use purchase terms to estimate (future) payments.
9. Analyze expense & payment patterns to complete operating & cash flow budgets.

Budgeting Material Purchases & Payments

    Units sold
+   Budgeted increase in finished goods
−   Budgeted decrease in finished goods
    Units to be manufactured
×   Units of raw material per unit of finished goods
    Units of raw material required for production
+   Budgeted increase in raw materials
−   Budgeted decrease in raw materials
    Budgeted raw material purchases
+   Budgeted decrease in accounts payable
−   Budgeted increase in accounts payable
    Budgeted payments for raw materials

Production Budget

    Budgeted (or projected) sales
    + desired ending inventory of finished goods
    Total needs
    − beginning inventory of finished goods
    Number of units to be produced

Note: Budgets must be prepared in the following order:
- Sales budget
- Production budget
- Direct/Raw materials purchases budget
- Cash Disbursements budget
- Budgeted financial statements (budgeted - Income statement, cash flow, balance sheet)

Flexible Budgeting

In contrast to static budgets, flexible budgets may be adjusted for changes in volumes. When organizations prepare budgets for internal use, they often use the direct costing method, since variable and fixed costs behave differently.

For example:

Sales (in dollars, not number of units)	1,000
-Variable costs	600
Contribution margin	400
-Fixed costs	300
Operating profit	100

If sales for a period turn out to be $1,500, one can readily modify the above statement. Sales increased from $1,000 to $1,500, or by 50%, and would be expected to also increase variable costs by 50%. One would not expect fixed costs to be affected. Thus:

Sales	1,000	× 1.5 =	1,500
-Variable costs	600	× 1.5 =	900
Contribution margin	400		600
-Fixed costs	300	=	300
Operating profit	100		300

Alternatively, the mathematics underlying a **flexible budget** can be most readily expressed using a linear function:

$$Y = a + (b * X)$$

- The "Y" is referred to as the **dependent variable**, or the item whose value is being estimated—in our example: expected total costs.
- The "a" is referred to as "the constant" (or the intercept), and in our example stands for **fixed costs.**
- The "X" is referred to as the **independent variable**, or the item whose changes may have an impact on the value of the dependent variable (Y). In linear functions applied to flexible budgeting, the independent variable is often called the **cost driver**. In our example, the cost driver is sales. In other settings, the independent variables are often called "predictors" or "determinants."
- The "b" is referred to as "the slope," and in our example stands for a **variable rate**, or the multiplier that reflects the effect of change in one unit of X on Y.

In our example, when sales were $1,000, variable costs were $600, implying a variable rate (b) of 0.6 (ie, variable costs / sales = $600 / $1,000, or 60% of sales). Fixed costs (a) are $300. Thus:

$$Y = 300 + (0.6 * X)$$

When sales are $1,000:

Expected total costs = 300 + (0.6 * 1,000) = 300 + 600 = 900

When sales are $1,500:

Expected total costs = 300 + (0.6 * 1,500) = 300 + 900 = 1,200

The **advantage of flexible budgets** is that they can readily adapt to changes in variable costs that result from changes in sales levels.

Lecture 8.02 – Correlation & Regression Analysis

To develop more relevant flexible budgets, companies may seek to identify which predictors to use as the X's for which Y's in their linear functions. For instance, sales might be the best predictor for a company's total costs. In contrast, direct labor hours might be the best predictor for manufacturing overhead costs. Managers may use a variety of techniques to assess the best predictors of their dependent variables.

Using **Correlation Analysis**, one may calculate the **Correlation Coefficient** (or coefficient of correlation, ρ, or the lower-case Greek letter, Rho) between (only) two variables at a time (ie, one's dependent variable and only one independent variable at a time). Values for ρ range between -1.0 and +1.0.

- The closer ρ is to -1 or to +1, the stronger the relationship between the two variables.
- A ρ close to -1 signals a very strong *inverse* relationship.
- A ρ close to +1 signals a very strong *direct* relationship.
- A ρ close to 0 signals a negligible relationship, and likely *no reliable relationship*, between the variables.

What is the relationship between the X & Y variable?

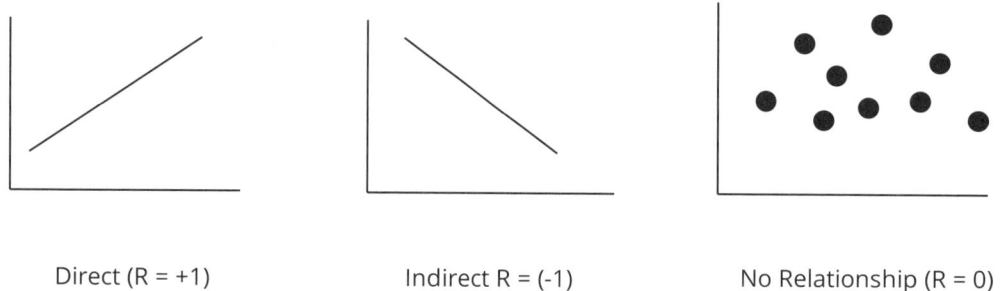

Direct (R = +1)   Indirect R = (-1)   No Relationship (R = 0)

Using **Regression Analysis** (ie, a mathematical or statistical technique), one may test the relationship between one dependent variable and several independent variables (ie, multivariate or multiple regression analysis). One can also perform regression analysis with the dependent variable and only one independent variable (ie, univariate or simple regression analysis).

Regression analysis provides a streamlined approach to test which, among various independent variables, is the best predictor of the dependent variable. Regression analysis may also reveal that several independent variables are simultaneously each relevant (ie, statistically significant) predictors of the dependent variable.

Using regression analysis to determine the best determinants, managers are likely to experiment with a variety of combinations of independent variables (ie, a model specification). To compare model specifications, managers may use a variety of measures. One of the key measures of a model specification's "goodness of fit" is its **coefficient of determination** (R^2, pronounced R squared). R^2 is defined as the percentage of variation in the dependent variable explained by the variation in the independent variables, and is commonly expressed with values ranging between 0 and 1.

The **F-statistic** (with the "F" always a capital letter) is a measure of the statistical significance (relevance) of the model specification. The p-value (with the p always a lower-case letter) attached to an F-statistic is the probability that the overall predicted relationship simply occurred by chance.

Regressions yield **t-statistics** (with the "t" always a lower-case letter) (and attached p-value) for each independent variable, which indicate their individual statistical significance (or relevance) in predicting the dependent variable p-value.

Analysts using regression analysis customarily to interpret p-values smaller than 0.01 (1%) as associated with relationships that are very reliable; p-values between 0.01 and 0.05 as reliable; p-values between 0.05 and 0.10 as somewhat, perhaps, or borderline reliable; and p-values larger than 0.10 as not reliable.

Regressions also yield **coefficients** for each independent variable which may be readily interpreted (if statistically significant) as the impact of a change of unit in the independent variable on the dependent variable (ie, the "b" in linear functions, or the variable rate in our earlier example). Thus, a coefficient of 0.6 would imply that one (or ten) extra dollar(s) of sales would yield 0.6 (or 6) dollars in total expected costs.

Responsibility Accounting

To reduce or eliminate defective units, to increase efficiency in the manufacturing process, and to reduce costs, companies seek to identify which parties within their organization are responsible for which tasks and seek to establish mechanisms to evaluate their performance. To evaluate managers' and divisions' performance, companies often apply responsibility accounting. In this terminology:

- The manager of a **cost center** is responsible for the costs incurred by that center.
- The manager of a **profit center** is responsible for both (1) the revenues earned and (2) the costs incurred by that center.
- The manager of an **investment center** is responsible for all (1) the revenues earned, (2) the costs incurred, and (3) the capital investments from each center.

Economic Value Added

One way in which the performance of an investment center is evaluated is based on its **economic value added** (EVA). The EVA is equal to the earnings of the investment center in excess of its cost of capital. It is calculated by first multiplying the cost of the investment center by the entity's weighted average cost of capital to determine the cost of capital, which is generally the minimum return that the investment center is expected to yield. Subtracting that amount from the investment center's operating profit gives the amount by which profits exceed the cost of capital and by which the investment center adds economic value to the entity.

Ideally, a manager should not be held responsible for costs that the manager cannot affect, such as costs that have somehow been allocated to that department, but that are directed by and incurred on behalf of either the corporate level or other divisions. Similarly, if the manager's own salary is determined by someone other than the manager, the manager should not be held responsible for that cost.

Activity-Based Costing

Modern budgets seek to identify cost drivers as accurately as possible (ie, what variables affect what costs). An example of these efforts is the technique called activity-based costing (ABC). ABC seeks to group together costs that are affected by common factors. For example, depreciation, repairs, and maintenance might be grouped together as activities affected by machine hours (ie, the usage of machines). In contrast, payroll taxes, employee wages, and benefits might be grouped together as activities affected by direct labor hours.

Under ABC, companies segregate manufacturing overhead into numerous overhead cost pools. Each pool will include costs that have common elements, usually the particular activity that will result in an increase in the costs included in that pool. The activity is the cost driver, or allocation base. One advantage of segregating costs in this manner is that it enhances the usefulness of **multiple regression analysis**, since it will yield both a greater number of potential cost drivers (which commonly enhances regression's ability to yield relevant results) and by ensuring that the boundaries across costs drivers are more sensible.

Costs may also be classified as either **Value-adding** or **Nonvalue-adding**. Value-adding costs are those that actually make the product itself or make it better for customers (such as engineering activity, direct manufacturing costs, the operation of production machinery, modifying products to better meet customers' specifications, or expenses that improve the product's endurance or performance, such as research & development). Costs are ultimately value adding if they result in specific outcomes that customers perceive as increasing the worth of a product or service, for which they would pay more. Nonvalue-adding costs (such as moving, handling, and storage of raw materials, factory utilities, or depreciation of manufacturing equipment) are costs that increase the cost of a product but that customers do not specifically value.

Service Department Costs

Large firms may include various **service departments** that incur overhead costs providing support to the production (or manufacturing) departments. Under the ABC approach, the firms seek to allocate the overhead costs incurred by service departments to the appropriate production departments.

- Under the **direct allocation** method, the firm allocates costs from each service department directly to, and only to, the production or operating departments.

- Under the **step allocation** method, the firm may allocate costs from a service department both to production/production departments and "temporarily or as a step" to the other service departments.

- The **reciprocal allocation** method is similar to the step allocation method except costs are allocated simultaneously among service departments. The high degree of complexity makes it unlikely that the CPA exam will test this method.

Under the **step allocation method**, the costs of individual service departments are allocated as follows:

1. The service departments are ranked, from the one performing services for the most other service departments to the one that performs the least.
2. The costs of the first service department are allocated to the remaining service departments and production/operating departments using appropriate allocation bases. Once the costs of a service department are allocated, that department is eliminated from the process.
3. The costs of the next service department are allocated to the remaining service and production departments. The process is repeated until the costs of the last (and thus of all) service departments have been allocated to production departments.

Most forms of regression analysis are too complicated for exam testing, but a simple technique known as the two-point, **high-low method** is occasionally tested. Under this method, a series of values of an independent and dependent variable (eg, the monthly observations for one year) are reduced to the two data points associated with the high and low value periods for the cost driver (or independent variables). For instance, assume the highest month of sales was March and the lowest month July, with the following sales and cost figures:

Month	Sales	Total costs
March	600	400
July	500	360
Difference	100	40

Based on the differences (ie, sales range from 500 to 600, or by 100, and total costs range from 360 to 400, or by 40), total costs change by 40/100 = 40% of the change in sales from the low to the high period. This method yields an estimate of the variable rate, or b. Using the data from March, with sales of $600, variable costs are 40%, or $240. Since total costs in March are $400, variable costs of $240 mean fixed costs are $160, and the resulting linear function is $Y = 160 + (.4 \times X)$.

Forecasting

Firms may use a wide variety of statistical techniques to assist them in developing the values and assumptions included in budgets. Some of these techniques are often referred to by several overlapping names.

- Regression analyses that incorporate not only company data, but also industry and/or economy-wide measures to estimate future sales and costs for a company are sometimes referred to as **econometric models** (economists use the terms *regression analysis* and *econometric models* interchangeably).

- The subset of regression (or econometric) techniques (or models) focusing on analyzing and forecasting data for a single firm over time (eg, its sales or costs) are commonly referred to as **time series analysis (or models)**.

When adequate data is not available, or budgets are being developed where there is little or no historical information to use, the judgment of various experts may be thought through a method known as **Delphi** (this is a somewhat bemused reference to The Oracle at Delphi, who in Ancient Greece was sought out by those looking for the advice of the gods). Experts are questioned individually and the judgments of the experts are then examined, combined, and sent back to the experts recursively until a consensus arises.

In the Delphi technique, the experts do not meet with each other (except sometimes in the final stage), so that their independent judgments aren't biased by the views of the other "oracles" interviewed. The Delphi technique avoids experts meeting to minimize the possibility of **groupthink**. Groupthink is the tendency of people at meetings to come to a consensus because of the pressures of conformity and fear of embarrassment, such that the consensus may fail to actually represent the best judgment of these same people individually.

Probability Analysis

Most planning techniques require estimates of the revenues and costs that will result from various decisions. In the real world, many decisions may lead to many different possible outcomes. Managers may use **probability theory** to develop the most sensible possible single estimates from the range of possibilities. A *probability distribution* describes the possible outcomes relating to a single action and the likelihood of occurrence of each possible outcome. To turn a probability distribution into a single expected value, one would multiply each of the possible outcomes by its likelihood (or probability, weight, or percentage) and sum the amounts.

> For example, if the decision to market a product is believed to have a 10% probability (chance) of resulting in sales of $100, a 40% probability of $200, a 30% probability of $300, and a 20% probability of $400. The calculation of expected value is as follows:
>
> | Revenue | Probability | Weighted Value |
> |---|---|---|
> | $100 | 10% | $10 |
> | 200 | 40% | 80 |
> | 300 | 30% | 90 |
> | 400 | 20% | 80 |
> | **Expected value** | 100% | $260 |

Lecture 8.03 – Performance Measures

Organizations use performance measures to monitor and manage various aspects of their performance for the organization as a whole and across its various subparts.

Balanced Scorecards

Organizations often use Balanced Scorecards to help ensure that they are following and implementing their mission and strategic plans. Balanced Scorecards commonly include **performance measures** that are generally grouped across **four perspectives** (see below).

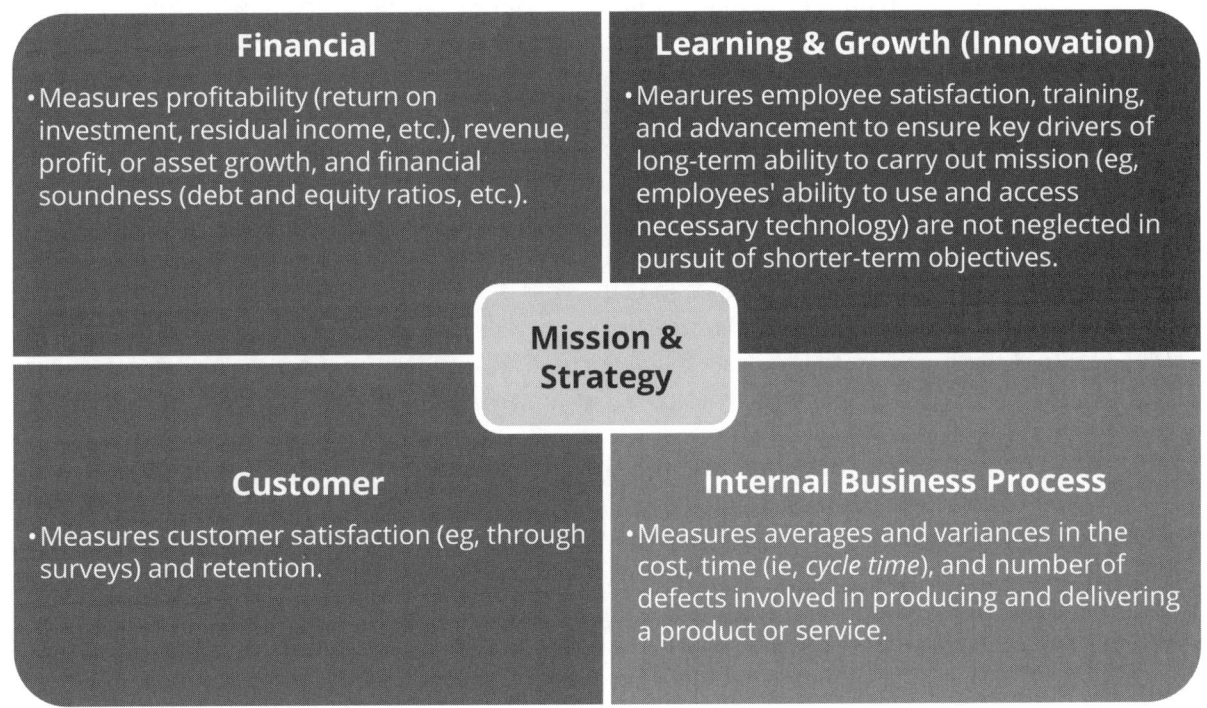

A balanced scorecard commonly includes:

- **Strategic objectives** – A statement of the firm's goals and what is needed to achieve them.
- **Performance measures** – The quantitative methods to be used to determine how much of the strategic objectives are being reached (yardstick).
- **Baseline performance** – How well the firm is doing under each performance measure.
- **Targets** – The amount of improvement being sought for each performance measure.
- **Strategic initiatives** – Specific changes the firm will make to achieve its objectives (and targets).

Organizations may seek to identify **cause-and-effect linkages** across their initiatives and changes in various performance measures. These efforts may help to identify which performance measures are actually **performance drivers** (leading indicators) and which are **outcome performance measures** (lagging indicators). Organizations would thus be better able to focus on the drivers that are most critical to achieving their strategic objectives.

Data mining may also be used, which is the sorting through data to identify patterns and establish relationships, to bring to light previously unidentified relationships. Some of the parameters include association, sequence or path analysis, classification, clustering and forecasting (predictive analytics).

Sunk costs are current costs associated with past decisions that are largely unavoidable, and that are thus largely irrelevant to such analyses.

Organizations using the balanced scorecard framework use **strategy maps** (ie, diagrams) to help identify cause-and-effect relationships:

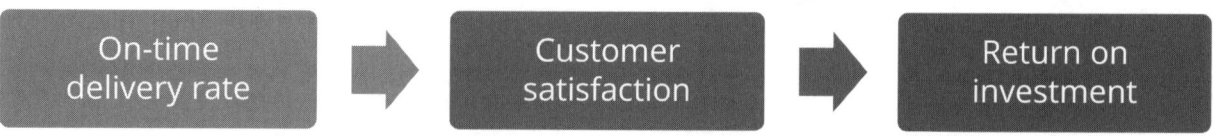

Decision Trees - Managers constantly face decisions for which they cannot have all relevant information initially. As any project evolves, managers have to respond to changing prices, to sales and costs that differ from their initial projections, and to all sorts of new developments, including new investment alternatives, and whether to expand the project further or to retrench. Managers may use decision trees as graphical aids to highlight the chains of decisions that will or will not happen under various scenarios (eg, if X happens, then the choices about Y are…).

Value-Based Management (VBM) seeks to examine all aspects of a company (as in a **financial scorecard**) to identify the **economic value added (EVA)** that different activities contribute. (EVA is defined as net operating profit after taxes minus the cost of capital). VBM seeks to determine each activity's financial value (or contribution) to the firm. However, if misapplied, VBM may focus on the activities for which it is easiest to link costs to value creation, and fail to reflect that some activities do lead to value creation, even if the links from cost to value creation are less easy to identify.

For instance, cost cutting may yield value in the short term, but not in the long term. Similarly, research expenditures may yield value in the long term, or erratically, or through improvements that are shared with other departments but with enhancements in revenues never clearly credited to the research expenditures.

A *value chain* is the sequence of business processes through which a product or service becomes more valuable (or useful), by converting inputs into outputs.

Real Options Techniques treat each business investment decision (ie, project) as the purchase of a series of options to be exercised as the project evolves. The value of these chains of options is not reflected when managers focus solely on expected cash flows.

Profitability Ratios

- **Return on Investment (based on assets)** = Net income / Average assets or Average invested capital
- **DuPont ROI analysis:** ROI = Return on sales × Asset turnover
    - **Return on sales** = Net income / Sales
    - **Asset turnover** = Sales / Total assets
- **Residual income** = Operating profit – Interest on investment
    - **Interest on investment** = Invested capital × required rate of return
- **Economic Value Added:** EVA = Net operating profit after taxes (NOPAT) – Cost of Financing
    - **Cost of financing** = (Total assets – Current Liabilities) × Weighted average cost of capital
- **Free Cash Flow** = NOPAT + Depr + Amort – Capital expenditures – Net increase in working capital

Benchmarking

Benchmarking involves evaluating performance (producing products, delivering services, etc.) on an ongoing basis across subdivisions within an organization and relative to historical and current performance within and outside the organization. Organizations engage in benchmarking in part to identify "best practices" that may then be adopted more widely across the subdivisions of the organization. Common types of benchmarking include:

- **Internal benchmarking:** To track, for instance, how well various subdivisions within one firm carry out one task. Generally, the information is relatively easy to obtain. The disadvantage is that improvement may be limited to the best that one subdivision is doing; *external benchmarking* may result in more dramatic improvements. For instance, reducing the employee time to process a vendor invoice and issue a check from 29 minutes to 14 minutes is impressive, until compared with 2 minutes to process an electronic funds transfer (EFT).

- **Competitive benchmarking:** To track how well one firm performs relative to its most direct competitors. This may yield dramatic improvements, but the information often is difficult to obtain; while some of this information is directly observable by the public, obtaining this information typically is very difficult as competitors have little incentive to assist and many incentives to protect their competitive advantages.
  - Cross-sectional analysis: exploring data for one time period for multiple firms (ie, including one's firm and other firms) in the same industry.
  - Time-series analysis: exploring data for one firm over time.
  - Panel data analysis: exploring data for multiple firms over time (ie, panel data analysis uses both multiple firms and multiple time periods).

- **Industry benchmarking:** To track one firm against its industry as a whole, instead of against only its direct competitors.

- **Generic benchmarking:** To track one firm against all firms, even if outside its industry. Benchmarking is likely to be more relevant the more alike the firms are that one compares against. Of course, obtaining data is usually easier the broader the category of firms one uses.

Quality Control

The International Organization of Standards (ISO) has developed a series of **ISO Quality Standards**).

- **ISO 9000 Series** – including five parts (9000 to 9004) focusing on the *quality* of products and services provided by firms.
- **ISO 14000 Series** – focusing on environmental goals.

According to the **Pareto Principle,** 80% of quality problems result from only 20% of the possible causes. Thus, firms should first focus on the most important causes of problems, and only later address less important cases.

Six-Sigma Quality is a statistical measure of the percentage of products that are in acceptable form (ie, achieve the firm's quality goals), based on standard deviation measures (hence the name sigma). To achieve one sigma, 68% of products must be acceptable. To achieve six sigma, 99.999997% of products must be acceptable. Six-sigma constitutes the practical hypothetical goal of perfection in manufacturing, with only 3.4 defects per million units.

Total quality management (TQM) is an entity-wide effort to continuously improve the ability to deliver high quality products and services by attending to systematic analysis; thus, it includes insights from suppliers as well as employees. It now is largely supplanted by six sigma and ISO programs; however, concepts from TQM often appear (in more evolved and formal versions) in implementation of these later perspectives.

Businesses may apply the **theory of constraints (TOC)** to maximize their operating income and overcome bottlenecks in their operations. Under TOC, if demand exceeds capacity for a resource, the resource is defined as a **bottleneck resource**. If capacity exceeds demand, the resource is defined as a **nonbottleneck resource**. TOC seeks to simultaneously maximize throughput contribution and minimize investment and operating costs.

- **Throughput contribution** equals revenues minus the direct materials cost of goods sold (COGS).
- **Investment** equals the cost of materials, work in process, inventories; research and development expenses; and (upfront) expenses on equipment and buildings.
- **Operating costs** equals employee compensation, rents paid, utilities (electricity, garbage collection, etc.), and depreciation (eg, of equipment and buildings).

Cost of Quality

This philosophy argues that failures have causes, that preventing failures is cheaper than having to address failures after they take place, and that measuring a firm's performance in implementing the cost of quality philosophy can help the firm. The costs related to addressing quality issues rise the later in the production process that the firm deals with the quality problems. There are *four different stages* at which costs can be addressed:

- **Prevention costs** – seeking to prevent quality failures
  - Using high-quality materials
  - Inspecting the production process
  - Focusing engineering and design to improve quality
  - Providing training to employees that focuses on improving quality
  - Quality circles
  - Maintenance of equipment (machines, etc.)
- **Appraisal (or detection costs)** – expenses on detecting quality failures
  - Inspecting samples of materials, in-process, and finished goods
  - Obtaining information from customers
- **Internal failure costs** – expenses addressing quality failures that were detected after production but before they were shipped to customers
  - Disposing of scrap resulting from wasted materials
  - Reworking units to correct defects
  - Re-inspecting and retesting after rework
- **External failure costs** – expenses addressing defective products that reached customers
  - Warranty costs
  - Expenses addressing customer complaints
  - Product liability costs
  - Cost of product returns
  - Marketing to help maintain and/or improve the firm's image
  - Losses of future sales, reputation

Planning, Control & Analysis — BEC 8

Costs of conforming to quality control standards are called **Conformance costs** = prevention + appraisal costs. Costs of failure of quality controls are called **Nonconformance costs** = internal + external failure costs.

Lecture 8.04 – Business Process Management (BPM)

This operations management approach seeks to align all aspects of an organization with the wants and needs of its clients. BPM is often called a "process optimization process." Business processes are the structured activities of an organization that produce a product or service. BPM promotes business effectiveness and efficiency while striving for innovation, flexibility, and integration with technology.

Business processes are strategic assets that must be *understood, managed, and improved*. Under BPM, managers seek to recognize that processes have **human and technological aspects** and that the two aspects interact. BPM argues that understanding these interactions play a key role in improving processes. The life cycle of business process management includes:

1. **Design**
   This first phase identifies current processes and designs improvements for them. Of course, proper design may prevent problems later.

2. **Modeling**
   During this second phase, processes are tested under various "what if" scenarios before rolling them out to full production so that issues may be identified and addressed (ie, redesigned).

3. **Execution**
   During the third phase, equipment and software are installed, employees are trained, and the new processes are implemented at full-production levels.

4. **Monitoring**
   Once new processes are implemented, they continue to be monitored (tested) yielding performance data.

5. **Optimization**
   Performance data (from the modeling or monitoring phases) is analyzed to identify areas for improvement (ie, bottlenecks) that may be re-designed further. Re-design may variously involve centralizing or de-centralizing some activities as appropriate (some purchases may be cheaper in large quantities; others may require specialized knowledge or be subject to particular time constraints). Re-design may also involve bringing some processes inside the firm (ie, acquiring a supplier) or outside the firm (**out-sourcing**) or outside the country (**off-shoring**, whether inside or outside the firm). Any re-design choice involves benefits, costs, and risks. For instance, the benefits of out-sourcing and off-shoring might include lower employee compensation and some tax benefits. However, they might also open the firm to the following risks:

   o Quality risk (less control over quality).
   o Language risk (eg, customer service).
   o Information security risk (potential loss of control over confidential customer and company info).
   o Intellectual property risk (potential loss of control of information about the company's products and processes).
   o Public opinion risk (potential loss of reputation).
   o Social responsibility risk (concerns about the ethics of organizations the firm may work with in other countries).

Re-design is an on-going process. Each change opens the doors for new benefits, new risks, and the eventual need for further re-designs. For instance, firms may seek to minimize the risks listed above by setting up various procedures, such as operating agreements with their domestic and international partners.

Final Review

Table of Contents

Lecture 9.01 – BEC Final Review   1

Lecture 9.01 – BEC Final Review

YOU FINISHED YOUR BEC COURSE...NOW WHAT?
A quick guide to the final days leading up to, and following, the exam

I. FINAL REVIEW
Now is the time to make connections and solidify your understanding of the topics you found most challenging, and to review the most heavily tested topics on the exam.

- ❑ Review your SmartPath data to ensure you have hit all targets. Revisit any areas marked "Needs Improvement."
- ❑ Reread your course notes and review your digital flash cards.
- ❑ If it is included in your program package, use the Cram Course to do a final review of the most heavily tested topics.
- ❑ Take at least one Full CPA Practice Exam in your QBank to hone your test-taking skills in an environment that follows the same 5-testlet, 4-hour structure of the exam.
- ❑ Checkout an AICPA Sample Test at www.cpa-exam.org to familiarize yourself with the exam format and welcome (instruction) screens.

II. DAY OF THE EXAM
- ❑ Get a good night's rest before heading into your exam.
- ❑ Arrive to the Prometric testing center at least 60 minutes before your appointment so you have time to park, check-in, and use the restroom before your exam begins.
- ❑ Bring your Notice to Schedule (NTS) and two forms of acceptable identification (see Intro for more details).
- ❑ Proceed through check-in: store belongings, get fingerprinted, have photo taken, sign log book, get seated, write your Launch Code (from your NTS) on your noteboard.
- ❑ Don't stress. You've prepared for this; now, just breathe and power through!

III. DURING THE EXAM
- ❑ Remember your BEC Exam time strategy, and jot down the times at which you want to be at your benchmarks:
    - o Allocate 75 seconds per multiple choice question
    - o Allocate 10 - 15 minutes for each written communication question
    - o Allocate 15-25 minutes for each task-based simulation, depending on complexity
    - o Take the standard 15-minute break after the 3rd testlet – it does not count against your time
    - o (Remember that any other break will count against your time)

BEC: 4 Hour Exam					
Testlet 1	Testlet 2	Testlet 3	Break	Testlet 4	Testlet 5
31 MCQs	31 MCQs	2 TBSs		2 TBSs	3 WCs
45 min	45 min	50 min		50 min	50 min

- ❑ You will be given 10 minutes to review the welcome screens and exam instructions. You should already be familiar with these screens after taking the AICPA Sample Test, and can bypass them during your exam.

- ❑ Once you begin testing, make sure to read each question carefully, paying close attention to the keywords that dictate the question's intention (e.g. *except, is greater than*).

- ❑ Take note if your questions are getting more difficult. That's a good sign! A progressively harder exam indicates that you are performing well.

IV. AFTER THE EXAM

- ❑ Remember, it is normal to not feel great afterwards. It's a tough exam and designed to challenge your confidence and competencies.
- ❑ Relax and celebrate! You've earned it.
- ❑ Your scores will be released within a couple of weeks.
- ❑ GOOD LUCK!!!